# Recent Technological Advancements in Finance, Economics and Management

# Recent Technological Advancements in Finance, Economics and Management

*Editors*

Dr. B.B. Tiwari
Dr. S. Ranjith Kumar
Dr. Rajeena Syed
Dr. Eshwar Reddy

ALLIED PUBLISHERS PVT. LTD.
Noida • Mumbai • Kolkata • Chennai • Bangalore

**ALLIED PUBLISHERS PRIVATE LIMITED**

D-5, Sector-2, **Noida**–201 301
Ph. Nos.: 0120-4320295/2542557/4352866 • E-mail: delhi.books@alliedpublishers.com

17 Chittaranjan Avenue, **Kolkata**–700072
Ph.: 033-22129618 • E-mail: cal.books@alliedpublishers.com

15 J.N. Heredia Marg, Ballard Estate, **Mumbai**–400001
Ph.: 022-42126969 • E-mail: mumbai.books@alliedpublishers.com

No. 25/10, Commander-in-Chief Road, Ethiraj Lane (Next to Post Office)
Egmore, **Chennai**–600008
Ph.: 044-28223938 • E-mail: chennai.books@alliedpublishers.com

P.B. No. 9932, No. 15, 3rd Floor (Next to Vijaya Bank), 5th Cross, Gandhinagar,
Karnataka, **Bangalore**–560009, Ph.: 080-41530285 / 22386239
E-mail: bngl.books@alliedpublishers.com

**Website: www.alliedpublishers.com**



ISBN: 978-93-89934-69-4



Published by Sunil Sachdev and printed by Ravi Sachdev at Allied Publishers Pvt. Ltd.,
D-5, Sector-2, Noida–201 301

# Contents

*Foreword* .......... *vii*

*Chairman's Message* .......... *ix*

*Chancellor's Message* .......... *xi*

*Pro-Chancellor's Message* .......... *xiii*

*Provost's Message* .......... *xv*

*Registrar's Message* .......... *xvii*

*Presidential Address (Inaugural Session)* .......... *xix*

*Inaugural Address by Prof. Prem Vrat* .......... *xxi*

*Inaugural Address: Guest of Honour by Prof. Prahlad Kumar* .......... *xxiii*

*Keynote Address: Valedictory Session by Prof. S. Indrakant* .......... *xxvii*

*Needonomics for Management of Fintech with Needo-use of Artificial Intelligence (AI) by Prof. M.M. Goel* .......... *xxxi*

*Editorial Remarks* .......... *xxxv*

## Economics

1. Empowering Rural Women: Theoretical Foundations of E-Governance Strategies for Digital Economy and Sustainable Rural Development .......... 3
   *Farhatnida Unnisa, Nilaish and Bhupendra Bahadur Tiwari*
2. Empowering India: Unveiling Government Schemes .......... 23
   *G. Manisha, M. Harshith and Santha Ganesh Iyer*
3. A Study on ITC's Social Investment Initiatives .......... 28
   *K. Neha, L. Kiran and Santha Ganesh Iyer*
4. The Impact of Exchange Rate Fluctuation on India's Agricultural Exports Using Bounds Test Approach .......... 35
   *Jyoti Tripathi*
5. Cashless Economy with Reference to Micro and Small Enterprises.... 47
   *Pratima Katti*
6. Exploring Music Consumption Trends in the Digital Age: Insights from Kerala .......... 58
   *Bindu Balagopal and P. Chacko Jose*
7. A Study on College Students' Perception Towards Digital Finance in Bengaluru City .......... 72
   *M.K. Shwetha and Suma Singh*

8. A Study of Various Schemes Available for SME's: A Case Study in State Bank of India ..... 86
*Neha Banu and S. Ranjith Kumar*

## Finance

9. Socio-Economic Impact of MGNREGA: A Paradigm Shift with Special Reference to Women Senior Citizens ..... 109
*I.B. Cirappa and J. Shivanna*

10. The Green Imperative: Financing a Sustainable Future ..... 124
*Manisha Vikas Jagtap*

11. Beyond The Hype: A Critical Examination of the Dual Nature of Social Media's Influence on Financial Literacy ..... 136
*Diksha, Sania Bassi and Abheeti*

12. Navigating Financial Markets: A Study of Investors Rationality and Behavioral Finance ..... 148
*G. Kavitha and P. Suryadevi*

13. The Association between Financial Literacy and Income Inequality—A Study on the Salaried Individual of Lucknow ..... 158
*Avnare Singh and Alka Singh*

14. Job Burnout and Psychological Well-being: A Study on Academicians of Higher Educational Institutions ..... 171
*Manjeet Kaur, Rekha Khosla and Masood Siddiqui*

15. Relationship between Product Differentiation and Brand Equity ..... 179
*T.D. Hemamalini and M. Kamaraj*

## Management

16. Consumers' Perceived Risk to Visit Restaurants: A Perspective from Theory of Planned Behaviour ..... 195
*Prachi Patil*

17. Analysis of Switching Intentions of Customers between Click and Brick Using Machine Learning Approach ..... 216
*Anuradha Yadav and Vijay Prakash Sharma*

***Author Index*** ..... 227

***Applauds*** ..... 229

# Foreword

It is a great pleasure and honor for me to write this foreword for the book on **"Recent Technological Advancements in Finance, Economics and Management"**, edited by the School of Economics and Commerce (SOEC) of CMR University, Bengaluru.

The contemporary world is witnessing a profound transformation driven by rapid technological advancements, reshaping the very foundations of finance, economics, and management. This book, Recent Technological Advancements in Finance, Economics and Management, provides an insightful exploration of these transformative trends. It delves into the multifaceted impact of technology, offering a nuanced understanding of its implications for financial systems, economic policies, and management practices. Through a diverse array of perspectives and analyses, this book bridges the gap between theoretical frameworks and practical applications, making it an invaluable resource for academics, professionals, and policymakers.

The chapters in this book collectively illuminate how technology fosters innovation, enhances sustainability, and addresses complex global challenges. From redefining traditional business models to promoting inclusive economic growth, the contributions underscore the critical role of technology in shaping a resilient and equitable future.

As we navigate this dynamic era, this book serves as a beacon of knowledge, inspiring thought leadership and informed action. It is with great enthusiasm that I present this compendium to the readers, confident that it will spark intellectual curiosity and meaningful dialogue.

This book, I am sure, will serve as a vibrant platform for the exchange of ideas and insights. It brings together the works of leading academicians, scholars, and practitioners who have shared their research outcomes, offering valuable perspectives to fellow readers and researchers. The discussions and analyses presented in this book provide a comprehensive glimpse of recent advances in the fields of Economics, Finance, Management, and Technology, aimed at fostering a robust environment for achieving the goals of "Amrit Kaal."

My best wishes are with the authors and editorial team for the resounding success of this book. May it inspire and guide readers in their pursuit of knowledge and innovation.


**Dr. H.B. Raghavendra**
*Vice Chancellor*
CMR University Bangalore

# Chairman's Message

I am truly exultant that CMR University has consistently been dedicated to fostering excellence in education, research, and innovation, believing in nurturing a dynamic learning environment that empowers our students and researchers to become leaders and change-makers in their respective fields.

The School of Economics and Commerce (SOEC) of CMR University has brought together a collection of invaluable insights in the book "Recent Technological Advancements in Finance, Economics and Management", which addresses topics that are currently capturing the attention of academicians, researchers, and industries on a global scale. The book emphasizes the latest trends in Economics, Finance, Management, and Technology, exploring all dimensions of these fields with a focus on achieving the Sustainable Development Goals (SDG) set by the UNDP.

I extend my warm greetings and felicitations to the authors and contributors of this book. I wish the book great success and hope it inspires readers to engage deeply with its content, advancing knowledge and innovation in the fields it covers.

**Dr. K.C. Ramamurthy**
Former Member of Parliament, Rajaya Sabha
Inspector General of Police (Retd.)
Chairman, CMR Group of Institutions and CMR University

# Chancellor's Message

*Dear Faculty Members, Students, and Esteemed Guests,*

I am delighted that CMR University's School of Economics and Commerce (SOEC) is presenting this insightful book on 'Recent Technological Advancements in Finance, Economics, and Management'. We live in an era where rapid changes in these fields are reshaping economies, businesses, and societies. In such a dynamic landscape, it is crucial for academic institutions like CMR University to nurture interactions with experts, instil a spirit of research in young minds, and create platforms that inspire research-oriented learning.

This book is a testimony to our combined pursuit of knowledge and innovation—key drivers in addressing complex economic challenges faced by nations across the globe. By exploring emerging trends and concepts, it serves as a treasured resource for students, researchers, and professionals, providing fresh perspectives which can influence both classrooms and workplaces.

I am confident that the ideas and discussions summarized in these pages will spark meaningful discourse and contribute to a deeper understanding of the evolving landscape of finance, economics, and management.

I extend my best wishes for the grand success of this book and hope it inspires ceaseless exploration and innovation in these critical spheres.

**Dr. Sabitha Ramamurthy**
*Chancellor*
CMR University

# Pro-Chancellor's Message

As the Pro-Chancellor of this esteemed CMR University, I am thrilled to witness the convergence of brilliant minds from across the globe, coming together to engage in intellectual discourse, exchange innovative ideas, and foster collaborative efforts towards advancing the frontiers of knowledge in the fields of Economics, Finance, Management, and Technology.

I extend a warm welcome to all the readers of this insightful book compiled by the School of Economics and Commerce (SOEC). The themes underscore the fact that areas like economics, finance, and technology are undergoing rapid and transformative changes. I am confident that the high-quality research and perspectives presented in this book will provide valuable insights for policymakers, contributing to the accelerated economic growth of the country. This book will undoubtedly serve as a significant milestone in the nation's journey toward achieving the $5 trillion economy target.

I congratulate the editorial team for curating such a remarkable collection. I wish all the readers a deeply enriching experience and success in their future endeavors.

**Shri K.R. Jayadeep**
*Pro-Chancellor*
CMR University

# Provost's Message

It is with great pride that I acknowledge the publication of this academic volume, which brings together fresh perspectives and scholarly contributions in the fields of economics, finance, management, and technology. This compilation stands as a testament to the intellectual curiosity, research rigor, and collaborative spirit that define our academic community.

In an era defined by rapid technological evolution and shifting economic paradigms, the role of research in shaping inclusive and adaptive financial systems has never been more critical. This compilation of selected papers captures both the urgency and opportunity of our times—bringing together insights that can inform policy, transform practice, and inspire innovation.

My heartfelt congratulations to all the contributors, faculty, and organizers who made this endeavour possible. May this volume serve as a valuable reference for scholars, practitioners, and students alike, and continue to advance the collective pursuit of knowledge for the public good.

**Dr. Tristha Ramamurthy**
*Provost*
CMR University

# Registrar's Message

As the excitement builds, it is my honor to extend a heartfelt welcome to the upcoming book on "Recent Technological Advancements in Finance, Economics and Management" edited by the School of Economics and Commerce at CMR University, Bengaluru, India. This book promises to be a dynamic collection of insights from global scholars, researchers, and practitioners, sharing ground-breaking ideas and exploring the latest advancements in Economics, Management, and Technology.

The book presents enlightening contributions, thought-provoking discussions, and a diverse array of research papers, providing a platform for the exchange of innovative ideas and the exploration of current trends in these fields. I extend my sincere appreciation to all the editors, authors and contributors for their enthusiastic support and commitment.

**Dr. Praveen R.**
*Registrar*
CMR University

# Presidential Address
## *(Inaugural Session)*

***Dear Faculty Members, Students, and Esteemed Guests,***

It is an absolute pleasure to stand before you today and address this gathering of bright minds and passionate learners. This conference brings together distinguished professors and experts who share their invaluable insights on Economics, Management, Technology, and various other fields that shape the world we live in. These discussions serve as more than just academic discourses; they provide us with the opportunity to reflect on our roles and responsibilities in an ever-evolving global landscape.

As students, you are driven by curiosity, ambition, and the desire to excel in your chosen fields. However, true education extends far beyond textbooks and classroom instruction. It lies in the ability to stay updated with the world around you, to engage in interdisciplinary conversations, and to participate in conferences & discussions that broaden your perspective. A law student, for example, can benefit greatly from understanding economic policies, just as a management student can gain significant insights from advancements in technology. The ability to connect different domains of knowledge will be your greatest asset in a complex, interconnected world.

In alignment with the National Education Policy (NEP), our university has introduced a range of courses designed to provide a holistic and well-rounded education. These programs offer you the opportunity to explore diverse fields, identify your strengths, and to be well-informed decisions about your future. Whether you choose to pursue postgraduate studies, engage in internships, or step into the professional world, self-awareness and adaptability will play a crucial role in your success. The future belongs to those who are not only knowledgeable but also flexible in their thinking and approach.

Beyond academic excellence, it is necessary to reflect on your values, ethics, and responsibilities toward society. Ask yourself: *What impact do I wish to create? How can I contribute meaningfully to my community, my nation, and the world?* In the past, career choices were often limited to conventional fields such as engineering, medicine, banking, or teaching. Today, the landscape has evolved, presenting countless opportunities that integrate business, research, and innovation into various industries. The challenge now is not the lack of opportunities but the ability to identify where your true potential lies and how best to harness it.

Rather than merely criticizing institutions and industries, I encourage you to take time and understand them—how they function, the challenges they face, and the role you can play in shaping them for the better. Developing this mindset will allow you to grow not only as professionals but also as individuals capable of driving meaningful change in society.

As India continues to rise as a global leader in various sectors, it is imperative for us to take pride in our achievements while also recognizing our responsibilities. Even as students, you have the power to make a difference. Service-learning programs, internships or active community engagement, reflect on what you have contributed each month. Cultivating this habit of giving back will shape you into responsible and compassionate leaders who contribute positively to society.

The COVID-19 pandemic brought along many challenges, particularly for students who were unable to experience social interactions and real-world exposure. However, it also reinforced the importance of resilience, adaptability, and community engagement. As you move forward, I urge you to embrace a mindset of continuous learning. Take advantage of the wealth of knowledge available through AI, digital platforms, and research tools. Delve deep into subjects that spark your curiosity, and never stop seeking knowledge.

Most importantly, amidst your ambitions and aspirations, do not forget the significance of inner peace. Self-reflection and mindfulness are essential in guiding you towards clarity and satisfaction. Just as we explore external knowledge, we must also explore ourselves. Once you embark on this journey of self-discovery, you will find your path, your purpose, and ultimately, happiness.

Wishing you all success in your pursuit of knowledge, and personal growth.

Thank you

**Dr. Sabitha Ramamurthy**
*Chancellor*
CMR University

# Inaugural Address (Prof. Prem Vrat)

Dr. Sabitha Ramamurthy, Chancellor, CMR University, Dr. KC Ramamurthy, Prof. Prahlad Kumar, Prof. MM Goel, Shri Jayadpeep K.R. Reddy, Dr. Trisha Ramamurthy, Prof. HB Raghvendra, Dr. Praveen R., Dr. B.B. Tiwari; delegates to the conference; faculty, students, ladies and gentlemen.

I greet you all in this inaugural session of the International conference at CMR University and thank Prof. HB Raghvendra, Vice-Chancellor for inviting me to the conference as the Chief Guest at the inaugural session. The theme of the conference though looks all-encompassing yet is very relevant to focus on integrated systems approach in problem solving in a highly inter-connected world where there is interplay of various aspects in influencing system behavior.

It is an honor for me to address on the theme that resonates profoundly with the very essence of our contemporary world: Economics, Finance, Management, and Technology in 2024. These four pillars not only define the landscape of our societies but also hold the key to unlocking the potential for a future of unprecedented progress and prosperity. Every system has these four aspects as well as the situational context in which it operates. The current business environment is called as VUCA (Volatile, Uncertain, Complex and Ambiguous) and in line with systems thinking and contingency theory of management; as decision makers we need to consider the interplay of economics; finance, technology and management and the situation to determine right policy options to achieve our organizational objectives. Since each of these four pillars of knowledge society are evolving; the recent advances in each of these will enable us to find the right solution to our problems using the latest knowledge on the subject.

As we gather here, we find ourselves at a pivotal juncture in history, where the convergence of these disciplines is reshaping the fabric of our existence. In every corner of the globe, technological innovation is driving economic growth, revolutionizing financial systems, transforming management practices, and fundamentally altering the way we live, work, and interact with one another.

In the realm of economics, we are witnessing a profound shift towards a knowledge-based economy driven by innovation and digitalization. Traditional industries are being disrupted, and new paradigms are emerging, presenting both challenges and opportunities. As economies navigate this transition, it is imperative that we foster environments that nurture creativity, entrepreneurship, and inclusive growth. Behavioural economics is addressing issues concerning rationalist theoretical economics.

Similarly, the domain of finance is undergoing a seismic transformation fueled by advancements in technology. From the proliferation of fintech solutions to the rise of decentralized finance (DeFi) and digital currencies, the financial landscape is evolving at an unprecedented pace. As stewards of financial systems, we must embrace innovation while ensuring stability, security, and equitable access to financial services for all. Blockchain technology is impacting supply chains to ensure safe financial transactions.

Furthermore, effective management practices are more critical than ever in navigating the complexities of our interconnected world. As organizations grapple with rapid change, leaders must possess not only technical expertise but also the ability to inspire, adapt, and drive meaningful change. Strategic management frameworks that prioritize agility, sustainability, and ethical decision-making are essential for navigating the uncertainties of the 21$^{st}$ century.

At the heart of this transformation lies technology, the catalyst that is driving progress across all fronts. From artificial intelligence and machine learning to blockchain and the Internet of Things, technological innovation is reshaping industries, redefining business models, and revolutionizing the way we approach challenges. However, with great power comes great responsibility, and it is incumbent upon us to ensure that technology is harnessed for the greater good, fostering innovation that is ethical, inclusive, and sustainable. It is the coordinated efforts in integrating people, process and technology for the good of human kind that is real challenge in management. Industry 4.0 concepts of managing cyber-physical systems can be a game changer if we can address concerns of cyber security.

As we contemplate the interplay of these disciplines, let us not forget the human dimension that underpins all our endeavors. Ultimately, the success of our collective efforts will be measured not only by economic metrics but also by the extent to which we improve the lives of people around the world.

In closing, I am filled with optimism for the future that lies ahead. By harnessing the transformative power of Economic, Finance, Management, and Technology in 2024 and beyond, we have the opportunity to build a world that is more prosperous, more equitable, and more sustainable for generations to come.

Thank you!

**Prof. Prem Vrat**
*Pro-Chancellor,*
The NorthCap University, Gurugram
Chairman, BoG, IIT (ISM) Dhanbad

# Inaugural Address: Guest of Honour (Prof. Prahlad Kumar)

*"Aa no bhadrah krutvoh yantu vishwatah"*

*Rigveda sanhita, Mandal 1, suktam 89*

**"May noble thoughts come to us from every side."**

In the present era of globalization where countries are fighting or are engaged in fighting with each other either on territorial issues, political ideology, supremacy of their religion or race or to show off their military and economic power, the guiding Indian philosophy for development is:

*"Vasudheve kutumbkam"*

**i.e., the whole earth is our family.**

This Sanskrit verse has its roots in *Maha Upanishad* and this was aptly adopted in, the 18th G-20 Summit held in September 2023 in New Delhi. It was translated into English as, "**One Earth, One Family, and One Future**." This translation captures the essence of global togetherness and shared aspirations. It highlights that actions in one part of the world have far reaching effects globally. It also necessitates a commitment to environmental conservation, and encourages sustainable practices and the protection of bio-diversity.

The presence of eminent personalities, academic administrators, educationists, technocrats, policy makers and game changers in the Conference and their thought-provoking ideas would definitely ignite the young minds to shape the destiny of "Vikasit Bharat" by 2047. The New Education Policy 2020 emphasizes on developing the hidden talent and potential in children and youth by incorporating and inculcating the ideas of self-esteem, confidence, constructiveness, innovation and entrepreneurship. The education system should produce such youths who are not job-seekers but are job-providers. We are aware that our country, Bharat has the largest reservoir of *'demographic dividend.'* The demographic dividend shows the potential for economic gains when the share of working-age population (15–64 years) is higher than the non-working age population (14 and younger, and 65 and older).According to the Economic Survey 2018–19, India's demographic dividend would peak around 2041, when the share of working age i.e. 20–59 years (lesser band), population is expected to hit 59 percent. It means, with more in the labour force and fewer children to support, India will have a window of opportunity for achieving higher economic growth. It is interesting to note that India had one of the youngest populations in an aging world. It was estimated that the median age in India in 2020 was around 28 years while it was 37 years in China and US, 45 years in Western Europe, and 49 years in Japan. By 2030, India's working age population is expected to be 1.04 billion i.e. 104 crore with a dependency ratio at 31.2 percent. This would be the lowest in its history. Since 2018, this bulge in the working age population is going to last till 2055 or 37 years from its beginning in 2018. It would be of interest to know the findings of a study on demographic dividend in India by United Nations Population Fund (UNFPA) which mentions:

- The window of demographic dividend opportunity in India is available for five decades from 2005–06 to 2055–56, longer than any other country in the world.
- This demographic dividend is available at different times in different states because of differential behavior of the population parameters.

The question arises why demographic dividend has become so important for the rapid economic growth of the countries. Historically, it was found that demographic dividend has contributed up to 15 percent of the overall growth in advanced countries. Japan was among the first major economies to experience rapid growth because of changing population structure. Its period of demographic dividend was 1964–2004. The changing age structure resulting in higher working age population & lower dependent population during this period enhances labour productivity, raises the women's workforce accompanied by a decline in fertility, diverts resources from spending on children to investing in physical and human infra-structure, increases the savings rate besides there is a massive shift towards middle class society, that is, the rise of aspiration class. Naturally, this situation simultaneously poses challenges before the economy. The asymmetric demographic situation in a large country like India concentrates this dividend in poorest states; they have lack of skills, are low in human development parameters, the nature of the economy being mostly informal and are likely to have jobless growth.

It is pertinent to throw more light on employment aspect. Less than half of urban workers have full time jobs while far too much of India's employment is in under-productive informal sectors. **Education, skill-building, and health care are grossly inadequate**. As per NSSO Periodic Labour Force Survey 2017–18, India's labour force participation rate for the age-group 15–59 years was around 53 percent, that is, around half of the working age population was jobless. In another Report by the NCAER (2018), out of more than 5 lakh final year bachelor's students aged 18–29 years (who were surveyed), around 54 percent were found to be "unemployable". The India Skills Report, 2023 found only half of young Indians are employable. More so, according to World Bank Report (June, 2022), female labour participation rate has been in a steady decline, having dropped from 32 percent in 2005 to 19 percent in 2021. To overcome this problem, cultural and organizational changes are needed to create on-ramps for women in the work-force and retain them. We know that The NEP 2020 addresses this issue of employment in the organized/unorganised sector – of the male/female employment. In a latest Report, it was disclosed that 36 percent fresher students of IIT, Mumbai this year, could not be placed till date. The figure for IIT, Delhi was 40 percent and IIT, Kanpur 31 percent. These students are struggling to be placed in the job market. What has emerged from the employers is that they require specific degrees rather than generic degrees. Here comes the role of the Government, private investors, institutions/ universities and the industry. The Government and other parties are required to invest in the training for emerging jobs and skills. Similar was the case with MBA degrees that till January 2024, 55 percent of degree holders could not be placed appropriately. To deal with such a problem, the need is to build human capital by:

(i) Identifying the emerging skills, and
(ii) Creating institutions for them.

The emerging skills for example may be related to:

1. Sustainability skills,
2. Data analytics,
3. Machine learning and AI modeling,
4. Synthetic Biology and Bioengineering,
5. Cyber security: protecting systems and data etc.

The United Arab Emirates (UAE) has taken a lead and established first

Artificial Intelligence College, than why India cann't emulates this? The above description clearly emphasizes on the fact that the theoretical knowledge of the subjects such as Economics, Commerce, Management and Technology is not sufficient to achieve the goal of Vikasit Bharat @ 2047 unless we address to the

Above issues seriously and create an environment of optimism, and invest in training in emerging skills and create suitable institutions. We Bhartiya have that zeal, and can transform the economy into a Vikasit Bharat by 2047, or even earlier.

*Yada bhawam, tad bhawati* |

i.e., you become as you think. It means that your inner thoughts create your reality.

I take an example of Artificial Intelligence (AI) and how it may affect business operations. AI powered automation and optimization algorithms have streamlined production processes, supply chain management, and resource allocation. Businesses can now operate more efficiently, reduce costs, and increase productivity, resulting in boosting economic output. Secondly, AI, in fact, create new job opportunities and transforms existing ones. Ai has created a demand for skilled professionals who can develop, implement, and maintain AI systems. Moreover, AI augments human capabilities, allowing workers to focus on more creative and high value tasks while AI handles repetitive and mundane work.

Innovations in healthcare, finance and manufacturing have led to the creation of entirely new job categories. For example, AI has driven the growth of Tele- health industry, creating opportunities for remote medical professionals and AI specialists. The financial sector also benefits from AI powered trading algorithms, leading to the rise of quant analysis and AI engineers. AI is also assisting the Government in policy-formulation, implementation, and evaluation.

In the foregoing discussion, I have restricted myself to two issues only and highlighted the importance of population dividend for our country but this advantage has poised challenges on building human capital i.e. investing in people through quality education, skill development, healthcare and jobs. A minimum of 10 million jobs per year are to be generated in the economy to reap the benefits of demographic dividend. The NEP 2020 along with the readiness of the economy to accept, adapt and adopt the emerging technological changes will convert these challenges into an opportunity to become a *Vikasit Bharat.* The education system should be flexible and should respond to the emerging areas in scientific and technological fields. The 21$^{st}$ century is the century for knowledge, innovation and research, and these should be utilized for sustainable steady growth of Bharat. Our aim is to move from *Amrit Kaal* to *Kartavya Kaal i.e.* to make *"India a developed nation by 2047."*

In the end, I would like to thank the organizers, especially Prof. B.B. Tiwari and his entire team along with the Registrar, Finance Officer & other officials of the University for organizing such an excellent event on the recent advances in Economics, Commerce, Management & Technology. These areas are very crucial for Bharat to become a developed country by 2047. Our period of **Kartavya Kaal** is extremely critical and important for all the Bhartiya.

**Prof. Prahlad Kumar**
*Ex-Dean,*
Faculty of Commerce,
University of Allahabad

# Keynote Address: Valedictory Session (Prof. S. Indrakant)

## THE JOURNEY OF THE ECONOMISTS

The path travelled by the Economists is characterised by many ups and downs coupled by sharp turnings in response to the changes in World Economy. Interestingly different Groups of Economists took different routes based on their perception of the Economy which resulted in the evolution of different Schools of Thought.

Physiocrats, who were popular in France perceived that land and land alone has the capacity to produce Surplus as it gives more output than what it consumes. In due course of time, Mercantlists dominated the scene and argued that the Trade was the Engine of the Growth. A country having larger exports and lower imports is bound to grow faster.

Adam Smith, who is considered as Father of Economics by the Continental Economists, taking more comprehensive view of the Economy made an inquiry into the nature and causes of Wealth of Nation. David Ricardo examined the dynamic Laws of Distribution of output among different factors of production namely workers, capitalists and rentiers. He argued that due to the increase in population, the cultivation of food grains is extended to less fertile land and the rent on the intra-marginal land will increase. As a result rentier class benefits while entrepreneurs suffer due to decline in land productivity. Wage rate cannot be reduced below the subsistence level. With passage of time, the rate of profit will tend to zero and there will be decline in investment. He concluded that due to scarcity of fertile land, the economy will reach Stationary State. The Technical Progress at the best will postpone the attainment of Stationary State. That is why Economics was referred as Dismal Science. T.R. Malthus, comparing the growth rate of food grains with that of population arrived at similar conclusion. He believed that food grains will grow in arithmetic progression while population grows in geomagnetic progression. In literature, these Economists are generally referred to as Classical Economists.

Thanks to the fruits of Technical Progress, no serious economic crisis were encountered by the advanced countries. So the Mainstream Economists shifted their attention from the working of the whole economy to the rational behaviour of individual economic agents like consumers, producers, workers and interaction among them. Implicit belief was that interaction among the economic agents will lead to a equilibrium situation which is optimal and beneficial to all the stake-holders. Jevons, Menger and Walras made important contribution in this Area. Marshall tried to syntheses the differences which existed among the Mainstream Economists.

However, a good number of Economists had a different view about the dynamics of the World Economy. Marx visualised that the Economy is composed of Classes having conflicting interest in which one Class (Capitalist) benefits at the expense of another Class (Workers). In other words, the Economy is composed of Classes having conflicting interest. Structralists argued that countries at the core developed at the cost of countries at the periphery. Others focused on institutional factors in the process of Development. At the same time, some Economists like Lewis, Nurkse, Rostow, and Hirschman took interest in issues relating to Growth and Development.

The honeymoon period of the Mainstream Economists came to an end in 1929 when the World Economy encountered Great Depression. Keynes looking from macro perspective diagonised that a lack of Effective Demand was the cause for the Depression and advocated for Government Intervention to boost effective demand and the capability of markets was questioned.

In due course of time the focus shifted to examination of the determinants of Long-run and Steady Growth. The works of Harrod, Domar, Kaldor, Solow and Von Neumann are worth-noting.. Building big macro-level, multi-sectoral and long-run plan models became the order of the day on account of availability of Computer Facilities. In this regard, the contributions of Leontief, Timberland, Mahalanobis, Gautam Mathur and Chakravarty were some of the important works. However, in the Era of Liberalisation, Privatisation and Globalisation, the role of these models seems to have reduced.

In the recent years, a new branch of Economics called Behavioural Economics has emerged. It is argued that people make decision based on perceived gains and losses, often valuing losses more than gains. In this respect, the contribution of Psychologists is substantial. In fact, Kahneman, a Psychologist, was awarded Nobel Prize in Economics in 2002 for his work in the field of Behavioural Economics.

Interestingly money as a medium of exchange was introduced into the Economy to overcome the difficulties like double-coincidence of Wants faced under Barter System, a system in which goods were exchanged for goods. Under Barter System, if a farmer wants to sell Milk to buy fodder for his cattle then he has to look for a person who is willing to buy milk and sell fodder. It is very difficult task. Money as a medium of exchange has simplified the operation. The farmer first sells the milk to a person Interested in buying milk for cash and with that cash buys fodder from a person selling fodder. This has smoothened the process of transaction. However, cash transaction becomes risky when the volume of transaction is large and the number of transaction is large. So on-line payment are becoming popular. Further, financial inclusion of so far unreached segments of the population is taking place at a rapid pace. Economy is getting digitalised. No doubt, it is not an unmixed blessings. Innocent persons are becoming victims of cyber crimes. In addition, old institutions like Planning Commission are being replaced by new institutions like NITI Aayog. Simultaneously financial and Fiscal Reforms having far reaching implications have been introduced. All these items have entered into agenda of Economists.

Not only the areas of Research changed with time, even the tools of analysis have undergone a radical change. The use of Mathematical and Statistical tools has become very common. Sophisticated Econometric Techniques are being used to estimate the parameters of Policy- oriented models. Availability of packages and computer facilities has enabled the the Economists to carry out a large number of simulation exercises. Articles appearing in some journals are highly mathematical in nature. In such articles, there are more equations and symbols than the number of sentences without symbols. It makes one to wonder whether it is a article in Economics or in Mathematics. Without the knowledge of quantitative techniques, it is difficult to understand the content of such articles. Long time back Walras had predicted that people without the knowledge of Mathematics have no role in Economics. It appears we are fast reaching that stage.

It is not out of place to make a few observations on Technology. In fact Technical Progress is a double-edged sword. It must be encouraged so long as it is environment-friendly but Technical Progress which adversely affects the environment should be avoided.

Release of waste water and used chemical detergent from the conventional washing machine pollutes our water bodies. A startup company in Chandigarh has come up with a new washing machine which uses less chemical detergents and water and kills bacteria by using radio frequency based microwaves.

The immense capacity of technology can be grasped by the fact Netherland with land equivalent to 2% of that of India produces 3 times the foodgrains production of India by using drone, robots, mobiles, greenhouse cultivation etc. India can also explore the possibility of a) enhancing the production of fish and other marine products by deep sea fishing, b) increasing the milk production by providing better quality of fodder at subsidised rate and thereby making livestock breeding more economical.

Perseverance and sustained interest is essential to enjoy the fruits of innovation. A factual information brings clarity on this issue. Kothilwa village near Gaya in Bihar State, is inhabitated by 700 persons and there is only one well which provides drinking water to the villagers. Farmers cultivate jowar solely depending on the scanty rainfall as the tank in the village usually gets dried up. People in the working age-group migrate to Gaya for labour work. In contrast, Loungi Bhuiyan, a farmer daily early in the morning goes to the top of the near-by hill and starts digging Canal. He pleaded with fellow villagers to join their hands in his work. Instead of helping him, they laughed at him. Even his wife and children drove him out of house accusing him as mad person and left for Gaya. Unmindful of all these things, he continued with his daily routine of going to the top of the hill early in the morning and start digging Canal single-handedly. Once the work was completed, the rain water from the hill started filling up the tank. Farmers started cultivating their land. Loungi Bhuiyan completed the work not for money or any award but only for his villagers. In recognition of his achievement, Chief Minister of Bihar, Prime Minister of India, other political leaders and Press Reporters visited the village to appreciate his work. He is called Inspiration Man of Bihar. The people who ridiculed him once as mad man have erected his statue. The country which is blessed with persons like Loungi Bhuiyan will definitely become a super power by 2047.

Dear participants perseverance and sustained interest are essential to do good Research. The conference has provided good food both to mind and body. You should be ready with your Research findings in the next Conference.

With best wishes

**S. Indrakant**

*Visiting Professor,*

Centre for Economics and Social Studies,

Begumpet, Hyderabad-500016

# Needonomics for Management of Fintech with Needo-use of Artificial Intelligence (AI)

## KEYNOTE ADDRESS
## (Prof. M.M. Goel)

**Professor Madan Mohan Goel***

Needonomics (economics of needs) and essentially refers to the study or understanding of human needs and how they drive economic behavior. In the context of the management of fintech (financial technology), understanding needonomics is crucial for developing products and services that cater to the genuine needs of consumers. India has seen significant growth in its fintech sector in recent years, with numerous companies emerging to offer a wide range of financial services leveraging technology. Some prominent fintech companies offering digital payment solutions, e-commerce services and Unified Payments Interface (UPI) ecosystem in India includes Paytm, PhonePe, MobiKwik, CRED etc. Razorpay provides payment gateway solutions, payment processing services, and business banking services for businesses of all sizes. It offers a range of products including payment links, subscription billing, and online store payments. Policybazaar is India's largest online insurance aggregator, allowing users to compare and purchase various insurance products including health insurance, life insurance, and car insurance. It provides a platform for users to research, compare, and buy insurance policies online. Zerodha is a fintech company that operates as a discount brokerage firm offering online trading services in stocks, commodities, and mutual funds. It is known for its low-cost trading model and innovative trading platforms. Lendingkart is a fintech platform that provides working capital loans and business loans to small and medium enterprises (SMEs) in India. It uses technology and data analytics to assess the creditworthiness of borrowers and streamline the lending process. CRED is a members-only platform that rewards users for paying their credit card bills on time. It offers various benefits such as cashback, discounts, and access to exclusive rewards and experiences. These are just a few examples of the many fintech companies operating in India, showcasing the diversity and innovation within the fintech ecosystem of Bharat to be Viksit by 2047.

### Needonomics applies to fintech as under:

- **Understanding Consumer Needs:** Fintech companies must deeply understand the financial needs and pain points of consumers. This involves studying their spending habits, saving patterns, investment goals, and overall financial well-being.

- **Personalization and Customization**: Fintech solutions should be tailored to individual needs as much as possible. This might involve personalized budgeting tools; investment advice based on individual risk profiles and customized savings plans.
- **Accessibility and Inclusion**: Needonomics in fintech also emphasizes making financial services accessible to all, including those who are traditionally underserved or marginalized. This might involve developing solutions for people with lower incomes, limited access to traditional banking services, or those with disabilities.
- **Affordability**: Fintech solutions should be affordable for users across different socio-economic backgrounds. This means considering pricing models that are transparent and fair, with minimal fees that don't disproportionately impact those with lower incomes.
- **Financial Education:** Educating consumers about financial literacy and empowering them to make informed decisions is a key aspect of needonomics in fintech. This might involve providing resources, tools, and educational content to help users improve their financial knowledge and skills.
- **Security and Trust**: Building trust is essential in fintech, particularly when handling sensitive financial information. Fintech companies must prioritize security measures to protect user data and transactions, thereby fulfilling the need for safety and trust among consumers.
- **Innovation with Purpose**: Fintech innovation should be driven by a genuine desire to address real consumer needs rather than simply chasing technological trends. By focusing on solving actual problems faced by consumers, fintech companies can create more meaningful and impactful solutions.

To incorporate needonomics into fintech involves a human-centered approach that prioritizes understanding and addressing the genuine needs of consumers, thereby creating more inclusive, accessible, and beneficial financial services and products.

## NEEDO-USE OF ARTIFICIAL INTELLIGENCE (AI)

AI plays a significant role in revolutionizing the fintech industry, offering innovative solutions to various challenges and enhancing efficiency, accuracy, and customer experience. Some key uses of AI in Fintech include:

- **Risk Assessment and Fraud Detection:** AI algorithms analyze large volumes of data to assess credit risk, detect fraudulent activities, and identify potential security breaches. Machine learning models can detect anomalies in transactions, flagging suspicious activities in real-time to prevent financial losses.

- **Customer Service and Chatbots**: AI-powered chatbots and virtual assistants provide personalized customer support, answer queries, and guide users through various financial processes. Natural Language Processing (NLP) enables chatbots to understand and respond to customer inquiries effectively, improving user experience and reducing wait times.
- **Credit Scoring and Underwriting:** AI algorithms analyze diverse data sources, including transaction history, social media behavior, and alternative data, to assess creditworthiness and streamline the under-writing process. This enables lenders to make more accurate lending decisions and offer tailored financial products to customers.
- **Algorithmic Trading and Investment Management**: AI-driven trading algorithms execute trades autonomously, leveraging vast datasets and complex models to identify market trends, predict price movements, and optimize investment strategies. AI-powered robo-advisors offer automated portfolio management services, providing personalized investment advice based on individual risk profiles and financial goals.
- **Personalized Financial Recommendations:** AI analyzes user data, including spending habits, income levels, and financial goals, to offer personalized financial recommendations and insights. This could include budgeting advice, investment suggestions, or customized insurance plans, enhancing financial literacy and helping users make informed decisions.
- **Fraud Prevention and Anti-Money Laundering (AML)**: AI algorithms analyze transaction patterns and behavior to detect suspicious activities indicative of money laundering or fraudulent behavior. By monitoring transactions in real-time and flagging potential risks, AI helps financial institutions comply with regulatory requirements and mitigate financial crime.

Predictive Analytics and Market Insights: AI algorithms analyze historical data and market trends to generate predictive insights, forecast market conditions, and identify investment opportunities. This enables investors and financial institutions to make data-driven decisions and stay ahead of market fluctuations.

Regulatory Compliance and Risk Management: AI automates compliance processes, helping financial institutions navigate complex regulatory frameworks and ensure adherence to legal requirements. By monitoring regulatory changes and analyzing compliance data, AI helps mitigate compliance risks and avoid costly penalties.

AI technologies continue to drive innovation and transformation across the fintech industry, offering powerful tools to improve decision-making, enhance operational efficiency, and deliver superior customer experiences.

Management of the contemporary world calls for the stakeholders to become street SMART (simple, moral, action-oriented, responsive and transparent) in understanding and using Gita-based needonomics. To achieve success in the endeavors, the stakeholders (C,P,D,T) must convert monkey mind (misuse of AI) to monk mind ( use of SI).

## CONCLUSION

To address the entire domain of the issues in economics, finance, management & technology in present times, we must understand and adopt needonomics as ethical and environmental friendly approach. Needo-adopt Gita-based Needonomics for the solutions of the contemporary problems caused by Greedonomics. Like a honey bee collecting just enough to sustain but not too much to destroy, economic practices should align with the principles of managing society responsibly. To fetch the fortunes in present times of global competition, we need to create business environment for Intellectual Property Rights (IPR) with its understanding and implications for converting into business proposition. The stakeholders must think out – of-the-box solutions on different aspects of the economy including needo-consumption, needo-saving, needo-production, needo-investment, needo-distribution, needo-altruism, needo-trade for ensuring needo-wealth, needo-health and needo-happiness of the people. To achieve success in all the endeavors of contemporary world, the stakeholders must convert monkey mind (misuse of AI) to monk mind (use of SI). We must become street SMART (simple, moral, action-oriented, responsive & transparent) with needonomics as a common sense approach.

***The writer Prof M.M. Goel is three-time Vice-Chancellor known as Propounder Needonomics School of Thought superannuated Professor of Economics from Kurukshetra University, Kurukshetra.**

**E-mail: mmgoel2001@yahoo.co.in**

# Editorial Remarks

Research a journey of exploring and experiencing the new insights to the existing theories and bank of knowledge in the selected area of study. School of Economics and Commerce, CMR University made an humble effort in this direction by joining the hands and getting connected with industry and academia people to bring in new outlook from research perspective by organizing an International Conference "ICREFMT-2024", an platform to meet both expert and intellectual minds, discuss, interact and contribute, the solution and path way for finding solutions to research questions raised, debated through this platform. Intellectuals, industrialist and research across India and Abroad participated to make this event special. Economics, Finance, Management and Technology were the key Buss-words areas for research papers and their presentations. The research papers were presented on the various themes and sub themes of the subjects selected for the conference.

It is with great pleasure that we present this Edited Volume, which encapsulates the rich and diverse research contributions from the recent conference dedicated to the fields of Finance, Economics, Management, and Technology – "ICREFMT-2024". This book stands as a testament to the vibrant academic discourse and cutting-edge research that continues to shape these dynamic fields.

The conference, which brought together scholars, practitioners, and thought leaders from around the globe, served as a platform for exploring the intersections between Finance, Economics, Management, and Technology. The papers compiled in this volume reflect the depth and breadth of current research trends and innovations, providing valuable insights into the evolving landscape of these following disciplines.

## Economics Section

The economics papers address a range of critical issues, from Macro-economic policies to Micro-economic behavior. They offer nuanced analyses of economic phenomena and policy implications, enriched by empirical data and theoretical advancements. This section reflects the ongoing dialogue about economic stability, growth, and equity.

The research papers presented in area of Economics are of varied in nature. Covering the Marco element as "Strategies for Digital Economy and Sustainable Rural Development" by Farhatnida Unnisa, Nilaish and Dr Bhupendra Bahadur Tiwari to Micro aspects like "The empowerment of rural women which is a critical component of inclusive and sustainable development, particularly in the context of India. The study of Cashless

Economy with Reference to Micro and Small Enterprises by Pratima Katti discusses about the major challenges like cyber fraud, lower digital literacy levels and attitude of people towards adoption have to be addressed to enhance penetration of cashless economy.

One more major study discusses about the perception towards "Digital Finance in Bengaluru City" by Mr. Chacko Jose P. Principal St Aloysius College, Elthuruth, Thrissur, Kerala and Ms. Neha Banu Assistant Professor CMR University, Bangalore.

Other scholars research papers discuss about Social and Economic Services Expenditure and Economic Growth, Unveiling Government Schemes leading to Empowering India, The Impact of Exchange Rate Volatility on India's Agricultural Exports Using Bounds Test Approach etc. The research papers have employed various new research methods, Statistical tools, models which were extensively discuss in the conference presentations.

## Finance Section

The contributions in the finance section delve into new methodologies, analytical tools, and empirical findings that offer fresh perspectives on financial markets, risk management, and investment strategies. The research highlights emerging trends and challenges, underscoring the need for adaptive financial models in a rapidly changing environment.

A Study of Various Schemes Available for SME's – A Case Study In State Bank Of India: by Prof. Shivanna J. discusses about the various schemes that bridges the Gap between the demand and supply of monetary support from the financial institutions particularly the SBI to its various Small and Medium Enterprises through its various schemes.

Connecting to the previous studies Ms. Sania Bassi, Research Scholar, School of Business Studies, College of Basic Sciences and Humanities, Punjab Agricultural University, Ludhiana, Punjab discusses through her research paper "Issues and Challenges of Crop Insurance" – A Conceptual Study" about the various challenges and issues that are faced by the agriculturists in the State of Punjab and how the Crop Insurance is supporting them and what are ground challenges they are facing in realizing the insurance claims. "Relationship between Product Differentiation and Brand Equity" T.D. Hemamalini1 and M. Kamaraj discuses about the Product differentiation which is instrumental in driving brand equity by creating a unique position in the marketplace.

Few more research papers discuss about the financial markets, behavioral finance, financial literacy and investment patterns. The papers put in-depth insight towards the functioning of financial markets, investment patters and investor's behavior towards information from the markets and decisions taken by the government and international institutions etc. and there impact on their investment decisions. The outcomes of studies highlighted the relationship between the financial literacy rate, information and psychological elements have positive correlation in investment decision making.

## Management Section

In the realm of management, the research presented explores innovative practices, strategic frameworks, and organizational dynamics. These contributions provide actionable insights for leaders and managers seeking to navigate complex business environments and foster sustainable growth.

The Management steams covered the varied areas of Management and decision making as the outcomes of the research papers presented at the conference. The research papers covered the wide areas of management including the research papers "Consumers' Perceived Risk to Visit Restaurants: A perspective from Theory of Planned Behaviour" by Dr Anuradha Yadav Assistant Professor IILM University, Gurugram in the area of Marketing, Analysis of Switching Intentions of Customers between Click and Brick Using Machine Learning Approach by Anuradha Yadav and Vijay Prakash Sharma covering areas of Consumer buying behavior which is a set of actions done over time.

This book not only captures the essence of the conference discussions but also contributes to the broader academic conversation by offering new perspectives and frameworks. We extend our gratitude to the authors, reviewers, and all those who contributed to the success of the conference and the creation of this book. Their dedication and scholarly rigor have ensured that this volume is a valuable resource for researchers, practitioners, and students alike.

We hope that this collection of research will inspire further inquiry and discussion, driving forward the boundaries of knowledge in Finance, Economics, Management, and Technology.

**Editorial Team**
CMR University, Bangalore

# Economics

# Empowering Rural Women: Theoretical Foundations of E-Governance Strategies for Digital Economy and Sustainable Rural Development

**Farhatnida Unnisa[1], Nilaish[2] and Bhupendra Bahadur Tiwari[3]**

[1]Research Scholar, School of Economics and Commerce, CMR University, Bangalore, India

[2]Assistant Professor And Research Supervisor, School of Economics and Commerce, CMR University. Bangalore, India

[3]Director, School of Economics and Commerce, CMR University, Bengaluru, India

E-mail: [1]nidafarhath@gmail.com; [2]Nilaish@cmr.edu.in; [3]drbhupendra.b@cmr.edu.in

***ABSTRACT:*** *The empowerment of rural women is a critical component of inclusive and sustainable development, particularly in the context of India. This paper delves into the transformative potential of e-governance in addressing the multifaceted challenges encountered by rural women in the country. Drawing from intersectionality theory, the capability approach, and institutional theory, the study explores how e-governance can serve as a catalyst for rural women's empowerment, gender equality promotion, and the attainment of sustainable development goals.*

*Through an extensive literature review, the paper elucidates key themes such as gender discrimination, sustainable livelihood strategies, and the role of information and communication technology (ICT) infrastructure. It underscores e-governance's capacity to enhance governance mechanisms, improve service delivery, and facilitate citizen participation, while also bridging the digital divide between urban and rural areas.*

*The proposed theoretical framework synthesizes these concepts, offering insights into policy implications and avenues for future research. It underscores the importance of prioritizing gender mainstreaming, narrowing digital disparities, and fostering collaborative models to empower rural women effectively.*

*In conclusion, the paper advocates for concerted efforts to invest in rural women's empowerment, recognizing it not only as a moral imperative but also as a strategic pathway to building more equitable and prosperous communities. By comprehensively understanding the unique challenges faced by rural women and leveraging technology strategically, e-governance emerges as a potent tool for fostering inclusive growth and empowerment in digital economies.*

**Keywords**: Challenges, E-Governance, Empowerment, Equality, ICT4D, Sustainability.

# 1. INTRODUCTION

*"Nothing, arguably, is as important today in the political economy of development as an adequate recognition of political, economic, and social participation and leadership of women." (AmartyaSen, 1999)*

Rural women, an important part of our communities, often face challenges that restrict their access to opportunities. Empowering rural women means helping them become more independent, make choices, and contribute to their communities. Despite progress, there are still gaps in education, healthcare, and jobs for rural women. This introduction lays the groundwork for exploring how technology-driven governance, known as E-Governance, can empower rural women. By understanding the unique challenges they face and using technology strategically, we aim to contribute to creating more inclusive and empowered rural communities. Through this research, we aim to unravel the theoretical underpinnings that guide effective E-Governance strategies tailored to the needs and aspirations of rural women, ultimately fostering inclusive growth and empowerment in digital economies.

## 1.1 Definition of Rural Women Empowerment

Women's empowerment describes the capability of women for self-determination: to take control over their own circumstances and to realize their aspirations in order to live a life they have reason to value. (A. Galièa, July 2019).

Women's economic empowerment Women's economic empowerment is the capacity of women and men to participate in, contribute to and benefit from growth processes in ways that recognize the value of their contributions, respect their dignity and make it possible to negotiate a fairer distribution of the benefits of growth. Women's economic empowerment increases women's access to economic resources and opportunities including jobs, financial services, property and other productive assets, skills development and market information. Women's economic participation and empowerment are fundamental to strengthening their rights and enables them to have control over their lives and exert influence in society (ILO, 2019)

## 1.2 Significance of Empowering Rural Women for Overall Community Development

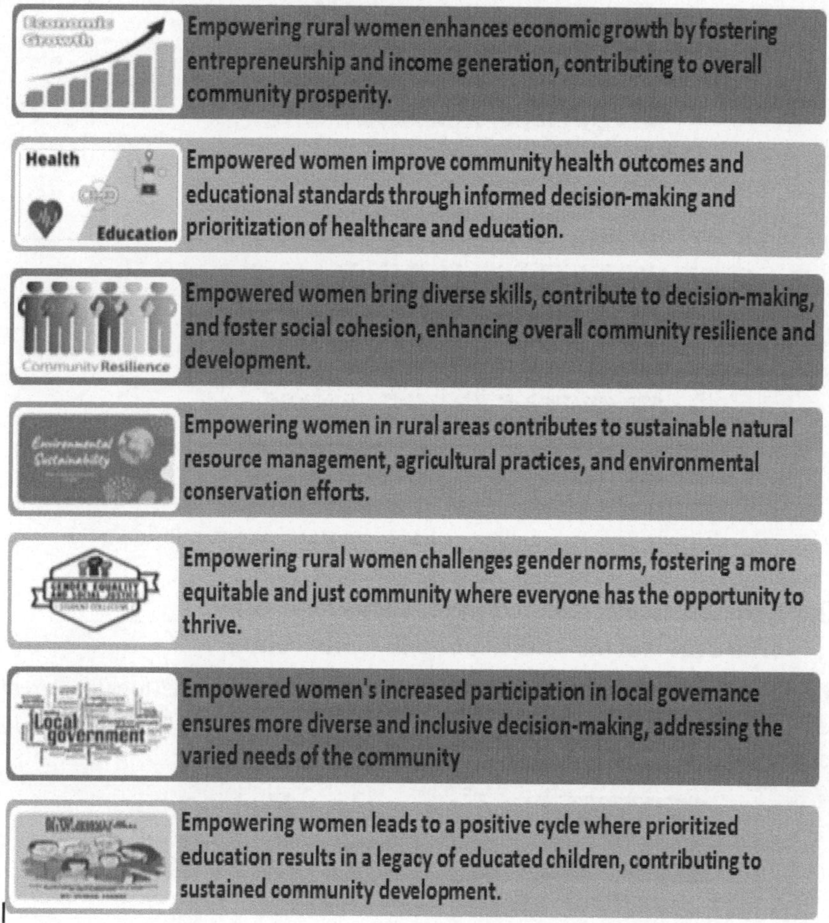


**Figure 1:** Significance of Empowering Rural Women for Overall Community Development

## 2. CHALLENGES FACED BY RURAL WOMEN IN INDIA

Indian Rural Women face several challenges that have adverse effect on their well-being, opportunities, and overall empowerment. These challenges are often interconnected and deeply rooted in Cultural, Social and economic factors. Above are some of the challenges faced by rural women in India. Addressing these challenges requires a holistic approach involving education, economic empowerment, legal awareness, healthcare, and efforts to challenges deeply ingrained gender norms. Various governmental and Non-governmental initiatives are working towards improving the conditions of rural women in India, but sustained efforts are needed to bring about lasting change.

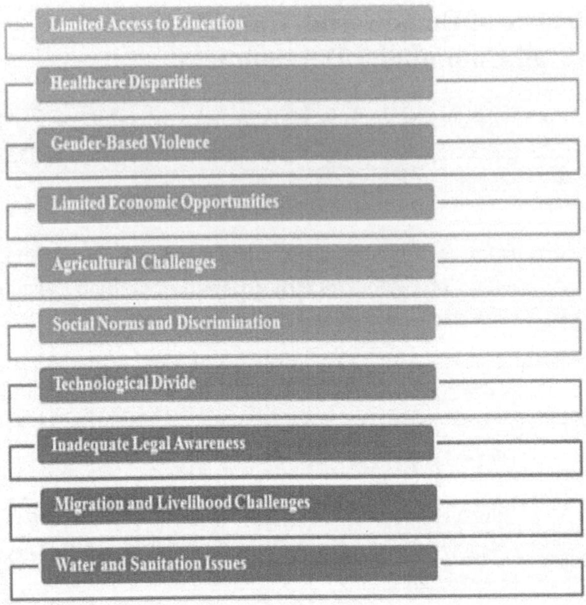


**Figure 2:** Key Challenges Faced by Rural Women in India

## 2.1 Specific Issues Related to Gender Disparities, Cultural Norms and Economic Constraints

Gender disparities, cultural norms and economic constrains together create challenges to rural women in India. Following are the issues related to the above mentioned factors

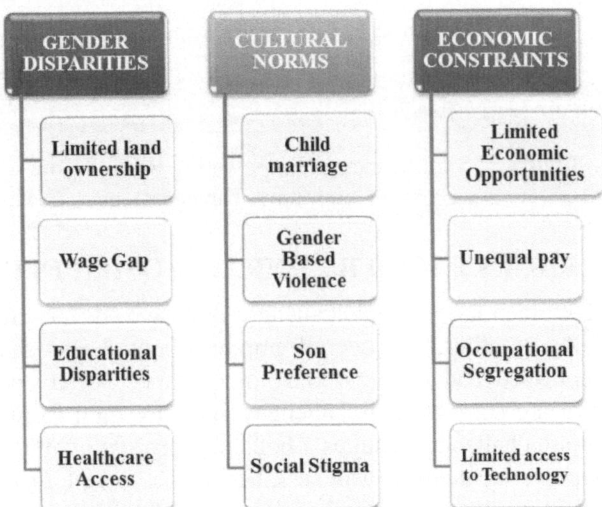


**Figure 3:** Issues Related to Gender Disparities, Cultural Norms and Economic Constraints

## 3. IMPORTANCE OF GENDER EQULAITY IN DEVELOPMENT

Gender equality ensures that development benefits all, fostering inclusive economic and social progress. Gender equality is fundamental to upholding human rights and promoting dignity, addressing systemic inequalities at their core. Achieving gender equality is integral to building just, stable, and resilient societies, fostering global progress towards shared development goals.

### 3.1 Importance of Gender Equality in Achieving Sustainable Development Goals

Gender equality is critical for achieving the Sustainable Development Goals (SDGs) as it guarantees that development efforts are inclusive, comprehensive, and sustainable. Here's why gender equality is of most important in the context of the SDGs:

1. ***Human Rights and Social Justice***: Gender equality is a basic human right, emphasizing fairness and equal treatment for everyone, aligning with principles of social justice.
2. ***Poverty Eradication (SDG 1):*** Gender equality is crucial for reducing poverty. Empowering women economically, closing wage gaps, and ensuring fair access to resources are key steps toward eliminating poverty.
3. ***Zero Hunger (SDG 2):*** Empowering women in agriculture, addressing land ownership disparities, and ensuring equal resource access contribute to food security and sustainable farming.
4. ***Good Health and Well-being (SDG 3)***: Ensuring gender equality in healthcare provides equal access for both genders, leading to improved health outcomes and overall well-being.
5. ***Quality Education (SDG 4):*** Promoting gender equality in education ensures equal opportunities for girls and boys, contributing to universal education goals.
6. ***Clean Water and Sanitation (SDG 6)***: Gender considerations in water and sanitation projects ensure that women, who often bear the primary responsibility for water-related tasks, benefit from improved access to clean water and sanitation
7. ***Decent Work and Economic Growth (SDG 8):*** Gender equality in the workplace, addressing wage gaps, and promoting equal opportunities contribute to sustainable economic growth and the well-being of communities.
8. ***Industry, Innovation, and Infrastructure (SDG 9)***: A diverse, inclusive workforce fosters innovation, contributing to sustainable industry and infrastructure development.

9. ***Reduced Inequality (SDG 10)***: Gender equality is key to reducing overall inequalities, contributing to a more just and equitable society.
10. ***Sustainable Cities and Communities (SDG 11)***: Inclusive urban planning considers the diverse needs of all genders, contributing to sustainable and resilient cities.
11. ***Responsible Consumption and Production (SDG 12)***: Gender equality initiatives contribute to responsible consumption and production by promoting inclusive decision-making in resource management and environmental conservation.
12. ***Climate Action (SDG 13):*** Gender equality is integral to effective climate action. Involving women in climate change initiatives ensures a more comprehensive and sustainable approach to environmental challenges.
13. ***Life below Water and Life on Land (SDG 14 and SDG 15)***: Gender equality contributes to the sustainable use and protection of marine and terrestrial ecosystems by incorporating diverse perspectives and practices
14. ***Peace, Justice, and Strong Institutions (SDG 16***): Gender equality in governance and justice systems fosters inclusive decision-making, contributing to peaceful and just societies.
15. ***Partnerships for the Goals (SDG 17)***: Promoting gender equality is crucial for building effective partnerships that encompass diverse perspectives and experiences, enhancing the overall success of sustainable development initiatives.

In summary, gender equality is not only a standalone goal (SDG 5) but a cross-cutting theme that amplifies the impact and effectiveness of efforts to achieve all SDGs. It is an essential prerequisite for building a more sustainable, equitable, and inclusive world.

## 3.2 Potential for Positive Impacts on Both Community Well-Being and Economic Growth

1. Empowered rural women significantly contribute to economic growth through income-generating activities, enhancing financial stability for households and communities.
2. Active participation of empowered women in decision-making processes fosters holistic community development, including improvements in infrastructure, education, and healthcare, enhancing overall well-being.
3. Empowered women often become entrepreneurs, driving local business ventures and introducing innovative solutions to community challenges, thereby stimulating economic activity and growth.
4. Empowered women prioritize family education and health, leading to improved literacy rates, better health outcomes, and an overall enhancement of community well-being.

5. Women's empowerment challenges gender norms, fostering social harmony and contributing to a more egalitarian community, creating a supportive environment for everyone.
6. Women's active involvement in agriculture, empowered by skills and resources, enhances food production, ensuring greater community food security and reducing the risk of hunger.
7. Empowered women play a key role in sustainable resource management and environmental practices, promoting a healthier environment for the community's long-term well-being.
8. Providing rural women with equal opportunities, access to resources, and economic agency through empowerment becomes a potent tool for poverty reduction, uplifting the entire community.
9. Educated and empowered women are more likely to prioritize their children's education, creating a positive cycle of knowledge and skill transfer for future community development.
10. Empowered women contribute to the cultural and social resilience of communities, preserving and enriching local traditions while adapting to changing socio-economic dynamics.

## 4. ROLE OF E- GOVERNANCE IN DEVELOPMENT

### 4.1 The Concept of E-Governance and its Potential to Address Development Challenges

E-Governance initiatives in India began in the late 1990s and early 2000s. One of the earliest and most significant initiatives was the launch of the National Informatics Centre (NIC) in 1976, which played a pivotal role in the development and implementation of e-governance projects across the country.

**Meaning:** Although the term e-governance is primarily used to refer to the usage of IT to improve administrative efficiency, this is argued to produce other effects that would give rise to increased transparency and accountability of government processes, reflect on the relationship between government and citizens and help build new spaces for citizens to participate in their overall development. (Madon.s, 2004)

### 4.2 Here are Some Key Milestones in the Introduction of E-Governance in India

These are just a few examples of the numerous e-governance initiatives undertaken in India over the years. India continues investing in digital infrastructure and services to enhance governance and citizen services.

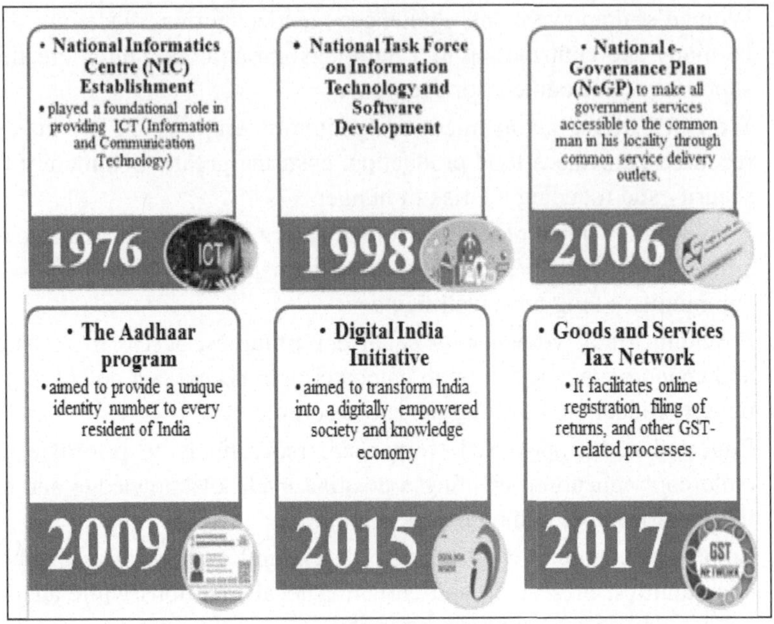


**Figure 4:** Key Milestones in the Introduction of E-governance in India

## 4.3 E-Governance Potential to Address Developmental Challenges

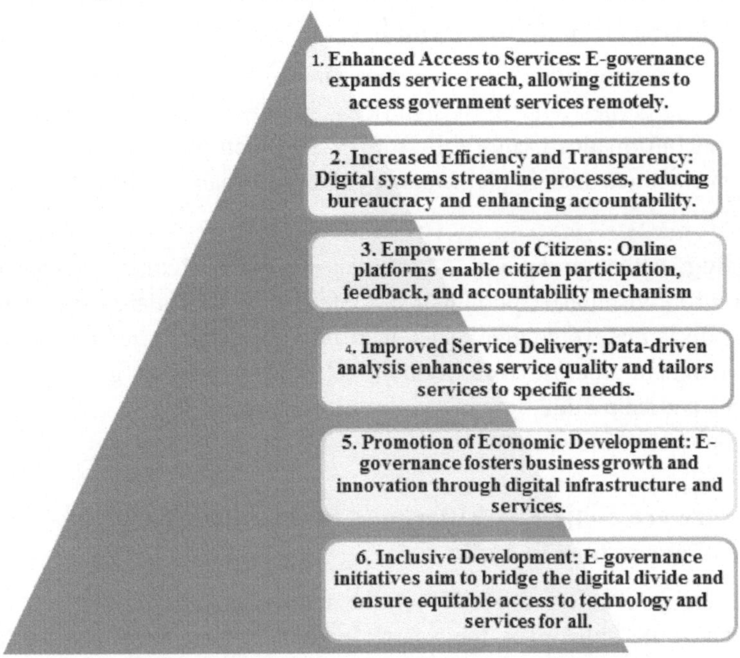


**Figure 5:** E-Governance Potential to Address Developmental Challenges

### 4.4 Enhanced Governance, Service Delivery and Citizen Participation Through Technology and Digital Solution

Technology and digital solutions can greatly enhance governance, service delivery, and citizen participation by providing efficient, transparent, and inclusive platforms for interaction between governments and citizens. Here's how:

1. ***Efficient Service Delivery***: Digital solutions automate administrative tasks, simplifying processes and reducing time and resource requirements, while online portals enable citizens to access government services conveniently from anywhere.
2. ***Transparency and Accountability***: Technology enables real-time monitoring of government activities and expenditure, fostering transparency, while open data initiatives empower citizens to scrutinize government actions, promoting accountability and reducing corruption risks.
3. ***Citizen Engagement and Participation***: Digital platforms facilitate citizen feedback and contributions to policymaking, enhancing democratic governance, while e-voting systems make electoral processes more accessible and inclusive, strengthening democratic participation.
4. ***Customized Service Delivery***: Data analytics enable governments to tailor services to specific needs, improving their effectiveness and relevance, while personalized service delivery enhances citizen satisfaction and outcomes in key sectors like healthcare and education.
5. ***Access to Information and Education***: Digital literacy programs and e-services centers empower citizens, particularly in marginalized communities, to access government information and services online, while mobile applications and multimedia tools provide educational resources and civic awareness, promoting informed citizenship.

"Technology and digital solutions can revolutionize governance, fostering efficiency, transparency, and citizen participation. By enhancing service delivery, promoting transparency, and empowering citizens, governments can advance trust, accountability, and inclusive development for societal welfare.

## 5. DIGITAL DIVIDE IN RURAL AREAS

The term 'Digital Divide' is used to describe situations in which there is a market gap in access to the use of ICT devices measured by, for example the number of fixed line phones per inhabitants, or the number of mobile users or the internet connections in the population. According to OECD (2001) the term 'digital divide' refers to "the gap between individuals, households, businesses and geographic areas at the different socio-economic levels with regard to their opportunities to access information and communication technologies (ICTs) and their use of Internet. It reflects differences among and within countries". This definition is exclusively focused at national and international level. Nevertheless, digital divide exists in variety of other levels; sector, community, and individual level. (Philip, 2017)

## 5.1 Existing Digital Divide between Urban and Rural Areas

**Table 1:** Existing Digital Divide between Urban and Rural Areas

| *Aspect* | *Urban Areas* | *Rural Areas* |
|---|---|---|
| Internet Access & Connectivity | Better internet infrastructure and connectivity | Limited internet access and slower speeds |
| Technological Infrastructure | More investment in broadband networks and digital infrastructure | Less investment in infrastructure |
| Digital Literacy & Skills | Higher digital literacy levels | Lower digital literacy levels |
| Access to Digital Services | Wider range of digital services | Limited access to digital services |
| Economic Opportunities | Better access to online job Opportunities and entrepreneurship resources | Limited access to economic opportunities. |
| Quality of Life | Better access to information, communication, healthcare, and government services | Limited access to information, healthcare, and government services. |

## 5.2 The Challenges Rural Communities Face in Adopting and Benefiting from Digital Technologies

**Table 2:** The Challenges Rural Communities Face in Adopting and Benefiting from Digital Technologies

| | | | |
|---|---|---|---|
| 1. | ***Limited Internet Access*** Lack of reliable internet infrastructure | 2. | ***Technological Infrastructure*** Limited access and affordability of technological devices and equipment |
| 3. | ***Digital Literacy*** Lack of skills and knowledge to use digital | 4. | ***Economic Constraints*** Limited financial resources technology adoption |
| 5. | ***Geographic Isolation*** Limited access to support services and technical assistance | 6. | ***Language and Cultural Barriers*** Language and cultural differences impact technology usability |

| | | | |
|---|---|---|---|
| 7. | ***Power and Electricity Issues*** Inadequate power supply and frequent outages disrupt technology access | 8. | ***Content Relevance*** Digital content and services may not always cater to rural needs and interests. |
| 9. | ***Security Concerns*** Lack of cyber security awareness infrastructure pose privacy and safety. | 10. | ***Limited Government Support*** Rural areas may receive less attention and investment in digital initiatives. |

## 6. RELEVANCE OF E-GOVERNANCE FOR RURAL WOMEN EMPOWERMENT

"E-Governance facilitates access to government services and information, empowering rural women with resources for education, healthcare, and economic opportunities. By bridging digital divides, e-governance can enhance rural women's participation in decision-making and socio-economic development, fostering empowerment and inclusion."

### 6.1 Specific Needs and Challenges Faced by Rural Women Tailored by E-Governance Strategies

General insights into the specific needs and challenges faced by rural women, along with potential e-governance strategies to address them:

While these strategies hold promise for addressing the specific needs and challenges faced by rural women, their effectiveness would depend on factors such as internet penetration, digital literacy levels, and socio-cultural contexts in rural areas. Gathering statistical data on the impact of these e-governance interventions would require comprehensive monitoring and evaluation efforts to assess their outcomes on rural women's empowerment and socio economic development.

**Table 3:** Specific Needs & Challenges Faced by Rural Women Tailored by E-Governance Strategies

| *Specific Needs and Challenges Faced by Rural Women* | *E-Governance Strategies* |
|---|---|
| Access to Healthcare | Develop telemedicine services.<br>Establish mobile health applications.<br>Create online healthcare portals tailored to rural women's needs. |
| Education and Literacy | Provide online education and skill development programs.<br>Offer virtual classrooms.<br>Conduct digital literacy training programs. |

| *Specific Needs and Challenges Faced by Rural Women* | *E-Governance Strategies* |
|---|---|
| Economic Empowerment | Establish e-commerce platforms.<br>Develop online marketplaces.<br>Provide digital banking services for financial inclusion. |
| Women's Safety and Security | Develop mobile applications for reporting incidents of violence.<br>Establish online counseling services.<br>Create digital platforms for legal aid and support. |
| Access to Social Welfare Schemes | Develop user-friendly online portals for welfare scheme information.<br>Establish mobile apps for easy access to scheme details.<br>Create community-based e-services centers for application assistance. |

## 6.2 Linking E-Governance, Sustainable Development, and Gender Equality

Emphasizing the theoretical linkages between e-governance, sustainable rural development, and gender equality while presenting the theoretical foundations supporting their integration.

Here are a few points elaborating on the theoretical linkages between e-governance, sustainable rural development, and gender equality, along with their supporting theoretical foundations:

- **Democratic Governance**: E-governance promotes citizen participation and transparency, aligning with principles of democratic decision-making. Sustainable rural development involves empowering communities to shape their own development agendas, ensuring inclusivity.
- **Environmental Sustainability**: Both e-governance and sustainable rural development aim to conserve natural resources and address climate change. Gender equality is crucial here, as women often play vital roles in environmental management.
- **Social Justice**: E-governance fosters equity in accessing services, while sustainable rural development aims to reduce inequalities and alleviate poverty. Gender equality ensures women have equal rights and opportunities.
- **Empowerment:** E-governance empowers citizens by providing information and platforms for engagement, while sustainable rural development empowers communities. Gender equality ensures women's empowerment by addressing barriers to their participation.

- **Holistic Approach**: Integrating e-governance, sustainable rural development, and gender equality requires a comprehensive approach, considering their interconnected nature and addressing development challenges holistically.

**Overall**, these points highlight the theoretical underpinnings of the ***linkages*** between e-governance, sustainable rural development, and gender equality, emphasizing their collective contribution to fostering inclusive, equitable, and sustainable development outcomes.

## 7. LITERATURE REVIEW

The literature covers a diverse range of topics related to development, gender, technology, and governance, with a particular focus on India and other developing countries:

1. **Gender Discrimination and Work Outcomes**: The study explores how contextual factors shape the link between perceived gender discrimination and work outcomes using relative deprivation theory. Findings indicate negative associations between discrimination and employee outcomes, with national differences in labor laws and cultural norms moderating these relationships, highlighting the importance of considering country context in addressing workplace gender bias. (Triana., 2018)

   **Research Gap:** The research lacks a detailed analysis of specific factors influencing the link between perceived gender discrimination and work outcomes. Additionally, there's limited exploration of strategies to address gender bias in diverse cultural and national contexts.

2. **Sustainable Livelihood Strategies**: The research in Andar District, Afghanistan, focuses on implementing sustainable livelihood strategies, including rural industrialization and solar energy use, to improve rural economies and living standards. Emphasizing empowerment of the rural poor, it underscores the significance of governmental and non-governmental efforts in addressing livelihood challenges for sustainable development in impoverished rural areas. (Miani., 2023)

   **Research Gap:** The literature overlooks potential barriers or challenges to the implementation of sustainable livelihood strategies in rural Afghanistan. Additionally, there might be a need for further investigation into the long-term sustainability and scalability of these strategies in diverse rural contexts.

3. **Critique of Economic Development Models:** The article critiques the 2019 Nobel Prize in economics, focusing on Esther Duflo's essay on women's empowerment and economic development. It highlights limitations in "randomista" economists' methods, suggesting they overlook historical context, and challenges the idea that economic development alone leads to gender equality. (Kabeer, 2020)

**Research Gap:** The critique did not fully explore alternative methodlogies or frameworks for studying women's empowerment and economic development beyond the "randomista" approach. Additionally, there could be a need for further investigation into the nuanced interplay between economic development, historical context, and gender equality outcomes.

4. **Gender Policies in India:** This book examines India's gender policies post-1990, evaluating their adoption of international gender mainstreaming and their impact. It argues that India's diverse state structure poses challenges and opportunities for feminists, shedding light on gendered development in the neoliberal era. It provides insights into development policymaking in India, addressing federalism, identity politics, and equality. (Spary, 2019)

   **Research Gap:** The literature did not sufficiently delve into the specific mechanisms through which India's diverse state structure influences the implementation and effectiveness of gender policies. Additionally, there could be a need for deeper exploration into the Intersectionality of federalism, identity politics, and gender equality within India's policy landscape.

5. **Feminist Resistance and Pleasure:** This article discusses how young urban Indian women use pleasure and fun as a form of feminist resistance, contrasting with past ideologies. It also explores how marginalized rural women discover pleasure and fun through involvement with an NGO, despite challenges. Their engagement in development work fosters new skills, revealing contradictions in neoliberal India's aspirations. (Roy, 2022)

   **Research Gap:** The literature overlooks the long-term impact of pleasure-based feminist resistance among Indian women in varied contexts. Further exploration is needed to understand how gender, pleasure, and resistance intersect within India's neoliberal development framework.

6. **Microfinance and Women's Empowerment:** This study investigates the impact of microfinance schemes on women's empowerment in Uttar Pradesh, India. Through semi-structured interviews, it examines the role of social capital in accessing financial resources and loan repayment. Findings suggest that while social capital facilitates access to resources, true empowerment is observed when women utilize these resources for entrepreneurial activities and self-determined goals. (Andriani, 2022)

   **Research Gap:** The literature did not thoroughly explore the nuanced pathways through which microfinance influences women's empowerment beyond access to resources. Additionally, further investigation is needed to understand the broader societal implications and sustainability of women's empowerment through microfinance in Uttar Pradesh, India.

7. **ICT4D Research and Practice:** several studies (Zheng, 2018; Chipidza, 2019; Schelenz, 2022; Kosec, 2020) delve into Information and Communication Technology for Development (ICT4D), discussing its theoretical foundations, criticisms, ethical considerations, and the need for nuanced interventions to achieve meaningful outcomes in rural settings.

   **Research Gap:** The literature lacks an integrated analysis of theoretical foundations and practical applications of ICT4D for rural development. Further research is needed to assess the long-term effectiveness and sustainability of ICT4D initiatives in rural settings.

8. **Rural Citizen Satisfaction with E-Health Care Services:** This study examines rural citizen satisfaction with e-health care services in Kancheepuram District during the COVID-19 pandemic. Utilizing a descriptive research design and neural network analysis, it identifies "Public Trust" as a key factor influencing satisfaction. The research offers insights for policymakers and healthcare providers to enhance e-health care services and meet the needs of rural populations effectively. (Bhuvana, 2020)

   **Research Gap:** The literature lacks comprehensive exploration into factors beyond "Public Trust" that influence rural citizen satisfaction with e-healthcare services. Further investigation is needed to understand additional determinants and barriers to effective e-healthcare delivery in rural areas during pandemics.

9. **Relationship between Economic Growth, Financial Inclusion, and ICT Infrastructure:** This paper investigates the relationship between economic growth, financial inclusion, and ICT infrastructure in 20 Indian states from 1991 to 2018. Employing Granger-causality analysis, it reveals significant temporal causality between these variables in both short and long terms. The findings underscore the importance of coordinated development in ICT infrastructure, financial inclusion, and economic growth strategies for sustainable development in Indian states. (Pradhan, 2021)

   **Research Gap**: The literature may not fully explore the nuanced dynamics and potential feedback loops between economic growth, financial inclusion, and ICT infrastructure in Indian states. Further research is needed to understand how these factors interact within specific socio-economic contexts to drive sustainable development effectively.

10. **Impact of National Cultural Forces on Gender Diversity in Corporate Boards:** This study investigates the impact of national cultural forces on gender diversity in corporate boards. Utilizing mixed

methods, it integrates gender schema and institutional theories to develop a mid-range theory. Findings shed light on the complex relationship between female empowerment, cultural dimensions, and board gender diversity. The research provides valuable insights for addressing the underrepresentation of women on corporate boards. (Lewellyn, 2019)

**Research Gap:** Existing research might overlook other cultural influences on gender diversity in corporate boards beyond gender schema and institutional theories. More investigation is necessary to understand how broader cultural contexts affect female empowerment and address the underrepresentation of women in corporate leadership.

11. **E-Governance and Public Service Delivery: Dhal (2020) and Singh (2020)** review E-Governance adoption in India, particularly in rural areas, highlighting challenges such as illiteracy and infrastructure gaps, and advocating for citizen-friendly approaches to enhance public service delivery.

    **Research Gap:** The research may overlook detailed approaches for citizen-friendly e-governance in rural India, and more study is necessary to effectively tackle issues like illiteracy and infrastructure gaps for improved public service delivery.

Overall, the literature underscores the complex interplay of gender, development, technology, and governance in shaping outcomes in diverse socio-economic contexts, with implications for policy and practice in fostering inclusive and sustainable development.

## 8. OBJECTIVES

1. Explore theories guiding e-governance for rural women's digital empowerment.
2. Investigate how e-governance can empower rural women for sustainable development.
3. Assess e-governance's role in promoting gender equality for rural women.
4. Formulate policy suggestions for empowering rural women through e-governance.

## 9. THEORETICAL FRAMEWORK

Based on the literature, we can formulate a theoretical framework that integrates key concepts and themes related to gender, development, technology, and governance in the context of India and other developing countries. Here's a proposed theoretical framework:

1. ***Intersectionality Theory:*** Recognizes how gender discrimination intersects with other forms of discrimination, influencing various outcomes like work, livelihood, and governance.

2. ***Capability Approach:*** Focuses on enhancing individuals' capabilities for economic empowerment, well-being, and agency, emphasizing sustainable livelihoods, resource access, and ICT.
3. ***Institutional Theory:*** Examines how institutions shape gender dynamics and development, including policies, cultural norms, and governance structures.
4. ***ICT4D Framework:*** Highlights ICT's potential for development, emphasizing context-specific factors, addressing digital divides, and promoting inclusivity.
5. ***Ethical Considerations:*** Considers equity, social justice, and human rights, ensuring development interventions uphold dignity and non-discrimination.
6. ***Agency and Resistance:*** Acknowledges individuals' and communities' agency in challenging gender inequalities, through activism, participatory approaches, and reclaiming autonomy.

This framework offers a holistic view of gender, development, technology, and governance interactions, providing insights into addressing inequality for more inclusive and sustainable development.

## 10. IMPLICATIONS AND SUGGESTIONS

1. Prioritize gender mainstreaming in development policies to address rural women's unique needs.
2. Bridge the digital divide by enhancing access to technology and promoting digital literacy among rural women.
3. Tailor e-governance solutions to rural women's specific needs for improved access to essential services.
4. Implement capacity building programs to empower rural women with skills for socio-economic advancement.
5. Strengthen institutional support for rural women's empowerment initiatives through policy frameworks and funding mechanisms.
6. Foster partnerships and collaboration among stakeholders to scale up interventions for rural women's empowerment.
7. Establish robust monitoring and evaluation mechanisms to assess the effectiveness and impact of empowerment interventions.
8. Advocate for gender-responsive policies and raise awareness about the importance of rural women's empowerment.

## 11. FUTURE RESEARCH DIRECTIONS

1. Study the lasting effects of gender equality policies on rural women's progress.

   Find solutions to bridge digital gaps for rural women, addressing connectivity and skills.

2. Assess e-governance programs' long-term benefits for rural women's access to services.
3. Evaluate the sustainability of programs boosting rural women's economic independence.
4. Investigate how institutions support or hinder rural women's empowerment efforts.
5. Explore collaborative models among government, NGOs, and communities for rural women's empowerment.
6. Develop effective monitoring methods for rural women's empowerment initiatives.
7. Research the impact of advocacy and community mobilization on rural women's rights.

## 12. CONCLUSION

In conclusion, addressing the multifaceted challenges faced by rural women requires holistic and collaborative efforts. By implementing gender-sensitive policies, bridging digital divides, and promoting inclusive governance, we can empower rural women to realize their full potential. Sustainable development hinges on the meaningful participation and empowerment of all members of society, and investing in rural women's empowerment is not just a moral imperative but a pathway to more equitable and prosperous communities.

## REFERENCES


[1] Al-Faham, H., Davis, A.M. and Ernst, R. (2019). Intersectionality: From theory to practice. *Annual Review of Law and Social Science*, 15, 247-265.

[2] Andriani, L., Lal, S.B. and Kalam, A.A. (2022). Entrepreneurial activities and women empowerment in rural India between microfinance and social capital. Strategic Change, 31(2), 227–237. https://doi.org/10.1002/jsc.2492.

[3] Bhuvana and Vasantha (2020). Rural Citizen Satisfaction on E-Health Care Services under E-governance Service Delivery Model during COVID 19. *International Journal of Management,* 11(05), IJM_11_05_150. http://www.iaeme.com/IJM/index.asp.

[4] Chipidza, W. and Leidner, D.E. (2019). A review of the ICT-enabled development literature: Towards a power parity theory of ICT4D. *The Journal of Strategic Information Systems,* 28(2), 145–174. https://doi.org/10.1016/j.jsis.2019.01.002.

[5] Del Carmen Triana, M., Jayasinghe, M., Pieper, J.R., Delgado, D.M. and Li, M. (2018). Perceived Workplace Gender Discrimination and Employee Consequences: A Meta-Analysis and Complementary Studies Considering Country context. *Journal of Management*, 45(6), 2419–2447. https://doi.org/10.1177/0149206318776772.

[6] Dhal, S. (2020). Empowering Women through e-Governance in the Indian province of Odisha: Capacity building as an enabling measure. In Springer eBooks (pp. 157–179). https://doi.org/10.1007/978-3-030-36012-2_8

[7] DeGregori, T.R. (2019). Resources are not; they become: An institutional theory. In Evolutionary Economics: v. 1 (pp. 291–313). Routledge.

[8] Galiè, A. and Farnworth, C.R. (2019). Power through: A new concept in the empowerment discourse. Global Food Security, 21, 13–17. https://doi.org/10.1016/j.gfs.2019.07.001

[9] Empowering Women in the Rural Economy. (2019). International Labour Organization.

[10] Kabeer, N. (2020). Women's Empowerment and Economic Development: A Feminist critique of Storytelling practices in "Randomista" Economics. *Feminist Economics,* 26(2), 1–26. https://doi.org/10.1080/13545701.2020.1743338

[11] Kosec, K. and Wantchékon, L. (2020). Can information improve rural governance and service delivery? World Development, 125, 104376. https://doi.org/10.1016/j.worlddev.2018.07.017

[12] Lewellyn, K. and Muller-Kahle, M.I. (2019). The Corporate Board Glass Ceiling: The role of Empowerment and Culture in shaping board gender Diversity. Journal of Business Ethics, 165(2), 329–346. https://doi.org/10.1007/s10551-019-04116-9

[13] Madon, S. (2004). Evaluating the Developmental Impact of e-governance Initiatives: An Exploratory framework. The Electronic Journal of Information Systems in Developing Countries, 20(1), 1–13. https://doi.org/10.1002/j.1681-4835.2004.tb00132.x

[14] Miani, A.M., Dehkordi, M.K., Siamian, N., Lassois, L., Tan, R. and Azadi, H. (2023). Toward sustainable rural livelihoods approach: Application of grounded theory in Ghazni province, Afghanistan. Applied Geography, 154, 102915. https://doi.org/10.1016/j.apgeog.2023.102915

[15] Philip, L.J., Cottrill, C., Farrington, J., Williams, F. and Ashmore, F. (2017). The digital divide: Patterns, policy and scenarios for connecting the 'final few' in rural communities across Great Britain. *Journal of Rural Studies*, 54, 386–398. https://doi.org/10.1016/j.jrurstud.2016.12.002

[16] Pradhan, R.P., Arvin, M.B., Nair, M., Hall, J.H. and Bennett, S.E. (2021). Sustainable economic development in India: The dynamics between financial inclusion, ICT development, and economic growth. *Technological Forecasting and Social Change*, 169, 120758. https://doi.org/10.1016/j.techfore.2021.120758

[17] Robeyns, I. (2021). The capability approach. In The Routledge handbook of feminist economics (pp. 72–80). Routledge.

[18] Roy, S. (2022). From feminist killjoy to joyful feminisms. Cultural Politics: *An International Journal,* 18(1), 12–27. https://doi.org/10.1215/17432197-9516897.

[19] Schelenz, L. and Pawelec, M. (2021). Information and Communication Technologies for Development (ICT4D) critique. *Information Technology for Development*, 28(1), 165–188. https://doi.org/10.1080/02681102.2021.1937473.

[20] Sein, M.K., Thapa, D., Hatakka, M. and Sæbø, Ø. (2019). A holistic perspective on the theoretical foundations for ICT4D research. *Information Technology for Development*, 25(1), 7–25.

[21] Singh, P. (2020). Challenges of E-Governance in Rural areas of Haryana. Studies in Indian Place Names, 40(3), 1583–1604.

[22] Spary, C. (2019). Gender, development, and the state in India. https://doi.org/10.4324/9780429022647.

[23] Zheng, Y., Hatakka, M., Sahay, S. and Andersson, A. (2017). Conceptualizing development in information and communication technology for development (ICT4D). *Information Technology for Development*, 24(1), 1–14. https://doi.org/10.1080/02681102.2017.1396020.

# Empowering India: Unveiling Government Schemes

**G. Manisha[1], M. Harshith[1] and Santha Ganesh Iyer[2]**

[1]Student of III-year BCom Honours, CMR University, Bengaluru, India

[2]Faculty, School of Economics and Commerce, CMR University, Bengaluru, India

***ABSTRACT:*** *We Citizens, as taxpayers, should maintain awareness of government-provided schemes and leverage them for personal benefit, underscoring the significance of informed utilization of public resources. So, this research article aims to present a detailed information of various government schemes implemented in India, focusing on their awareness, benefits, impacts and challenges. Through a systematic review of literature and analysis of available empirical data, the paper attempts to offer insights into the wide and diversified range of schemes initiated and implemented by the Indian government across sectors like healthcare, education, agriculture, and social welfare. Through analysis of secondary data and primary data, the research assesses the awareness level, the usage and the factors influencing the reach of government schemes contributing to a better understanding of government schemes and paving the way for informed citizen engagement and empowerment.*

**Keywords:** Agriculture, Education, Government Schemes, Healthcare, Social Welfare.

## 1. INTRODUCTION

The Indian government is always striving to better the lives of its citizens, especially the poor and disenfranchised, through a variety of policies and initiatives. These often innovative and multifaceted projects aim to empower individuals across several domains, foster equitable development, and tackle a spectrum of socioeconomic concerns. The government is involved in many different aspects of life, from social security maintenance to entrepreneurship promotion, from expanding access to healthcare to supporting education. These government programmes are the outcome of a concerted effort to maximise the nation's potential and steer it in the direction of sustainable development. They show how committed the government is to eradicating poverty while also encouraging innovation, creating employment, and building strong communities. These initiatives, which strongly emphasise inclusion and engagement, aim to transform challenges into opportunities so that every Indian may achieve their goals and help the nation progress.

## 2. RESEARCH PROBLEM

Since our country is determined to become developed economy by 2047, it is very important to strengthen today's youth. The government educational schemes help the youth to upgrade their skill and thus help them to be a part of developed country. The awareness of youth regarding these schemes is a crucial factor which is studied in this research article.

## 3. REVIEW OF LITERATURE

According to Singh & Mohanty (2012), firms should achieve a balance between education and instruction since training is a key tool for increasing employee productivity and will ultimately increase an organization's worth.

Okada (2012) identified the skills gap in India between the abilities that young people gain via vocational training and what industries want based on recent fast economic expansion. In order to encourage industrial development and ensure sustainable growth, he recommended that India increase its investment in youth education and training.

Shome (2018) discovered that, between 2016 and 2017, over 78% of the PMKVY trained and placed data were employed as wage earners and 22% were self-employed. Nonetheless, the statistics released for the years 2016–20 likewise show a placement breakdown in the same percentage. With 55% of women working, the top 5 sectors with the greatest placement rates were apparel, retail, electronics, beauty, and telecom. Thousands of young people who received training via PMKVY are said to have filed for Mudra loans via the Udyami Mitra site.

According to Halawi and Haydar (2018), the training would have an impact on employees' behaviour and productivity, leading to better results and positive improvements. Additionally, training plays a significant role in employee performance by imparting in them the critical abilities needed to carry out various responsibilities inside the company.

Divyaranjani & Rajasekar (2017) evaluated the benefits of training for the progress of workers in general and enumerated the results of the training programme that was provided. Primary data from 456 automobile industry personnel were evaluated for the study. The findings demonstrate the importance of training and development programmes as they improve employee productivity and performance by raising skill, competence, and ability levels.

## 4. RESEARCH OBJECTIVES

1. To summarise the data based on demographic variables.
2. To assess the perception of students regarding effectiveness of educational schemes.
3. To examine if the awareness of educational schemes differs from boys to girls.

## 5. RESEARCH HYPOTHESIS

H1a: There is significant difference between boys and girls regarding awareness of educational schemes offered by government of India.

H1b: There is significant difference between boys and girls regarding awareness of scholarship schemes provided by Indian government.

## 6. RESEARCH METHODOLOGY

This research article uses primary data to find out the awareness level among students regarding Pradhan Mantri Education schemes and scholarships. The collected data is summarised based on demographic variables and other parameters under study like perception on strength of educational schemes, benefits of schemes, accessibility of these schemes etc.

## 7. DATA ANALYSIS AND DISCUSSION

In this survey, 38 boys and 43 girls form undergraduate commerce and management responded.

1. Percentage frequency analysis on select parameters like awareness of schemes/scholarships, perception of students regarding accessibility of schemes, strength of schemes, communication and reach of schemes.

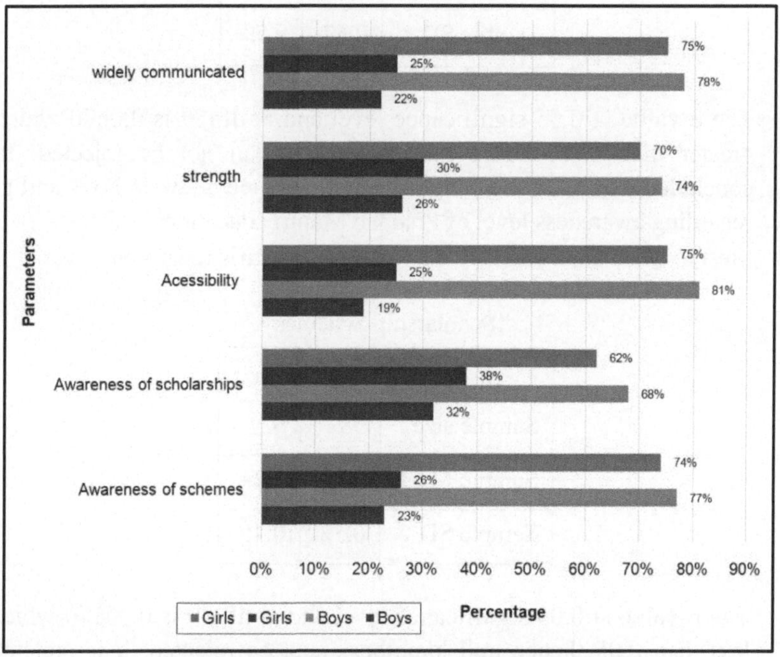


Awareness and Perception of Pradhan Mantri Education Schemes among Students

*Source:* Primary data.

| | *Boys* | | *Girls* | |
|---|---|---|---|---|
| Parameter | Yes | No | Yes | No |
| Awareness of schemes | 23% | 77% | 26% | 74% |
| Awareness of scholarships | 32% | 68% | 38% | 62% |
| Accessibility | 19% | 81% | 25% | 75% |
| strength | 26% | 74% | 30% | 70% |
| widely communicated | 22% | 78% | 25% | 75% |

*Source:* Primary data.

2. t-test to calculate awareness among boys and girls regarding Pradhan Mantri educational schemes.

| | *Boys* | *Girls* |
|---|---|---|
| Sample size | 38 | 43 |
| Sample Mean | 2.43 | 2.69 |
| Sample SD | 0.67 | 0.59 |

The p-value at 0.05 significance level and at df=79 is 0.0670 which is greater than 0.05, hence null hypothesis can not be rejected. It is concluded that there is no significant difference between boys and girls regarding awareness level of Pradhan Mantri educational schemes.

3. t-test to calculate awareness among boys and girls regarding government

Scholarship Schemes

| | *Boys* | *Girls* |
|---|---|---|
| Sample size | 38 | 43 |
| Sample Mean | 2.89 | 3.24 |
| Sample SD | 0.52 | 0.45 |

The p-value at 0.05 significance level and at df=79 is 0.00170 which is less than 0.05, hence null hypothesis can be rejected. It is concluded that there is significant difference between boys and girls regarding scholarship schemes.

## 8. FINDINGS

Following are the findings of this study.

1. The awareness level is very low among boys and girls regarding Pradhan Mantri educational schemes as well as scholarships.
2. The perception of students regarding schemes' accessbility, wider reach, easy availability is not satisfactory.
3. Boys and girls do not differ in their awareness level regarding Pradha Mantri educational schemes.
4. Boys and girls differ in their awareness level regarding Pradha Mantri scholarship schemes.

## 9. CONCLUSION

From the data analysis it can be concluded that awareness level is very low and hence some measures should be taken so that most of the students can take benefits from these schemes.

## REFERENCES

[1] Ansari, T. and Khan, M. (2018). Skill India Opportunities and Challenges - researchgate.net

[2] Divyaranjani, R. and Rajasekar, D. (2017). International Journal of Civil Engineering and Technology, 8(6), p. 19–30.

[3] Halawi, A. and Haydar, N. (2018). International Humanities Studies - researchgate.net

[4] Okada, A. (2012). Journal of International Cooperation in Education - core.ac.uk

[5] Singh, R. and Mohanty, M. (2012). Interscience Management Review (IMR), Researchgate.net

[6] http://www.pmkvyofficial.org

# A Study on ITC's Social Investment Initiatives

K. Neha[1], L. Kiran[1] and Santha Ganesh Iyer[2]
[1]Student of III-year BCom Honours, CMR University, Bengaluru, India
[3]Faculty, School of Economics and Commerce, CMR University, Bengaluru, India

***ABSTRACT:*** *ITC is a well-known private sector company in India with operations in a number of industries, including agribusiness, hotels, fast-moving consumer products, paperboard and packaging, and information technology. With a net profit of ₹ 18,753.31 crores as of March 31, 2023, the company was acknowledged as one of India's most valuable business organisations, with gross sales amounting to ₹ 69,481 crores. According to a Fortune India and Hay Group survey, ITC is the most admired corporation in India. This research study attempts to explore ITC's social investment initiatives, aiming to assess their impact, effectiveness, and alignment with global sustainability goals. It also examines the impact and effectiveness of ITC's social investment initiatives, evaluating key performance indicators and stakeholder perspectives. Through a comprehensive analysis, it provides insights for enhancing the company's corporate social responsibility strategies in alignment with global sustainability goals.*

**Keywords:** ITC, Social Investment Initiatives, Sustainability Goals.

## 1. INTRODUCTION

The current landscape of corporate responsibility and societal effect is mainly influenced by social investment initiatives. These initiatives show how business goals may be carefully matched with the broader goals of sustainable development, community welfare, and environmental stewardship. Compared to standard corporate philanthropy, which often consists of passive contributions, social investment efforts are distinct. In fact, social investment efforts entail corporations proactively allocating their funds, expertise, and to benefit the organisation as well as the society at large. These initiatives, which include everything from improving education and healthcare to supporting local communities and environmental preservation, are excellent representations of a paradigm shift towards ethical and comprehensive business operations. A company's social investment initiatives determine its long-term survival and reputation in an increasingly connected and socially conscious society. They also act as catalysts for positive change in this era of heightened awareness of stakeholder expectations and corporate accountability.

## 2. RESEARCH PROBLEM

Understanding social investment projects is crucial because they represent corporations' proactive efforts to address environmental and social challenges while advancing sustainability over the long run. These initiatives support stakeholders' accountability and engagement while also aligning nicely with the organisations' overall business strategies. By assessing their effectiveness, organisations may enhance their plans, identify best practices, and advance the area of corporate social responsibility. Since ITC holds significance in the realm of Corporate Social Responsibility (CSR), the attempt to study ITC's social investment initiatives may inspire other companies to adopt similar strategies for positive social impact.

## 3. REVIEW OF LITERATURE

ITC's e-choupal in India has helped to promote rural development via the effective development of organisational, individual, and collaborative competence in a multi-stakeholder framework. (Sindhi, S., Maurya, U., & Shukla, M, 2014)

Indian agriculture is now significantly more competitive because to ITC's corporate charity and its e-choupal initiative, which has reached 100,000 villages and created 10 million e-farmers. (Basavaraj, K., & Deene, S, 2011)

Across a wide range of industries, including paperboards and packaging, apparel, foods, hotels, information technology, and tobacco products, ITC is a prominent Indian conglomerate. The business asserts that it has attained the triple bottom line, which takes into account social, environmental, and economic factors. In fact, the business has received praise and awards for its environmental efforts. (Krishnamurthy, B., & Jalnawalla, D, 2012)

In order to foster inclusive innovation and social entrepreneurship in India, alternative financing programmes like micro venture capital and social company incubation can fill the gap between banks and microfinance. (Sonne, L., 2012).

In addition to involving people in the process of generating meaning and offering opportunities for engagement and transformation, social innovation initiatives craft narratives of change that challenge the dominant capitalist, neoliberal paradigm. (Wittmayer, J. *et al.,* 2019)

The CSR mandate in India has been aided by ITC's Mission Sunehra Kal, which has effectively matched commercial expansion with social, economic, and environmental development. (Ambasta, A, 2017)

Indian FMCG firms, such as Hindustan Unilever and Dabur India, are putting CSR into practice in a number of areas, including as the environment, healthcare, education, women's empowerment, and the care of young girls. (Jaiswal, N. *et al.*, 2016)

The triple bottom line, stakeholder engagement, and government involvement are the key drivers of the ITC's sustainability performance. (Anbarasan, P. *et al.*, 2018).

Since social investment programmes are in line with the principles of the welfare state, they have no detrimental effect on the protection of the impoverisher's income. Examples of these programmes are active labour market initiatives and childcare services. (Noël, A., 2018)

Social investment has the potential to serve as a model for welfare policy in the twenty-first century, even though its future depends on further budgetary austerity, the competitive knowledge economy, and the needs of modern family life. (Hemerijck, A., 2017).

## 4. RESEARCH OBJECTIVES

1. To identify best practices towards CSR from ITC's social investment initiatives.
2. To assess ITC's impact focussed program under MSK (Mission Sunehra Kal).
3. To assess awareness of ITC's social investment initiatives.

## 5. RESEARCH HYPOTHESIS

H1a: Awareness regarding ITC's social investment initiatives differ between male and females.

H2a: There exists a positive relation between perception of ITC's addressing social issues and satisfaction in buying ITC products.

## 6. RESEARCH METHODOLOGY

This article uses secondary as well as primary data. Secondary data is used from ITC portal, sustainability integrated reports, Impact reports and literature reviews. Primary data is collected from 123 respondents. Awareness and perception regarding ITC's social investment initiatives is measured through primary data.

## 7. DATA ANALYSIS AND DISCUSSION

1. ITC's social investment initiatives and their contribution to society.

| *ITC's Social Investment Initiatives* | *ITC's Contribution to Society* |
|---|---|
| Afforestation Programme | improving India's green capital through multi-stakeholder partnerships, reforesting damaged areas, and generating sustainable livelihoods |

| ***ITC's Social Investment Initiatives*** | ***ITC's Contribution to Society*** |
|---|---|
| Watershed Development Programme | A cooperative framework that encourages neighbourhood involvement to manage local water resources |
| Sustainable Agriculture | Boosting Farmer Adaptability to Climate Change via Collaboration |
| Livestock Development | Constructing partnerships with multiple stakeholders to improve cattle in order to diversify and raise farm revenues |
| Women Empowerment | Using multi-stakeholder partnerships to enable economically disadvantaged women to earn higher/independent incomes |
| Primary Education | Creating cooperative connections with a variety of stakeholders in order to improve learning outcomes, lower student dropout rates, and keep children in school |
| Skilling & Vocational Training | Enhancing the employability of youth from underprivileged backgrounds via collaborative partnerships |
| Health & Sanitation | Encouraging Dignity and Health and Putting an End to Open Defecation via cooperative multi-stakeholder partnerships |
| Solid Waste Management | Creating a Successful Waste Management Chain with Multi-Stakeholder Collaborations |

*Source:* ITC Sustainability Integrated Report.

2. ITC's Impact focussed program (part of Mission Sunehra Kal for Sustainable & Inclusive Growth)

**Grass-root Institutions (cumulative)**

| Intervention | Institution | Nos. | Members | Corpus Fund (₹ Million) |
|---|---|---|---|---|
| Watershed | Water User Groups (WUGs) | 3,856 | 62,154 | 14.6 |
| Social Forestry | Vanikaran Sanghas (VSs) | 1,792 | 43,856 | 18.3 |
| Agriculture | Agri-business Centres (ABCs)* | 613 | 13,147 | 44.0 |
| Women Empowerment | Self-Help Groups (SHGs) | 4,541 | 52,630 | 167.4 |
| Education | School Management Committees (SMCs)* | 1,293 | 7,758 | - |
| | | **12,095** | **1,79,545** | **244.3** |

*ABCs and SMCs are annual numbers

3. Government Partnerships towards social investment initiatives.

| Theme | State | Department/Programme | No. of MoUs | Ongoing | Completed |
|---|---|---|---|---|---|
| Agriculture | Karnataka, Rajasthan, Maharashtra, Bihar, Madhya Pradesh, Assam, Jharkhand, Uttar Pradesh, Odisha | NABARD Tribal Development Fund (TDF), NITI Aayog | 3 | 2 | 1 |
| Biodiversity | Maharashtra, Rajasthan, Telangana | Forest Department, Govt. of Maharashtra and Telangana; Wasteland & Pastureland Development Board (WPDB), Govt. of Rajasthan | 3 | 3 | - |
| Education | Karnataka, Assam, West Bengal, Andhra Pradesh | Department of State Education Research and Training – Karnataka and Assam; District Elementary Education/ Samagra Shiksha Mission, West Bengal; Women Development & Child Welfare Department AP; | 6 | 3 | 3 |
| Livestock | Andhra Pradesh, Madhya Pradesh | Livestock Development Agency (APLDA); NABARD | 2 | - | 2 |
| Sanitation | Rajasthan, Punjab | Zila Panchayats under Swachh Bharat Mission | 4 | - | 4 |
| Solid Waste | Uttar Pradesh, Andhra Pradesh, Tamil Nadu, Karnataka, Punjab, Maharashtra, Bihar, Uttarakhand, Telangana | Saharanpur Municipal Corporation; Guntur Municipal Corporation, Guntur Zila Parishad; Coimbatore - Karamadai Panchayat; Greater Chennai Corporation; Zila Panchayat, Mysuru; Municipal Council of Kapurthala; Zila Parishad, Ranjangaon; Nagar Palika Parishad, Shivalik Nagar, Haridwar; Ministry of Urban Development, UP; District Panchayat Office (DPO), TS; Hindu Religious and Charitable Endowments (HR&CE), Government of Tamil Nadu; Munger Municipal Corporation; Lohiya, Swachh Bihar Abhiyan, Bihar Government | 14 | 13 | 1 |
| Vocational Training | Madhya Pradesh, Andhra Pradesh | NABARD | 2 | 2 | - |
| Water Stewardship | Madhya Pradesh, Andhra Pradesh, Maharashtra, Rajasthan, Bihar, Telangana, Karnataka | Mukhyamantri Jal Swabhalamban Abhiyan (MJSA); MGNREGA; Integrated Watershed Management Programme/Watershed Development Programme; NABARD; Water Resources Department (WRD), Government of Maharashtra; Watershed Development Department, Karnataka; DRDA Munger; Rajiv Gandhi Jal Sanchay Yojana | 46 | 8 | 38 |
| Women Empowerment | Madhya Pradesh, Maharashtra, Bihar, Rajasthan | State Rural Livelihood Mission of Maharashtra and Madhya Pradesh; Bihar Rural Livelihoods Promotion Society; MGNREGS - Women Initiative for Self-employment and Empowerment project | 4 | 1 | 3 |
| Total | | | 84 | 32 | 52 |

*Source:* ITC Sustainability Impact Report.

4. Awareness and perception about ITC (products, packaging, CSR initiatives, impact on society, SDG goals alignment etc.).

| ***Awareness and Perception about ITC Regarding/Degree of Agreement*** | ***Very High*** | ***High*** | ***Moderate*** | ***Slightly Moderate*** | ***Not at All*** |
|---|---|---|---|---|---|
| Eco friendly packaging | 45% | 32% | 14% | 5% | 4% |
| Activities - Alignment with SDG goals | 41% | 37% | 15% | 6% | 1% |
| addressing social issues | 37% | 35% | 20% | 8% | 0% |
| transparent and well managed social activities | 40% | 25% | 15% | 11% | 9% |
| positively contribute to the society | 39% | 33% | 16% | 8% | 4% |
| Satisfaction in buying ITC products | 47% | 23% | 15% | 10% | 5% |

5. T-test calculation for research hypothesis

H1a: Awareness regarding ITC's social investment initiatives differ between male and females.

| | *Male* | *Female* |
|---|---|---|
| Mean | 3.238806 | 3.39622642 |
| Variance | 1.517865 | 0.78229318 |
| Observations | 67 | 53 |
| Pooled Variance | 1.193715 | |
| Hypothesized Mean Difference | 0 | |
| df | 118 | |
| t Stat | –0.78378 | |
| P(T<=t) one-tail | 0.217369 | |
| t Critical one-tail | 1.65787 | |
| P(T<=t) two-tail | 0.434738 | |
| t Critical two-tail | 1.980272 | |

Since p-value of 0.217369 greater than 0.05, null hypothesis cannot be rejected at the 0.05 significance level, indicating Awareness regarding ITC's social investment initiatives do not differ between male and females.

6. Corelation between perception of ITC's addressing social issues and satisfaction in buying ITC products.

| | *Perception of ITC's Addressing Social Issues* | *Satisfaction in Buying ITC Products* |
|---|---|---|
| Perception of ITC's addressing social issues | 1 | |
| Satisfaction in buying ITC products | 0.746579 | 1 |

The p-value for correlation coefficient r = 0.746579 is 0.00001 which is less than 0.05 at 0.05 level of significance and hence the result is significant, null hypothesis is rejected and it is concluded that there is a significant correlation between perception of ITC's addressing social issues and satisfaction in buying ITC products.

## 8. FINDINGS

Following are the findings of this research work.

1. ITC's social investment initiatives contribute positively to the society's sustainable development.
2. ITC's social investment initiatives are aligned with SDG goals.
3. From the sustainability integrated report, it can be concluded that ITC's interventions with government partnerships towards sustainability is progressive.
4. Awareness regarding ITC's social investment initiatives do not differ between male and females.
5. There is a significant correlation between perception of ITC's addressing social issues and satisfaction in buying ITC products.

## REFERENCES

[1] Ambasta, A. (2017). ITC Limited's Mission Sunehra Kal: Two Decades of Transforming Lives and Landscapes, 97–115. https://doi.org/10.1007/978-3-319-41781-3_8.

[2] Anbarasan, P. and S. (2018). Stakeholder Engagement in Sustainable Enterprise: Evolving a Conceptual Framework, and a Case Study of ITC. Business Strategy and The Environment, 27, 282–299. https://doi.org/10.1002/BSE.1999.

[3] Basavaraj, K. and Deene, S. (2011). Corporate philanthropy in India: a new business model of ITC Ltd. JIMS8M: The Journal of Indian Management & Strategy, 16, 15–21.

[4] Hemerijck, A. (2017). The Uses of Social Investment. https://doi.org/10.1093/oso/9780198790488.001.0001.

[5] Jaiswal, N. and Gautam, A. (2016). Corporate Social Responsibility: Entrepreneurial initiatives of Indian FMCG Industry, 2. https://doi.org/10.21844/SMSJEI.V2I2.11140.

[6] Krishnamurthy, B. and Jalnawalla, D. (2012). ITC and Sustainability. SRPN: Sustainable Business (Topic). https://doi.org/10.2139/ssrn.2026853.

[7] Noël, A. (2018). Is social investment inimical to the poor? Socio-Economic Review. https://doi.org/10.1093/SER/MWY038.

[8] Sindhi, S., Maurya, U. and Shukla, M. (2014). Analyzing Capacity Development Approaches in CSR Implementation and Their Societal Impact: A Case Study of ITC's E-Choupal, 31–44. https://doi.org/10.1007/978-81-322-1653-7_3.

[9] Sonne, L. (2012). Innovative initiatives supporting inclusive innovation in India: Social business incubation and micro venture capital. Technological Forecasting and Social Change, 79, 638–647. https://doi.org/10.1016/J.TECHFORE.2011.06.008.

[10] Wittmayer, J., Backhaus, J., Avelino, F., Pel, B., Strasser, T., Kunze, I. and Zuijderwijk, L. (2019). Narratives of change: How social innovation initiatives construct societal transformation. Futures. https://doi.org/10.1016/J.FUTURES.2019.06.005.

# The Impact of Exchange Rate Fluctuation on India's Agricultural Exports Using Bounds Test Approach

**Jyoti Tripathi**
Assistant Professor Amity University, Punjab, Indi0061

***ABSTRACT:*** *After the collapse of the Bretton Woods system, exchange rate market became highly volatile as the world started floating exchange rate systems instead of pegged ones. Since then, it became an important discussion to analyze the impact of exchange rate movements on trade performance but, their findings are ambiguous and confusing. Thus, we attempted to seek the answer in the Indian context, particularly to the export of agriculture and allied products which is not touched yet by many researchers. Our study will be an add-on to the current literature in this area. The study is based on quarterly data and spans the years 2004Q2 through 2018Q2 using the ARDL bound test procedure. The test results show that real exports are co-integrated with real exchange rate Fluctuation, real effective exchange rate, and world real GDP. Exchange rate Fluctuation has a positive and significant impact on exports in the long run, while it is negati-vely correlated in the short run. World GDP as a proxy of external economic activity has a positive and significant impact on agricultural exports in the long run. The real effective exchange rate is also positively correlated with the exports in the long run but, negatively correlated in the short run.*

**Keywords:** Agricultural Exports, Bounds Test, Exchange Rate Fluctuation, Exchange Rate.

## 1. INTRODUCTION

Agriculture is a crucial sector in India which employ approximately 58 per cent of India's population. Recently pandemic hits the world and every sector got badly affected but, India's agricultural exports rose 23.24 per cent during March 2020 to June 2020. Agriculture exports as a percentage of agricultural GDP in India rose from 9.4 per cent in 2017–18 to 9.9 per cent in 2018–19. Though agricultural imports as a percentage of agricultural GDP in India have decreased from 5.7 percent to 4.9 percent, reflecting an exportable surplus and reduced reliance on agricultural imports in India (Ministry of Agriculture and Farmers Welfare, 2020). The share of agriculture and allied products in India's total export is approximately 12 per cent though the share of this sector is less than the secondary and tertiary sector, its dependency on imports is also less than these sectors which shows the self-sufficient nature of this sector. As both the agriculture sector and its exports have great importance in the Indian context, recently government introduced the Agriculture Export Policy (AEP), 2018 to strengthen and increase agricultural export with proper policy instruments so that India can become globally powerful and the earnings of farmers can increase.

After the collapse of the Bretton Woods system, the exchange rate market became highly volatile as the world started floating exchange rate systems instead of pegged ones. Since then, it became an important discussion to examine the effects of exchange rate movements on trade performance. In 1991, India was amid a serious Balance of Payments (BoP) crisis, with low levels of external exchange reserves that were insufficient to cover import bills even for a month. Policymakers debated several approaches to deal with the crisis, which finally led to economic liberalization. Following this, India switched to a market-determined floating exchange rate system.

Many studies have investigated the effect of exchange rate fluctuations on trade performance both in developed and developing countries but if it comes to analyzing the effects of exchange rate movements on agriculture exports, very few studies have been done to date. An earlier study by Chambers R.G. and Just R.E. (1981) find out in their study that, the effect of exchange rate fluctuations is very significant and negative on U.S. commodity market of wheat, corn, and soybean. Caballero, Ricardo J., and Corbo Vittorio (1986) explain in their study that exchange rate Fluctuation has an unambiguous, negative, and strong significance on the exports of six developing countries: Chile, Colombia, Peru, Philippines, Thailand, and Turkey used for the study. Keith (1986) explained the effect of exchange rate fluctuations on sector-wise which are US imports and exports on agriculture, crude materials, and manufacturing goods from 1974–1984. He found that among the sectors chosen for the study agriculture was the most susceptible sector to influenced negatively by exchange rate Fluctuation during the study period. Pick D.H. (1990) also tells that exchange rate risk has a negative and strong effect on U.S. agricultural exports to three developing countries but it is insignificant for the remaining seven developed countries they have chosen for the study. Adubi A.A. and Okunmadewa F. (1999) analyze that exchange rate fluctuations have negative effects on Nigeria's agricultural exports during 1986 to 1993. Cho G., Sheldon I.M., and McCorriston S. (2002) calculated the impact of exchange rate fluctuation on agricultural exports among developed countries by gravity model. Their study suggests that exchange rate Fluctuation has a very significant negative impact on agricultural exports. Kargbo (2007) employed a vector error correction model to investigate the relationship between exchange rate Fluctuation and its impact on agricultural trade in South Africa from the period of 1960–2004. The results of the study indicate that exchange rate Fluctuation has strong significant and negative effect on agricultural trade. Wang and Barrett (2007) employed a rational expectation-based multivariate

GARCH-M model using monthly data of export of Taiwan to USA from 1989–1998. The study finds that high-frequency exchange rate Fluctuation has strong negative effects on agricultural exports. Kandilov (2008) tells that movements in exchange rate have strong negative impact on agricultural exports between member countries of the G-10. Toktas and Kiziltan (2020) employed an ARDL bound test model from the period 1997–2015 to investigate the relationship between exchange rate Fluctuation and agricultural and food product exports of Turkey to the European Union. The study found that exchange rate fluctuations negatively affected total agricultural and food product exports during 6the study period.

Another study by Essien E.B. Dominic A.O. and Sunday E.R. (2011) conducted study in Nigeria using agricultural export, particularly cocoa and explained that the effect of exchange rate movements has a positive and strong significance on exports. Fogarasi (2011) assessed a gravity model and analyzed that exchange rate Fluctuation has positive effects on Hungarian agricultural exports between 1999 to 2008. Erdal *et al.* (2012) employed the Johansen cointegration test to find out the relationship between exchange rate movements and agricultural export and import of Turkey between the period 1995–2007. Results of the study tells that exchange rate fluctuations have a positive long-term relationship with agricultural exports and a negative long-term relationship with agricultural imports.

Gautam V., Suresh K.G., and Tiwari A.K. (2013) employed a panel data model to find out the association between exchange rate Fluctuation on India's real exports of agricultural commodities to the Euro area, USA, UK, and Japan from 2002 to 2009. The results of the study explained that exchange rate fluctuations have mixed effects on India's agricultural exports.

Yanikkaya *et al.* (2013) employed a gravity model for panel data on exports of 46 countries and selected agricultural commodities consisting of 1840 observations. The results suggest that the exchange rate fluctuation does not have any significant effect on the agricultural exports. Gatawa N.M. and Mahmud A.A. (2017) conducted their study in Nigeria from 1981 to 2014 and revealed that exchange rate Fluctuation has negligible effects on agricultural export volumes. After a review of the literature, we can say that very few researchers have chosen agricultural and allied sector export to investigate the effect of exchange rate fluctuations. Thus, we attempted to seek the answer in the Indian context, particularly to the export of agriculture and allied products which is not explored yet by many researchers. Our study will be an add-on to the current literature in this area.

This article is organized as; the first section is an introduction; second is the existing review of literature, and the third section explains the data and methodology for the study. The fourth section provides the results and discussion. The last section concludes the study.

## 2. METHODOLOGY

### 2.1 Data Description and Sources

The study is based on quarterly data and spans the years 2004Q2 through 2018Q2. The data on India's total agricultural and allied product exports and the real effective exchange rate is taken from the Center for Monitoring Indian Economy's Economic Outlook database. The data for the indices of export unit value is collected from the Indian Economy Database of Reserve Bank of India. The study utilized indices of export unit value for estimating real exports. Data of World GDP is collected at constant prices from World Bank National Accounts Database. Indices of export unit value indices and World GDP were collected as yearly data and converted to quarterly data using the quadratic interpolation approach followed by Arize *et al.* (2000) as quarterly series were not available for both. The period of 2011–2012 is used as the base year for all the the data series in the model. All variables used in this study have converted into a natural log form to compress the scale on which they are measured (Gujrati, 1995).

### 2.2 Equations

We tried to assess that, Fluctuation in exchange rate has any impact on real exports. Thus, we have chosen real exports as a dependent variable, and to calculate real exports we have divided nominal exports by the unit value index of exports and multiplied it by 100.

$$x = \left(\frac{nx}{nxuvi} \times 100\right)$$

Where $x$ is domestic country's real exports to the world; $nx$ is domestic country's nominal export quarterly data to the world. The data is measured in US dollar; $xuvi$ is the index of unit value export of the domestic country.

The dependent and the main variable for our study is exchange rate Fluctuation which is calculated by Moving Average Standard Deviation of the exchange rate, the formula is:

$$ver = [\tfrac{1}{2}\Sigma_{i=1}^{2}(ler_{t+i-1}ler_{t+i-2})^2]^{\frac{1}{2}}$$

Where $vx$ is the Fluctuation in real exchange rate; $ler$ is the log-returns of the real exchange rate. The order of moving average standard deviation (MASD) is 2. MASD is chosen since it is appropriate for low frequency database (Poon and Granger, 2003).

Depends on the literature, in this study, we have added external economic activity and price competitiveness as control variables. We have employed world Gross Domestic Product (GDP) as an external economic activity and real effective exchange rate (REER) as a relative price in our study.

## 2.3 Model

The purpose of the research is to examine that Fluctuation in real exchange rate has any impact on real exports. Our research depends on the equation of long-term export demand followed by Arize (1997). In the flexible exchange-rate environment, where India's real export is the dependent variable and the exchange rate, real exchange rate fluctuation, and world's real income are the independent variables. Our model can be represented as:

$$x_t = \xi_0 + \xi_1 w_t + \xi_2 p_t + \xi_3 v_t + \varepsilon_t, \quad \ldots (1)$$

Where, $x_t$ denotes the Napierian log of real exports at time $t$; $w_t$ denotes the Napierian log of world income at time $t$ (a proxy measure for the importing country's economic activity); $p_t$ denotes the Napierian log of relative prices at time $t$ and the real exchange rate is used to measure it; $v_t$ denotes the exchange rate fluctuation at time $t$; and $\varepsilon_t$ denotes the disturbance term.

The current study employed the Autoregressive distributed lag (ARDL) bounds test approach of co-integration developed by (Pesaran and Shin, 1999; Pesaran *et al.*, 2001), for empirical analysis, to assess the impact of real exchange rate fluctuation on India's real export of aggregate manufacturing goods. ARDL has several advantages first, we may use it to evaluate the long-run relationship among variables whether the series is stationary at the level I(0) or stationary at the first difference I(1). The second advantage of the ARDL model is that it is more suitable for small samples (Boutabba, 2014). Although it does not matter if the variables are I(0), I(1), or a mixture of both, variables should not be I(2) in the ARDL model. To evaluate the stationary characteristics of each variable, the study used the Augmented Dickey-Fuller (ADF) test Dickey and Fuller (1981) of unit root. In addition to this, we have applied Bai-Perron multiple breakpoint Bai and Perron (1998) test to find out the unknown structural breaks in the model.

## 2.4 Estimation Strategy

The study utilized the ARDL bound test, for determining the optimal lag length which is based on the computed F-statistic and compared to the critical value tabulated by Pesaran, *et al.* (2001). The critical value of the F-statistic is based on two sets of assumptions: one set assumes that all of the model's variables are I(0), while the other set assumes that the variables are I(1). The null hypothesis of no co-integration can be rejected under three situations based on the F-statistic: first, if the computed test statistic exceeds the upper bound critical value. Second, the cointegration test becomes inconclusive if the calculated F-statistic falls into the bounds. If the bound test result is inconclusive, the error correction term can be used to check cointegration (Banerjee *et al.*, 1998). The third condition is that the null hypothesis of no cointegration cannot be rejected if the computed F-statistic is less than the lower bounds value. With the ARDL approach, Eq (1) is rearranged as follows to obtain the long-run relationship among variables:

$$\Delta\, ln(x_t) = q_0 + \sum_{i=1}^{j} q_1 \Delta\,(lnx)_{t-1} + \sum_{i=1}^{j} q_2 \Delta\,(lnw)_{t-1} + \sum_{i=1}^{j} q_3 \Delta\,(lnp)_{t-1} + \sum_{i=1}^{j} q_4 \Delta\,(v)_{t-1} + \delta_1 (lnx)_{t-1} + \delta_2 (lnw)_{t-1} + \delta_3 (lnp)_{t-1} + \delta_4 (v)_{t-1} + \epsilon_t \quad \text{... (2)}$$

In equation (2) Δ represents the first difference operator and the term with summation signs indicates the short-run error correction dynamics, whereas the second portion of the equation with $\delta$ corresponds to the long-run relationship and the other variables of the equation are as defined earlier. The time trend variable is included in this equation to reflect the autonomous time-related changes. The ARDL technique calculates the optimal lag length for each variable by estimating $(j+1)k$ number of regressions, where j is the maximum number of lags to employ and k is the number of variables in the model. The following short-run error correction model, Eq(3), is calculated after establishing the long-run relationship among variables in Eq. (1).

$$\Delta\, ln(x_t) = q_0 + \sum_{i=1}^{j} q_1 \Delta\,(lnx)_{t-1} + \sum_{i=1}^{j} q_2 \Delta\,(lnw)_{t-1} + \sum_{i=1}^{j} q_3 \Delta\,(lnp)_{t-1} + \sum_{i=1}^{j} q_4 \Delta\,(v)_{t-1} + \gamma ecm_{t-1} + \epsilon_1 \quad \text{... (3)}$$

ECM stands for error correction mechanism. The pace of convergence from the short-run to the long-run model is measured by the error correction term.

# 3. EMPIRICAL RESULTS AND DISCUSSION

## 3.1 Unit Root Test

The ADF test is used to examine the stationary properties of all the variables in the model. The results of the unit root test are shown in table 1. The tests

**Table 1:** Estimated Statistics of Unit Root Test

| *Augmented Dickey-Fuller Test Statistics* | | | | |
|---|---|---|---|---|
| *Variable* | *Test Type* | *Level* | *First Difference* | *Order of Integration* |
| ln$x$ | Intercept | –2.03967 | –8.55644* | I(1) |
| | Trend and intercept | –1.75019 | –8.61015* | I(1) |
| ln$w$ | Intercept | 1.20604 | –3.10334** | I(1) |
| | Trend and intercept | –2.10407 | –3.23669*** | I(1) |
| ln$p$ | Intercept | –2.56481 | –4.19020* | I(1) |
| | Trend and intercept | –3.94974** | –4.08545** | I(0) |
| $v$ | Intercept | –4.49498* | –6.08249* | I(0) |
| | Trend and intercept | –4.46648* | –6.09019* | I(0) |

*Source:* Authors' own.

*Note:* ***, **, and * denote the level of significance at 10 per cent, 5 per cent, and 1 per cent respectively.

are conducted with trend and intercept and without trend (only with intercept). The results demonstrate that variables are the mixture of stationary at I(1) and I(0), allowing us to use the ARDL model.

### 3.2 Structural Break

To discover unknown structural breaks in the model, the study used Bai-Perron multiple breakpoint test. This test is helpful to understand multiple breaks at unknown dates endogenously when we are unable to explain easily a structural break by referring to a well-known, major, and disruptive event. According to test results, we found one significant structural break in the model in March 2015. The break, in March 2015 might be the result of contemporary measures taken to overcome the global recession as well as a slowdown in the European Union which is a major export trading partner for India (Chandrashekhar and Ghosh, 2016). The result of the Bai & Perron multiple breakpoint test is shown in table 2.

**Table 2:** Results of Bai-Perron Multiple Breakpoint Test

| *Break Test* | *F-Statistic* | *Scaled F-Statistic* | *Critical Values* | *Break Dates* |
|---|---|---|---|---|
| 0 vs. 1* | 25.9348 | 103.7394 | 16.19 | 03/01/2015 |
| 1 vs. 2 | 1.5535 | 6.2143 | 18.11 | |

*Source:* Authors' own.

### 3.3 Bound Test

The study used a bound test model to assess the long-run connection between all of the variables. Akaike Information Criteria (AIC) (Akaike, 1976) is used to determine the proper lag length, and our model's lag order is ARDL (3, 0, 1, 4). Table 3 displays the results of the bound F-test, which demonstrates that the estimated value of the F-statistic is 9.6756, which is greater than the upper bound critical value of 4.66 at a 1 per cent significance level. The dependent variable is lnx, whereas the independent variables are lnw, lnp, and v in the model.

**Table 3:** Estimated Statistics of ARDL Bound Test

| *Significance (in per cent)* | *Critical Value* | | *F-Statistics* |
|---|---|---|---|
| | *Lower Bound* | *Upper Bound* | |
| 10 | 2.37 | 3.2 | 9.675 |
| 5 | 2.79 | 3.67 | |
| 2.5 | 3.15 | 4.08 | |
| 1 | 3.65 | 4.66 | |

*Source:* Authors' own.

### 3.4 Long-run Results

The outcomes of the long-run relationship between real exports of agricultural and allied products, real-world GDP, real effective exchange rate, and real exchange rate Fluctuation are reported in Table 4. The results show that the real-world GDP, real effective exchange rate, and exchange rate Fluctuation have a positive and significant impact on real exports.

**Table 4:** Estimated Long-run Coefficients

| *Variable* | *Coefficient* | *T-statistics* | *P-Value* |
|---|---|---|---|
| ln$w$ | 2.4303 | 5.2611 | 0.0000 |
| ln$p$ | 1.8021 | 2.2565 | 0.0299 |
| $v$ | 9.7958 | 3.3289 | 0.0019 |

*Source:* Authors' own.

### 3.5 Short-run Elasticity

Table 5 represents the results of the short-run dynamics relationship. The coefficient of the error correction term is negative and significant at the 1 per cent level, which indicates evidence of a long-run causal relationship among the variables. The speed of adjustment towards equilibrium is determined by the coefficient of the error correction model. As shown in the table, the ECM coefficient is –0.7958, implying that any disequilibrium in the present period will be corrected by 79% in the following period. Table 5 depicts the negative significant impact of real exchange rate fluctuation and real exchange rate on real exports.

**Table 5:** Estimated Short-run Coefficients

| *Variable* | *Coefficient* | *T-Statistics* | *P-Value* |
|---|---|---|---|
| D(ln$x$ (–1)) | 0.23881 | 2.55627 | 0.0147 |
| D(ln$x$(–2)) | –0.34632 | –3.63850 | 0.0008 |
| D(ln$p$) | –0.59520 | –0.98838 | 0.3292 |
| D($v$) | 4.53983 | 4.04313 | 0.0002 |
| D($v$ (–1)) | –3.32678 | –2.76308 | 0.0088 |
| D($v$ (–2)) | –2.91161 | –2.49970 | 0.0169 |
| D($v$ (–3)) | –3.20373 | –2.69076 | 0.0105 |
| D1503 | –0.50628 | –7.14233 | 0.0000 |
| CointEq(–1)* | –0.79581 | –7.31238 | 0.0000 |
| R-squared: 0.6935, DW-statistics: 2.1245. | | | |

*Source:* Authors' own.

### 3.6 Diagnostic Tests

To test the reliability of the model the study has employed some diagnostic tests. Breusch–Godfrey Lagrange multiplier test for the residual serial correlation, Breusch–Pagan–Godfrey test for heteroskedasticity in the model, and Jarque–Berra test for normality in table 6. The results explained that the study is free from serial correlation, heteroskedasticity, and non-normality.

**Table 6:** Diagnostic Test

| 6 | *LM-Version* | *P-Value* | *F-Version* | *P-Value* |
|---|---|---|---|---|
| Serial correlation | 3.0416 | 0.2185 | 1.1416 | 0.3306 |
| Heteroscedasticity | 11.3851 | 0.4952 | 0.9100 | 0.5460 |
| Normality | 3.5660 | 0.1681 | (Not Applicable) | |

*Source:* Authors' own.

Finally, CUSUM (cumulative sum of recursive residuals) and CUSUM of Squares tests were performed to examine the model's stability.

### 3.7 CUSUM and CUSUM of Squares Tests

Test results of CUSUM and CUSUM of Squares are shown in Figures 1 and 2. The test results are shown in the middle of the dotted lines and could not surpass the critical value at a 5% significance. As a result, we may infer that the model we calculated is reliable and stable.

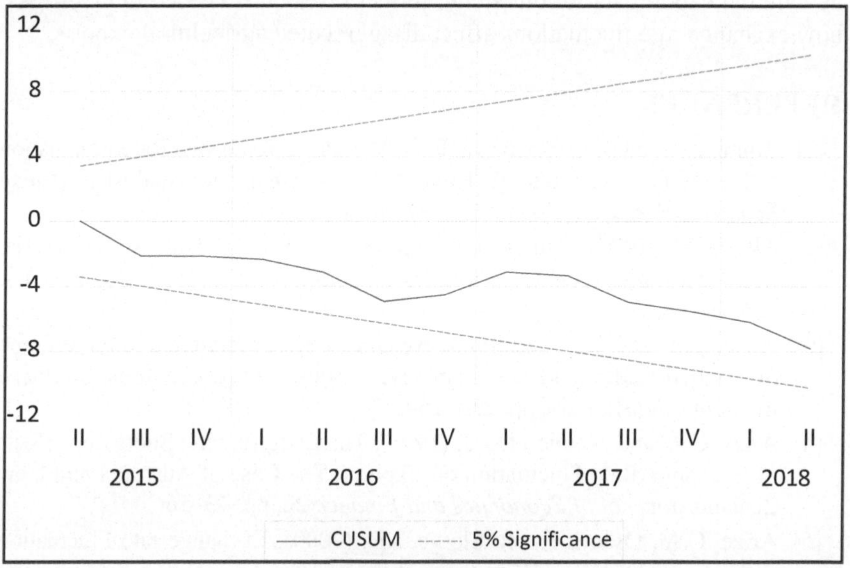


**Figure 1:** CUSUM Test

*Source:* Authors' own.

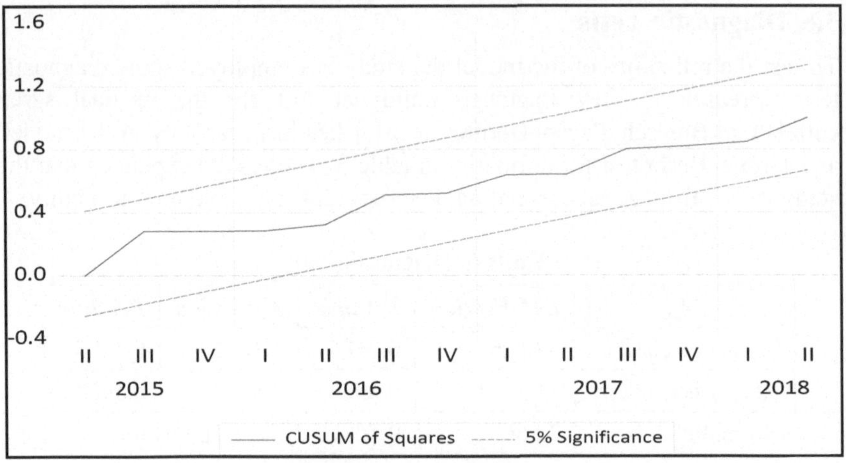


**Figure 2:** CUSUMQ Test

*Source:* Authors' own.

## 4. CONCLUSION

The study investigated the impact of exchange rate Fluctuation on exports using India's agricultural exports data and found a positive and significant impact of the exchange rate Fluctuation on exports in the long run, while it is negatively correlated in the short run. India needs to develop its external exchange market to a certain level that can provide traders with to hedge effectively against external exchange uncertainty. We have chosen aggregate agricultural export data for our study; further research is needed to investigate how exchange rate fluctuations affect disaggregated agricultural exports.

## REFERENCES

[1] Adubi, A.A. and Okunmadewa, F. (1999). Price, Exchange Rate Fluctuation and Nigeria's Agricultural Trade Flow: A Dynamic Analysis, *African Economic Research Consortium*, 87, pp. 1–41.

[2] Akaike, H. (1976). Canonical Correlation Analysis of Time Series and the Use of an Information Criterion, *Mathematics in Science and Engineering, 126,* 27–96.

[3] Arize, C.A. (1997). Conditional exchange rate Fluctuation and the volume of external trade: evidence from seven industrialized countries. *Southern Economic Journal,* 64, pp. 235–254.

[4] Arize, C.A. and Malindretos, J. (1998). The Long-run and Short-run Effects of Exchange-Rate Fluctuation on Exports: The Case of Australia and New Zealand, *Journal of Economics and Finance* 22, pp. 43–56.

[5] Arize, C.A., Osang, T. and Slottje, J.D. (2000), Exchange rate Fluctuation and external trade: evidence from Thirteen LDCs, *Journal of Business and Economic Statistics,* 18 (1), pp. 10–17.

[6] Bai, J. and Perron, P. (1998). Estimating and Testing Linear Models with Multiple Structural Changes, *Econometrica,* 66 (1), pp. 47–78.

[7] Banerjee, A., Dolado, J.J. and Mestre, R. (1998), Error-Correction Mechanism Tests for Cointegration in a Single-Equation Framework, *Journal of Time Series Analysis,* 19, pp. 267– 283.

[8] Boutabba, M.A. (2014). The impact of financial development, income, energy and trade on carbon emissions: evidence from the Indian Economy, *Econ Model,* 40, pp. 33–41.

[9] Caballero, Ricardo J. and Corbo, Vittorio (1986), The Effect of Real Exchange Rate Uncertainty on Exports: Empirical Evidence, *The World Bank Economic Review,* 3(2), pp. 263–278.

[10] Chambers, R.G. and Just, R.E. (1981). Effects of Exchange Rate Changes on U.S. Agriculture: A Dynamic Analysis, *Americal Journal of Agricultural Economics*, 32–46.

[11] Chandrashekhar, C.P. and Ghosh, J. (2016, November 21), *Understanding India's export collapse,* The Hindu Business Line.

[12] Cho, G., Sheldon, I.M. and McCorriston (2002). Exchange Rate Uncertainty and Agricultural Trade, *American Journal of Agricultural Economics,* 84(4), pp. 931–942.

[13] Dickey, D.A. and Fuller, W.A. (1981). Likelihood ratio statistics for autoregressive time series with a unit root, *Econometrica,* 49, pp. 1057–1072.

[14] Erdal, G., Erdal, H. and Esengün, K. (2012), The effects of exchange rate Fluctuation on trade: evidence from Turkish agricultural trade, *Applied Economics Letters,* 19(3), pp. 297–303.

[15] Essien, E.B., Dominic, A.O. and Sunday, E.R. (2011), Effects of Price and Exchange Rate Fluctuations on Agricultural Exports in Nigeria, *International Journal of Economic Development Research and Investment,* 2(1), pp. 1–10.

[16] Fogarasi, J. (2011), The Effect of Exchange Rate Fluctuation upon External Trade of Hungarian Agricultural Products, *Studies in Agricultural Economics,* 113, pp. 85–96.

[17] Gatawa, N.M. and Mahmud, A.A. (2017), Impact of Exchange Rate Fluctuations on Agricultural Exports (Crops) In Nigeria, *International Journal of Humanities and Social Science Invention,* 6(3), pp. 65–71.

[18] Gautam, V., Suresh, K.G. and Tiwari, A.K. (2013), Impact of Real Exchange Rates on Exports of Agricultural Commodities: Evidence from India, *Review of Economic and Business Studies,* 6(1), pp. 46–48.

[19] Gujarati, D.N. (1995), *Basic econometrics* (3rd ed.), New York: McGraw-Hill.

[20] Kandilov, I.T. (2008), The Effects of Exchange Rate Fluctuation on Agricultural Trade. *American Journal of Agricultural Economics,* 90(4), pp. 1028–1043.

[21] Keith, E.M. (1986), Exchange Rate Risk and U.S. Trade: A Sectoral Analysis, *Economic Review*, Federal Reserve Bank of Kansas City, 16–28.

[22] Kargbo, J.M. (2007), Exchange rate Fluctuation and agricultural trade under policy reforms in South Africa, *Development Southern Africa,* 23(1), pp. 147–170.

[23] Ministry of Agriculture and Farmers Welfare Government of India (2020), *Exports of agricultural commodities during March to June 2020 increased by 23.24 per cent* Public Information Bureau.

[24] Pesaran, M.H. and Shin, Y. (1998), An autoregressive distributed lag modelling approach to cointegration analysis, *Econometrics and Economic Theory in the 20th Century: The Ragnar Frisch Centennial Symposium*, 31, pp. 371–413.

[25] Pesaran, M.H., Shin, Y. and Smith, R.J. (2001), Bounds testing approaches to the analysis of level relationships, *Journal of Applied Econometrics,* 16(3), pp. 289–326.

[26] Pick, D.H. (1990), Exchange Rate Risk and U.S. Agricultural Trade Flows, *American Journal of Agriculture Economics*, pp. 694–700.

[27] Poon, S.H. and Granger, C.W.J. (2003). Forecasting financial market Fluctuation: A review, *Journal of Economic Literature,* 41(2), pp. 478–539.

[28] Toktas, Y. and Kiziltan, A. (2020). The Impact of Turkey's Real Effective Exchange Rate and its Fluctuation on Turkey's Agricultural Export to the European Union. In Y.A. Unvan, *Studies on Economic Sciences*. pp. 41–59. Lyon: Livre De Lyon.

[29] Wang, K. and Barrett, C. (2007). Estimating the Effects of Exchange Rate Fluctuation on Export Volumes, *Journal of Agricultural and Resource Economics,* 32(2), pp. 225–255.

[30] Yanikkaya, H., Kaya, H. and Kocturk, O.M. (2013). The effect of real exchange rates and their volatilities on the selected agricultural commodity exports: A case study on Turkey, 1971–2010, *Agricultural Economics,* 59(5), pp. 235–245.

# Cashless Economy with Reference to Micro and Small Enterprises

**Pratima Katti**
School of Economics and Commerce, CMR University,
Kalyan Nagar, Bangalore, Karnataka, India

***ABSTRACT:*** *Cashless economy is the essence of sound and sustainable economic growth. Several empirical studies have reviewed the challenges in the implementation and adoption of digital payments towards cashless economy. Major challenges like cyber fraud, lower digital literacy levels and attitude of people towards adoption have to be addressed to enhance penetration of cashless economy. The government and RBI_are working with tremendous efforts to achieve the success of cashless economy. Policy makers have to focus to maintain the integrity have in the digital systems while making and executing the policies. MSEs have adopted the digitization to the maximum extent. At a macro perspective cashless economy has achieved its growth but there is a need for additional research to address the hurdles at micro level of the economy to increase digitization to enhance the growth of the cashless economy.*

**Keywords:** Adoption of Digitalization, Banking Sector, Banking Technology, Cashless Economy, Cyber Security, Digital Literacy, Digital Payments, Impact on Small Enterprises, Micro and Small Enterprises, Net Banking.

## 1. INTRODUCTION

Indian Economy growing towards Cashless Economy. Banking sector is developing very fast due to technological evolution, internet and globalisation. The creation of service delivery options are trending in the banking sector. ATMs, mobile banking, NEFT etc different options. (Anand, 2015 Oct) At a macro level it is a good sign. But we need to understand at the micro level. Benefits and drawbacks are to be considered. There is a huge transformation in the banking sector and its technology (Sardana & Singhania, 2018). Customers have to drastically move to digitalisation and update their digital skills. We need to understand the difficulties faced by micro and small enterprises. Study of digital transformation and its challenges are the essence of today and need to find the solutions for the challenges.

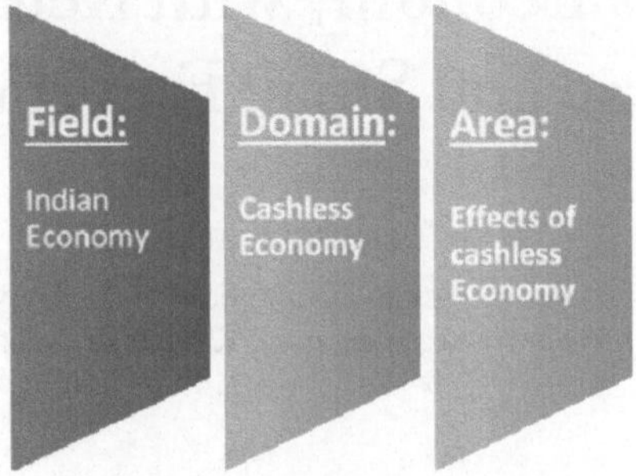


**Figure 1:** Cashless Economy

## 2. CASHLESS ECONOMY IN INDIA

In India is a in the transition period. Studying the merits and demerits of the system and finding the solutions for the challenges is today's necessity. Banking sector has to improve its technology in leaps and bond to meet the necessity of the customers and improvement of cyber security system should be on a higher priority. Digital literacy should increase. Common people and especially senior citizens are really getting affected. Central govt is encouraging for user friendly applications UPI and mobile payments. Digitalization is getting evolved continuously. Banks also have the pressure to introduce customer friendly services. Taking care of the safety measures in banking system is very important.

### 2.1 Benefits and Challenges of Cashless Economy in India

Preeti Garg and M Panchal Author *et al.* explain the views and experience of people on introduction of cashless economy in India. It shows how India is able to control black money and fight against terrorism. And it also explains the challenges in the implementation of digital payments. Major challenges like cyber fraud, illiteracy, attitude of people towards adoption of new system are very well explained. Today's need is to cross the hurdles and achieve the growth. Ultimately, we can say that cashless economy is a positive indication of growth. (Garg & Panchal, 2016)

### 2.2 Effects of Cashless Payment Methods

M. Tirupati elaborate that "The Digital India "is a showcasing scheme of government of India. Paperless and Cashless is the moto of this scheme. Government is pushing the people to adopt towards cashless transactions. It will help India to achieve growth. (Tirupati, 2019)

### 2.3 Cashless Transaction and its Perception in Indians

V. Podile, P. Rajesh Author *et al.* showcase how Demonetization initiate has geared the usage of electronic payments. Slowly India is moving towards cashless economy. This paper attempts to understand the perception of people towards cashless transactions and their problems during payments. Digital instruments and adopting to the usage of these instruments are highlighted in this paper. (Podile & Rajesh, 2017)

## 2.4 Technology Infrastructure and Digital India

Author D. Ghosh *et al.* explain the purpose of this paper is to understand the technology infrastructure proposed in the cashless economy initiative in India. The paper tries to explain the efforts taken by the Government to set up the huge infrastructure and to make it reachable to all sectors of the economy. So that it can be used by a small vendor and labourer also. The sweeping changes can be witnessed in the Indian Economy. The papers suggest the areas where the policy makers have to focus to maintain the fairness in the system while making and executing the policies. (Ghosh, 2021)

## 2.5 Cashless Transactions at a Micro Level of the Society

S. Venkatraman; PG Reddy Author *et al.* examine how aspects such as Trust, Economic and Social values influence on their everyday transactions. There has been study is done which is more focused on Macro level of the society and micro level is ignored. The paper focuses more at a Micro level and tries to understand the influence of social values and trust on the day today transactions. Suppose when person pays by cash, he feels the pinch of spending whereas when a person pays by plastic card, doesn't realise the pinch. The person ends up spending more with credit and debit cards. Trust is a major factor in money transactions. Some traditional minded people may not trust digital payments or it might take more time for them to accept. Many old people might feel insecure to do digital payments. Some religious thoughts also influence on cash transaction. (Venkatramanan & Reddy)

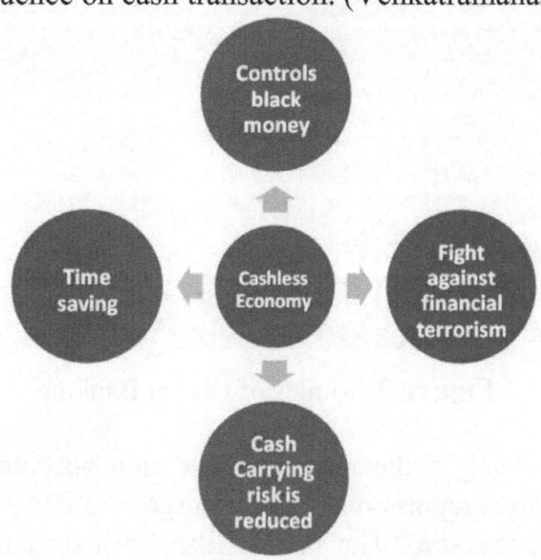


**Figure 2:** Benefits of Cashless Economy

## 3. DIGITAL PAYMENTS AND ONLINE BANKING TECHNOLOGY IN INDIA

PP Patil; NP Rana; YK Dwivedi *et al.* Analysed on digital and mobile payments adoption and usage. Digital payments have changed lives of millions of people in the modern world. Internet has changed the way business is conducted in recent years. It has become as a most powerful emerging trend in the modern era. The rate of adoption is very fast compare to any other consumer technology adoption. The wide penetration of mobile usage has given the opportunity to transform quickly. Another aspect we need to consider is covid era has created the urge to use contactless transactions. (Patil, Dwivedi, & Rana, 2017)

Benedict J. *et al.* Explain how banks are dependent on Fintech in transforming their business module. Banks have to adopt more technology to meet their customers requirement Technology is the only way for banks to reshape their growth. Banking has got a new idea in the tech world. Banks are able to give a greater number of services to its customers due to technology. Integration of fintech into banking sector has transformed the financial sector. (Benedict, 2018)

Bansal *et al.* Writes that The Economic Prosperity and Growth of a Nation depends upon accessibility to financial product and services. Government and RBI are making tremendous effort to bring all sections of the economy into the mainstream financial system. There is an urge to develop tools to Bridge the gap and bring every section from rural as well as urban population. High amount of technology usage will cut the cost to the banker and increase the comfort level to the customer. (Bansal, 2014)

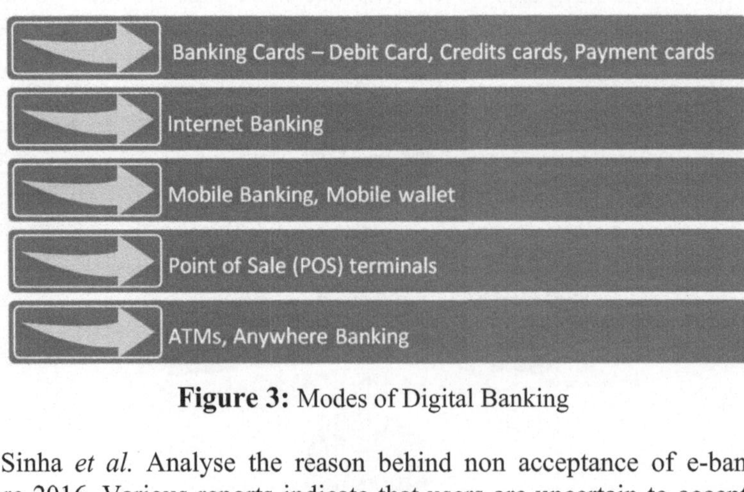


**Figure 3:** Modes of Digital Banking

Sinha *et al.* Analyse the reason behind non acceptance of e-banking before 2016. Various reports indicate that users are uncertain to accept and use the electronic banking. The factors like Trust on bank, complexity in technology make people hesitant to make use of e-banking. The growth of banking sector in the physical form is very limited. Only e-banking can increase the number of transactions which will lead to more profit. E-banking Technology can prosper the business activities. It saves the time of consumers as well as bankers. (Sinha & Indrajit) Agarwal *et al.* Explain that customer perception and attitude towards e-banking is the key to banking strategy formulation process. To understand the customer satisfaction, a study was conducted in northern part of India. The study concludes that the customers are influenced by the type of account they hold, their profession and age. Trust and security aspects are the most important factors in e-banking. (Agarwal & Rastogi, 2009)

## 4. DIGITAL LITERACY OF THE POPULATION IN INDIA

Prema Nedungadi *et al.* demonstrate a inclusive Digital Literacy framework for lower sections of the society and propose a model to educate the masses using tablet based Mobile technology. The Educational framework helps overcome the financial literacy levels, E-safety and addresses the low internet band width etc in remote areas. The research and the framework propose to involve Civil societies, schools and Govt agencies to increase the reach The framework when implemented helps improve the Digital literacy levels amongst the vulnerable society (PNedungadi, 2018)

Khokhar, A.S, discusses the current levels of digital literacy in India and ways to improve at the national level. India with largest working population needs to embrace the digital inclusion of the masses for development, rapid growth, elimination of poverty. The digital literacy of the people enables access to information and is a powerful tool for inclusion, empowerment. The challenges to improve the digital literacy include low level of literacy amongst rural areas /women population and lack of internet facilities in many areas. The Indian Govt has implemented policy initiative like Digital India program. The critical success factors to digitally skill the population depends on the collaboration of Govt, Industry bodies and social organizations. The role of teachers in enabling the masses is highly important. (Khokar, 2016)

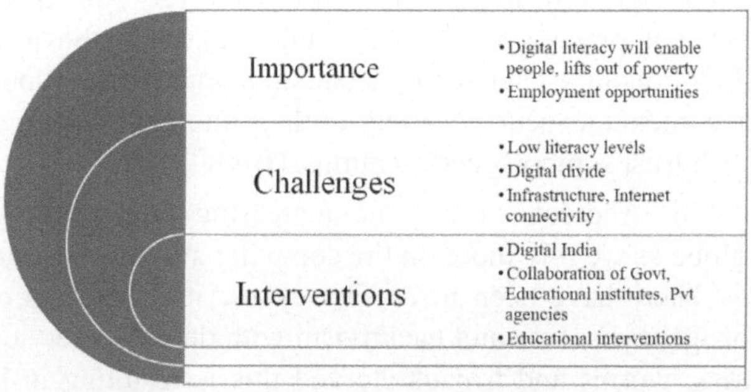


**Figure 4:** Digital Literacy: Current State, Challenges and Interventions

Siriginidi Subba Rao studies the reasons for Digital divide in India and opines that creation of the knowledge society is important to bridge the digital divide and help deprived and disadvantaged. Compared to developed countries like USA, India suffers from a digital divide due to constraints like Internet penetration, Lower tele density, IT knowledge of the population. The research suggests methodology consisting of ICT Infra creation, digital content creation as a remedial action. It proposes a national agenda for bridging the digital divide, consisting of 8 core action areas consisting content creation, competence building, core technologies creation, connectivity provision, community participation, commitment, capacity augmentation and cost reduction (S. Subbarao, 2005)

In their research Prasad, H. *et al.* observed that digital financial literacy/adoption has increased post demonetisation and Covid 19 outbreak. In the survey of 268 sample households in Udaipur city of Rajasthan state, India found that the males have higher digital financial literacy. The survey clearly established that the population involved in Service class i.e. the formal Job sector have adopted digital financial systems than the Non service class, which is due to lack of awareness and many a times have not disclosed their income. (Prasad, 2018)

Abdul Azeez N.P. Et El through their research conclude that digital financial literacy is a basic prerequisite for financial inclusion of the people. They did the research based on the survey of 500 households in rural Aligarh district. The research concluded that education, Age, Gender and occupation of the person are the key determinants of the digital financial literacy. (Azeez, 2021)

## 5. CYBER SECURITY IN CASHLESS ECONOMY

Bomil Suh and Ingoo Han did the research effect of trust on customers' acceptance of the internet banking. They state that apart from the ease of use and usefulness of the product, the third factor that decides on the acceptance is the trust factor. They did a survey and analysed the responses of the 845 users of internet banking to establish the effect of trust on adoption of internet banking. Their research imply that customers rely on trust in online environments that process the sensitive information in the internet online banking. They conclude that internet banking practitioners should educate their end customers on security/ safety of their internet banking systems and should publish trust symbols/ certifications. (Bomil, 2002)

Bendovschi, Andreea studies the increasing number of cybercrimes across the globe as we rely more on the computer systems for our day-to-day transactions. There have been increasing cybercrimes such as cyber-crime, cyber espionage, cyber war and hacktivism with denial of service, malicious codes, viruses, worms and trojans etc and this is resulting in loss of info, business disruptions, revenue loss etc Author recommends the three main solutions to reduce the cybercrimes – Increase the cybercrime awareness, address international legal aspects pf cybercrime and individual responsibility of end users. (Bendoschi, 2015)

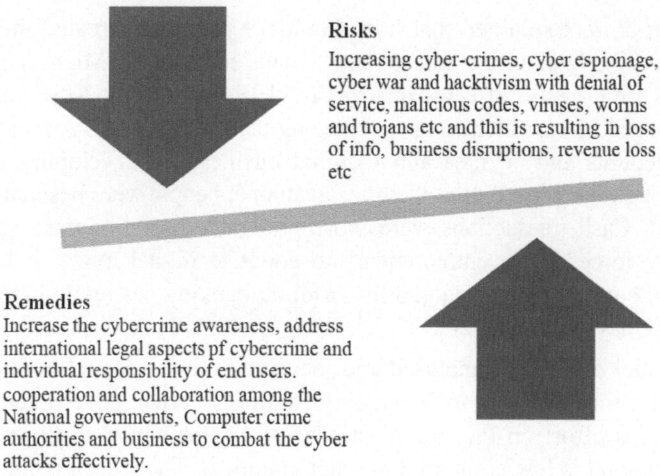


**Figure 5:** Cyber Security in Cashless Economy: Risks and Remedies

Srinivas, *et al.*, discuss about the cyber-attacks and the cyber security arrangements/ measures to be taken to protect against cybercrimes. They detail out the security policies of governments of leading countries to deal with cyber-crimes prevention and management. The research recommends governments to integrate standardisation as part of cybersecurity policy. They suggest that National regulatory bodies to utilise greater application of the standard as a point of reference in order to impose cyber security regulations. (Srinivas, 2018)

Nir Kshetri analyses that synergy between crime gangs and internet has resulted in higher number of cybercrimes. With higher computerisation/ digitisation of processes and increasing number of cyber-attacks, the organisations are concerned about the security of their networks. The motivations behind the attacks may be due to intrinsic motivation or extrinsic motivation. The paper concludes that there should be cooperation and collaboration among the National governments, Computer crime authorities and business to combat the cyber attacks effectively. (Kshetri, 2005)

Mehta, S., Sharma *et al.*, did the research on need for cyber security in secure systems and what are the Govt. policies and frameworks to address the cyber security concerns like establishment of Cyber-Crime-Investigation-Centre-Of-India, Cyber-Security-Research-AndDevelopment-Centre Of-India-(CSRDCI), National Critical Informati and CERT-In: The development in The Indian Computer Emergency Response Team (CERT-In), which operates as the national agency for handling the rate of cyber-attacks on the government network on Infrastructure Protection Centre (NCIIPC) Of India. (Soni, 2021)

## 6. ADOPTION OF DIGITAL PAYMENTS BY MICRO AND SMALL ENTERPRISES

Quayson *et al.* Explained that how Covid-19 pandemic created the urge to adopt to digitization by Micro and Small enterprises. Micro and Small business are the most affected during Covid 19. Most of the MSE enterprises are managed by low literates. Many among them are women. And don't have bank accounts and no idea about digital business. In developing countries even though there are digital facilities available, people were hesitant to make use of it. Cash transactions were more preferable mode of transaction. But covid 19 forced these entrepreneurs to adopt to digital mode. It became a matter of survival and sustainability. Mobile banking has really helped these MSEs. (Quayson & Bai, 2021)

Samuel *et al.* have analysed and identified the drives and hurdles in the growth of e- governance in developing countries. Indian government has put tremendous effort on the growth model of e-governance at all levels. But adoption level is low compared to other countries. The reason is literacy and digital literacy level of Indian citizens is low. It's very challenging to make them use the new technology. It's a major hurdle in the digital transformation of the economy. (Samuel, 2020)

Mukherjee S. *et al.* have examined how the MSEs are lagging behind compared to other neighbouring countries. MSEs are like footprints of the economy. If they don't adopt a updated technology, they can't compete and grow. Author has done an empirical study on the jute industry of India. Its facing lot of competition from synthetic products from neighbouring countries. Jute industry has not adopted new technology which leads to more cost of production. (Mukherjee, 2018)

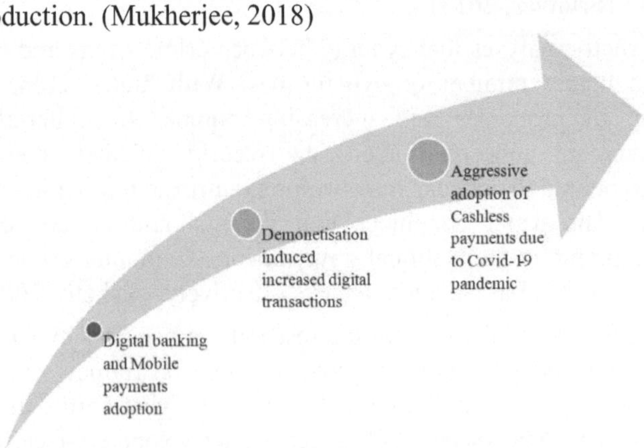


**Figure 6:** Drivers for Adoption of Cashless Economy by Micro and Small Enterprises

Patwardhan *et al.* examine the Financial Inclusion of unbanked population to achieve economic growth. Financial inclusion is nothing but providing reasonably priced financial services to the poor people by the sound institutions. So, the unbanked poor person can start and expand his own business which will lead to economic growth of the country as well. Financial inclusion can also help the poor person to get credit and expand his business. It naturally gives a good income status and builds confidence in the individuals which leads to a good mental health also. (Patawardhan, 2018)

Author Anshika *et al.* have done research on the determinants of general financial literacy, overall financial literacy and specific financial literacy of Micro and Small enterprises in Punjab state. The research reviews that the age has the significant role in the adoption of new technology. The firms have to spend some portion of their profit on Digital literacy training for their employees. Government also should conduct some regular training programmes for MSEs workers which will lead to the success of digitization. (Anshika, 2021)

## 7. CONCLUSIONS

Indian Economy is a fast-growing economy towards digitization. Government has taken significant interest in the success of Cashless Economy by setting up a huge infrastructure and make it reachable to all the sectors of the economy.

Banking sector plays a pivotal role in transforming and reshaping the modern digital economy. Integration of fintech in a large scale into banking sector will boost the economy. MSEs should be under the digital umbrella. Government should encourage more Financial digital literacy programmes which will promote the cashless economy.

## ACKNOWLEDGEMENTS

Authors thank directorate of research and Innovation (DORI), CMR University for training and support. The research is funded by CRU Student research & Innovation fund.

## REFERENCES

[1] Anshika, S.A. (2021). Determinants of financial literacy: Empirical evidence from micro and small enterprises in India. *Asia Pacific Management Review.*

[2] Agarwal and Rastogi (2009). Customers' perspectives regarding e-banking in an emerging economy, *Journal of retailing consumer.*

[3] Anand, H. (2015). E-banking trends in India. *shanlax International Journal of Management.*

[4] Azeez, A. (2021). Digital financial literacy and its determinants. *South Asian journal of social studies and economics*, 8–22.

[5] Bansal (2014). Perspective of Technology in Achieving Financial Inclusion in Rural India. *Procedia Economics and Finance, 2014 - Elsevier,* 472–480.

[6] Bansal (2014). Perspective of Technology in Achieving Financial Inclusion in Rural India. Procedia Economics and Finance, 11(), 472–480. doi:10.1016/S2212-5671(14)00213-5. *Procedia Economics and Finance,* 472-480.

[7] Bendoschi (2015). Trends, Pattern and security contermeasures. *Procedia Economics and Finance*, 24–31.

[8] Benedict, J. (2018). Integrating the troublemakers: A taxomony for cooperatin between banks and fintech. *Journal of Economics and Business*.

[9] Bomil (2002). Effects of trust on customer acceptance of internet banking. *Procedia Economics and Finance*, 247–263.

[10] Garg, P. (n.d.). Cshsless economy in India. *Journal of business and management.*

[11] Garg, P. and Panchal, M. (2016). Study on Introduction of Cashless Economy in India 2016. *IOSR Journal of Business and Management (IOSR-JBM)*.

[12] Ghosh, D. (2021). The commercialization of bias in cashless India. *ScienceDirect.*

[13] Khokar (2016). Digital literacy: How India is prepared to embrace it. *International Journal of Digital Literacy and Digital Competence (IJDLDC) 7(3)*.

[14] Kshetri (2005). pattern of global war and crime. *Journal of international management*, 541–562.

[15] Mukherjee (2018). Challenges to Indian micro small scale. *Journal of Global enterprenuership Research*, 8–28.

[16] Patawardhan (2018). *Handbook of blockchain, digital financial inclusion.* Elseiver.

[17] Patil, P., Dwivedi, Y. and Rana, N. (2017). Digital Payment Adoption: An Analysis of Literature.

[18] *international federation for information processing*, 61–70.

[19] PNedungadi (2018). *Towards an inclusive digital literacy framework for digital India.* Retrieved from www.emeraldinsight.com

[20] Podile, V. and Rajesh, P. (2017). Public Perception on Cashless Transactions in India. *Asian Journal of Research in Banking and Finance.*

[21] Prasad (2018). digital financial literacy: a study of households in Udaipur. *Journal of business and management*, 23–32.

[22] Quayson and Bai (2021). Covid–19 pandemic digitization lessons for sustainable development of micro and small enterprises. *Sustainable Production and Consumtion.*

[23] S. Subbarao (2005). Bridging digital divide efforts in India. *Telematics and informatics*, 361–375.

[24] Samuel (2020). Druvers and barriers to e-government adoption in Indian cities. *journal of urban management.*

[25] Sardana and Singhania (2018). Digital Technology in the realm of banking. *international journal of research in finance and management*, 28–32.

[26] Sinha and Indrajit (n.d.). Acceptance of technology, related factors in use of off branch e-banking: An Indian. *The Journal of High Technology Management Research.*

[27] Soni, M.A. (2021 ). The Urgency of cyber security in secure networks. *international conference on intelligent computing and control systems.*

[28] Srinivas, J. (2018). Government regulations in cyber security framework, standards and recomendations.

[29] Tirupati, M. (2019). Effects of cashless payment methods. *International Journal of Scientific & Technology Research.*

[30] Venkatramanan, S. and Reddy (n.d.). Cashless transactions in local context.

# Exploring Music Consumption Trends in the Digital Age: Insights from Kerala

**Bindu Balagopal[1] and P. Chacko Jose[2]**

[1]Professor, Department of Economics, Government Vitoria College, Palakkad, Kerala

[2]Principal, St Aloysius College, Elthuruth, Thrissur, Kerala, India

E-mail: [2]chackojosep@gmail.com

***ABSTRACT:*** *The music industry in India has undergone a significant transformation due to the digital revolution. The industry is undergoing a change, shifting from a tangible to a virtual platform. The consumption of music differs from the consumption of other things. Music is a cultural and entertainment commodity, and so its consumption differs from that of other things. This research utilises primary data gathered from the state of Kerala to examine the consumption trends of music in the digital age. The results were obtained via a sample survey administered to persons who both purchase and listen to music. Individuals' music consumption might differ depending on criteria such as their income, age, gender, and education. These characteristics are evaluated against specific variables that have an impact on music consumption. The chosen variables are the frequency of music consumption, music consumption during travel, method of music consumption, expenditure on music purchases, utilisation of mobile music, and consumption of online music. The test results indicate that the number of music purchases is not affected by any of the criteria examined, such as age, gender, education, and income. The transition from tangible to virtual music has resulted in profound alterations in the pattern of music consumption.*

**Keywords:** Cultural Good, Cultural Industry, Digitalisation, Entertainment Good, Music Industry.

## 1. INTRODUCTION

India ranks as one of the leading entertainment markets globally, with music playing a fundamental role within this industry. The music sector holds a significant position within India's economy. Unlike other goods, the consumption of music is distinct. Music serves as both a cultural and entertainment commodity, thereby exhibiting consumption patterns unique from other goods. The value derived from music as a consumption good is perceived as a social phenomenon rather than through individual consumption.

The advent of digitalization has fundamentally transformed the essence of music. Within the music industry, the focus of change lies not in expenses, demands, or revenues, but rather in the essence of music itself. Prior to the widespread adoption of digital technology, music was mostly consumed by the end user. It possessed the characteristic of being a completely exclusive commodity. Music, being classified as a pure private item, can be purchased by the customer and utilised purely for their own benefit. For example, ownership of a CD is vested in the consumer who has purchased it, and the pleasure derived from it is solely reserved for that individual. Consumption is characterised by rivalry, meaning that when one person consumes a good, it reduces the amount available for others to consume. Additionally, excludability applies, which means that access to the good can be restricted to only those who have the right to consume it. However, the advent of digitalization has altered the nature of music as a commodity. Digital music possesses the defining characteristics of a public good, as it is both non-rivalrous and non-excludable within a peer-to-peer network. The absence of these traits can be attributed to its inherent lack of spatial dimensions (Hubbs, 2015, p. 4). After digitalisation, music exhibits the properties of a public good. Consumption is now non-rival and exclusion is not always feasible. The merging of the MP3 format with peer-to-peer networks has rendered music non-excludable, a crucial aspect in comprehending the economics of the music industry. In fact, as the customer base approaches infinity, the average payment per customer decreases to zero (Hougaard, 2009, p. 11).

## 2. MUSIC AS A CULTURAL GOOD

Cultural industries revolve around the point of genesis of creative ideas and expand outward when these ideas are merged with additional inputs to provide a broader array of products. Therefore, the fundamental basis of this industry model is rooted in the conventional definition of creative arts, encompassing music, dance, theatre, literature, visual arts, crafts, video art, performance art, computer art, multimedia art, and more.

Thus, the term "music industry" encompasses a vast array of participants, such as composers, performers, publishers, record companies, distributors, promoters, retailers, and collecting societies. However, the fundamental essence of the industry still revolves around the original musician. Expanding outward, the concentric circles defining the cultural industries include sectors producing goods with cultural significance alongside other non-cultural products. This broader category encompasses areas like advertising, which demands creative input in its operations; tourism, where certain market segments are rooted in cultural elements; and architectural services, where designs may transcend mere functionality. Nevertheless, these industries can be considered integral components of the cultural sector. (Throsby, 2008, p. 151)

In Throsby's model, the pattern represents a concentric circles of the cultural industries with the arts lying at the centre, and other industries forming layers or circles located around the core, extending further outwards as the use of creative ideas is taken to wider production contexts.

Cultural commodities, such as music, possess distinct and unique attributes. The marketing of these commodities is carried out by recording firms, but, their significance and ultimate worth are contingent upon the consumer's discernment and personal tastes. Music is considered an experiential good, meaning that buyers need to personally experience it in order to evaluate its worth. When we classify music as an experiential good, we are venturing into a more ambiguous realm.

As widely recognized by diligent cover artists worldwide, individuals typically have a strong preference for music they are already acquainted with. This tendency is evident in the fact that a significant proportion of professional musicians sustain their livelihood by repeatedly performing well-known tunes that are commonly heard in live concerts, on radio broadcasts, and are widely available on recordings in numerous households (Madison Guy, 2017, p. 2).

The listener's appreciation and enjoyment of music are influenced by factors such as their mood, personal preferences, level of expertise, familiarity with the genre, and recognition from their peers. Another facet of music is that its pleasure amplifies with repeated exposure. A music that may initially fail to captivate or be disregarded can be better appreciated by repeated listening or when accompanied by visual representation on screen. This assertion does not hold true to the same degree when it comes to films or novels.

Pandora in 2004, introduced a system where users are proactive in their experience. When faced with a multitude of options, consumers attempt to streamline the process by engaging with familiar artists or songs, listening to tunes they are already acquainted with. Spotify's inception in 2008, following Pandora's debut in 2004, offered a user-centric approach that allows users to actively engage in their music experience (Pagnin, 2016, p. 9).

Decisions about production and consumption in the music industry are ultimately influenced by the public inside a social network. These social networks operate as marketplaces. The advent of digitalization has led to a decline in the function of music firms as music promoters, as individuals with musical content can now independently promote themselves through social media platforms. Intermediaries become obsolete. In the conventional music industry, an artist needs the support and financial resources of a record label. Labels and brand names hold significant importance.

Aspiring artists can promote their work by bypassing music labels. Social networking websites, forums, and YouTube serve as their current promotional methods. Uploading a music production on these platforms is an efficient and free method of promotion (Margounakis Dimitrios, 2013, p. 782).

Music has the ability to influence our emotions. For example, fast-paced music with a strong focus on rhythm can make a person feel more energetic and alert. On the other hand, melancholic music can evoke feelings of nostalgia or regret. Sad songs, which may bring tears to our eyes, can serve as a means of emotional release or catharsis. Music is chosen either to fulfil one's mood or to modify it.

Emotional states are frequently the outcome of numerous interconnected and underlying factors, with music being one of them. Music is a powerful medium that has the ability to impact emotions, alter moods, and leave a lasting impression on human feelings (Ahmad, 2015, p. 1).

Music possesses a myriad of facets. Occasionally, a musical composition gains popularity far beyond its intrinsic merit, experiencing a surge in acclaim. There exists a phenomenon akin to a bandwagon effect in the appraisal of such music, as an increasing number of individuals become captivated by its allure. In the realm of goods like music, significance and worth predominantly arise from communal encounters. Individual preferences are shaped by informational feedback and social networks rather than inherent inclinations and price indicators.

## 3. MUSIC CONSUMPTION

The consumption pattern associated with conventional goods typically correlates with income levels. However, due to the cultural attributes inherent in music consumption, this relationship with income may not consistently hold. Given this context, the current study endeavours to examine the patterns of music consumption during the era of digital transformation.

The present paper uses primary data collected from the state of Kerala. The data were collected through a sample survey conducted among individuals who purchase music and listen to music. Samples were identified with the help of music shops. To include possible geographical diversity in music consumption, data were collected from five districts namely Thiruvananthapuram, Ernakulum, Thrissur, Palakkad and Kozhikode in the state of Kerala. Data were collected from a total sample of 200 individuals, with 50 from each district. The present study defined a sample only as an individual who listened to music.

## 4. CONSUMPTION PATTERN OF DIGITAL ENTERTAINMENT

In the digital space, various modes of entertainment are accessible digitally such as music, TV, movies, e-books and online games. Respondents were asked to rank their preferred mode of entertainment. The weighted mean rank method was used to analyse the preferred mode of entertainment of the respondents. Mean rank was found by giving due weightage to different groups (Table 1). The majority of the sample respondents ranked music as the primary mode of entertainment. Music has a mean score of 3.975 followed by TV with a mean score of 3.765 and movies with a mean score of 2.825. This shows that music is still the primary source of entertainment for the respondents. Very few people prefer reading and games as their preferred mode of entertainment.

**Table 1:** Mode of Entertainment Mean Rank

| *Mode of Entertainment* | *1* | *2* | *3* | *4* | *5* | *Score* | *Mean Score* | *Rank Position* |
|---|---|---|---|---|---|---|---|---|
| Music | 77 | 70 | 31 | 15 | 7 | 795 | 3.975 | 1 |
| Movies | 23 | 38 | 56 | 47 | 36 | 565 | 2.825 | 3 |
| TV | 61 | 62 | 51 | 21 | 5 | 753 | 3.765 | 2 |
| Reading | 27 | 25 | 44 | 73 | 31 | 544 | 2.72 | 4 |
| Games | 14 | 6 | 16 | 45 | 119 | 351 | 1.755 | 5 |

*Source:* Sample Survey.

Mode of listening to music is taken as the medium through which music is accessed by the respondents. The common mode of listening seemed to be radio, CD/MP3/DVD players, TV and mobile phones (Table 2). People did not depend on a single medium to listen to music. 76.5% of the respondents listened to music from different media. Majority of the respondents depended on mobile phones for hearing music much more than traditional music players.

**Table 2:** Mode of Listening to Music

| *Mode of Listening* | *Frequency* | *Percent* |
|---|---|---|
| Radio | 9 | 4.5 |
| CD/MP3/DVD player | 9 | 4.5 |
| TV | 3 | 1.5 |
| Mobile | 25 | 12.5 |
| More than 1 | 153 | 76.5 |
| All | 1 | 0.5 |
| **Total** | **200** | **100.0** |

*Source:* Sample Survey.

Respondents were asked about their music listening habits. 62.5% of the people listened to music daily. Only 3% said that they listened to music less than once a week. Respondents were also asked whether there was a change in the preferred type of music as age advanced. 57% opined that a shift in interest took place as age increased. Older people tended to prefer slow music compared to the fast-paced music preferred by the younger generation. But it is not always possible to generalize, as music lovers irrespective of age listened to all kind of music provided it is good.

In a family consisting of people of different age groups, a conflict in music listening may arise because old people may not be tolerant of loud rock or pop music. In the same way classical and devotional music are barely tolerated by younger generation. 42% of the respondents replied that there is conflict in music listening between family members.

Another interesting phenomenon was that 80% of the people listened to music while travelling. Before mobile phones and MP3 players became widespread, only people who had private vehicles with music players had the privilege of listening to music while travelling. Today with smartphones becoming universal, it is much easier to listen to music while travelling. This again showed how technological change was impacting the music consumption habits of people.

## 5. MUSIC CONSUMPTION PATTERN

There are several variables which affect the consumption pattern of music. Music consumption of individuals can vary based on variables like their income, age, gender and education. Similarly, various factors need to be tested to analyse the pattern of music consumption such as frequency of listening to music, listening to music while travelling, mode of listening to music, amount spent on music purchase, use of mobile music and listening to online music.

### 5.1 Music Consumption Based on the Income of the Respondents

Like in the consumption of any good, music consumption can also be a function of income. Respondents were categorized into different income classes. 52% of the respondents fell in the income category of Rs. 10,000 to Rs. 20,000 per month. 19.5% of the respondents belonged to the income category below Rs. 10,000 and 6% had income above Rs. 50,000. Based on the income of the respondents, the expenditure pattern on music was analysed. It was seen that irrespective of different levels of income, people generally purchased music from shops. It is seen that the amount spent on music purchases did not increase as income increased. The majority of the respondents spent below Rs. 300 per month for the purchase of music. People who had income above Rs. 50,000 spent less on music. To analyse the music consumption pattern of individuals, several factors were taken about the income of the respondent and tested for significance. Kruskal Wallis test is used for analysis.

Analysing the relation between the income of the respondent and music consumption using the Kruskal Wallis test it is seen that, there is no significant difference in the purchase of music as income increases (Table 3). The Chi-Square value is obtained as 3.857 which shows that income is not a significant factor influencing the purchase of music. Purchase of music essentially reflects the tastes and preferences of individuals. So, a person with a higher income need not necessarily buy more music

**Table 3:** Music Consumption Pattern Based on Income of the Respondent

| *Null Hypothesis* | *P value* | *Significance* | *Chi Square Value* | *Decision* | *Interpretation* |
|---|---|---|---|---|---|
| Frequency of listening is same across categories of income | .011 | significant at 5% level | 14.801 | Reject null hypothesis | Income is a significant factor in frequency of listening to music |
| Listening to music while travelling is same across income | .011 | significant at 5% level | 14.902 | Reject null hypothesis | Income is a significant factor in listening to music while travelling |
| Income is not a significant factor influencing mode of listening | .033 | significant at 5% level | 12.170 | Reject null hypothesis | Income is a significant factor influencing mode of listening |
| Music purchase is same across income of the respondent | .570 | Not significant at 5% level | 3.857 | Retain null hypothesis | Income is not a significant factor affecting music purchase |
| Use of mobile music is same across categories of income | .596 | Not significant at 5% level | 3.680 | Retain null hypothesis | Income is not a significant factor in use of mobile music |
| Listening to online music is same across income | .047 | significant at 5% level | 11.251 | Reject null hypothesis | Income is a significant factor in listening to online music |

*Source:* Sample Survey.

The most surprising result from the analysis of primary data is that income is not a significant factor influencing music purchases. However, income has a significant influence on the creation of circumstances congenial to enjoying music. For instance, with higher income, there is an increase in listening to music while travelling or better and more efficient ways of listening to music could be obtained. Income allows the listener to have a better mobile phone, better MP3 player and other accessories needed for music enjoyment. The mode of listening and listening to online music is also impacted by income; here the obvious influencing factor seems to be the ability to purchase the necessary electronic appliances. Income seems to confer certain privileges and better exposure to awareness of copyright laws. Thus, many of the peripheral factors involved in the consumption of music are influenced by income though income is not an influential factor in the purchase of music.

## 5.2 Music Consumption based on the Age of the Respondent

Another factor which influenced music consumption is the age of the respondent. The age of the respondents was classified into below 20, between 20 to 30, 30 to 40, 40 to 50, and 50 to 60 and above 60. People of all age groups purchased music. But people between the age group of 20 to 30 purchased music much more than people of other age groups. Data showed that below the age of 20 and above the age of 50, a smaller number of people purchased music. In the case of people below 20, it may be because they are more into file sharing and downloading than purchasing music from physical shops.

To analyse the music consumption pattern of individuals, several factors are taken about the age of the respondent and tested for significance. Kruskal Wallis test is used to test the significance (Table 4).

**Table 4:** Music Consumption Based on Age of the Respondent

| *Null Hypothesis* | *P-value* | *Significance* | *Chi Square Value* | *Decision* | *Interpretation* |
|---|---|---|---|---|---|
| Frequency of listening to music is same across age | .325 | Not Significant at 5% level | 5.812 | Retain null hypothesis | Age of the respondent is not a significant factor in frequency of listening to music |
| Listening to music while travelling is same for all age groups | .009 | Significant at 5% level | 15.353 | Reject null hypothesis | Age of the respondent is a significant factor in listening to music while travelling |
| Mode of listening is same for all age groups | .001 | Significant at 5% level | 21.759 | Reject null hypothesis | Age of the respondent is a significant factor in mode of listening to music |
| Amount spent on the purchase of music is same across all age groups | .110 | Not Significant at 5% level | 8.976 | Retain null hypothesis | Age of the respondent is not a significant factor influencing music purchase |

| *Null Hypothesis* | *P-value* | *Significance* | *Chi Square Value* | *Decision* | *Interpretation* |
|---|---|---|---|---|---|
| Use of mobile music is same across age | .000 | Significant at 5% level | 45.620 | Reject null hypothesis | Age of the respondent is a significant factor in the use of mobile music |
| Online music listening is same across age | .430 | Not Significant at 5% level | 4.883 | Retain null hypothesis | Age of the respondent is not a significant factor in listening to online music |

*Source:* Sample Survey.

The age of the respondent did not influence the amount spent on music purchase or type of music purchase or mode of music purchase. But it is a significant factor in the mode of listening to music, listening to music while travelling and listening to mobile music. The age of the respondent influenced the mode of listening to music, listening to music while travelling and use of mobile music but did not influence the amount of music purchased.

## 5.3 Music Consumption Based on the Gender of the Respondent

Music listening and music purchase need not be gender specific. The amount spent on music purchase, mode of listening, type of music purchase, time of listening to music, and frequency of listening to music all these reflect personal tastes rather than gender differences.

To analyse the music consumption pattern of individuals, several factors were taken in relation to the gender of the respondent and tested for significance. Mann Whitney U test is used to test the significance (Table 5).

The gender of the respondent did not influence the amount spent on music purchases or type of music purchase or awareness of copyright violation or any of the factors considered. It can be concluded that music consumption is gender neutral. Gender does not influence music consumption patterns.

Since technology is gender neutral and there is no difference between men and women in the use of mobiles and other electronic appliances it is understandable that gender does not influence any of the variables taken in primary data.

It was seen from the analysis that people used different kinds of music players including mobile phones to listen to music. Less educated people seemed to stick to traditional music players compared to more educated people.

**Table 5:** Music Consumption based on Gender of the Respondent

| *Null Hypothesis* | *P-value* | *Significance* | *Chi Square Value* | *Decision* | *Interpretation* |
|---|---|---|---|---|---|
| Gender is not a factor influencing frequency of listening to music | .985 | Not significant at 5% level | .000 | Retain null hypothesis | Frequency of listening to music is not influenced by the gender of the respondent |
| Listening to music while travelling is not gender specific | .235 | Not significant at 5% level | 1.411 | Retain null hypothesis | Listening to music while travelling is not influenced by gender of the respondent |
| Mode of listening is gender neutral | .366 | Not significant at 5% level | .818 | Retain null hypothesis | Gender does not influence mode of listening |
| Gender is not a factor influencing the amount spent on music purchase | .057 | Not Significant at 5% level | 3.615 | Retain null hypothesis | Amount spent on music purchase is not influenced by gender |
| Gender is not a factor influencing the use of mobile music | .948 | Not significant at 5% level | 3.998 | Retain null hypothesis | Use of mobile music is not influenced by the gender of the respondent |
| Listening to online music is gender neutral | .816 | Not significant at 5% level | .054 | Retain null hypothesis | Gender does not influence listening to online music |

*Source:* Sample Survey.

## 5.4 Music Consumption Based on Education of the Respondent

To analyse the music consumption pattern of individuals, several factors are taken in relation to the education of the respondent and tested for significance. Kruskal Wallis test is used to test the significance (Table 6).

The education of the respondent did not influence the amount spent on music purchase or type of music purchase or mode of music purchase. But it is a significant factor in the mode of listening to music, listening to music while travelling, listening to online music, and use of mobile music.

Education is a significant factor in the frequency of listening to music, in listening to music while travelling, in the mode of listening to music and listening to music online. But it is not significant in the amount of music purchased.

**Table 6:** Music Consumption Based on Education of the Respondent

| *Null Hypothesis* | *P-value* | *Significance* | *Chi Square Value* | *Decision* | *Interpretation* |
|---|---|---|---|---|---|
| Frequency of music listening is same across education | .006 | Significant at 5% level | 4.653 | Reject null hypothesis | Education is a significant factor in frequency of listening to music |
| Listening to music while travelling is same across education | .000 | Significant at 5% level | 28.848 | Reject null hypothesis | Education is a significant factor in listening to music while travelling |
| Mode of listening is same across education | .000 | Significant at 5% level | 22.603 | Reject null hypothesis | Education is a significant factor influencing mode of listening |
| Amount spent on music purchase is same across education | .747 | Not Significant at 5% level | 2.695 | Retain null hypothesis | Education is not a significant factor in the amount of music purchase |
| Education is not a factor influencing the use of mobile music | .000 | Significant at 5% level | 33.811 | Reject null hypothesis | Education is a significant factor influencing the use of mobile music |
| Education is not a factor influencing listening to online music | .083 | Significant at 10% level | 9.751 | Reject null hypothesis | Education is a significant factor influencing listening of online music. |

*Source:* Sample Survey.

## 6. DISCUSSION

When examining music consumption in relation to income, age, gender, and education, noticeable disparities emerge concerning how individuals listen to music, particularly in terms of online consumption. However, music listening habits, such as timing and frequency, are subjective and reflective of personal tastes and preferences. An analysis of music consumption based on income, age, gender, and education underscores the unique characteristics of music as a cultural good, distinguishing it from conventional goods. The absence of a correlation between income and music consumption corroborates this distinction. In a typical scenario, an increase in income would result in increased music purchases if music were considered a normal good. However, as a cultural good, music consumption is influenced by non-economic factors rather than income alone. Higher income levels do contribute to creating conducive circumstances for music enjoyment, such as affording better quality mobile devices and audio players. Income also affects the mode of listening and online music consumption, primarily by enabling the purchase of necessary electronic equipment. Furthermore, income levels often correlate with a heightened awareness of copyright laws, indicating a broader cultural influence. While income indirectly influences various peripheral factors related to music consumption, its direct impact on actual music purchases remains limited.

Testing various factors against age of the respondent led to the conclusion that, age of the respondent is a significant factor in listening to music while travelling, mode of listening to music and use of mobile music. The age of the respondent is not a significant factor influencing the amount of music purchased, frequency of listening to music and listening to online music.

The gender of respondents had no discernible impact on the amount spent on music purchases, the type of music purchased, the mode of listening, or engagement with online music. This suggests that music consumption exhibits gender neutrality, with no significant influence from gender on consumption patterns. This observation can be attributed to the gender-neutral nature of technology, as evidenced by the similar usage of mobile devices and other electronic appliances by both men and women. Consequently, gender does not exert influence over any of the variables examined in the primary data.

Despite the plethora of options available for purchasing music in today's digital age, including both physical and virtual formats, gender disparities in purchasing behaviour were not observed. Individuals of all genders displayed a propensity to purchase music from both physical and online outlets, as well as engage in music downloads. The analysis further revealed that respondents utilized various music players, with mobile phones emerging as the preferred mode for listening to music.

Moreover, the analysis unveiled a trend wherein individuals with lower levels of education tended to adhere to traditional music players, in contrast to their more educated counterparts who demonstrated a preference for mobile phones. This underscores the influence of education level on music consumption behaviour, with mobile phones emerging as the favoured medium across gender lines.

The level of education of the respondent does not impact the expenditure on music purchases, the type of music purchased, or the method of purchasing music. However, it does play a significant role in determining the manner in which music is listened to, particularly in terms of listening habits while traveling, accessing online music, utilizing mobile music platforms, and awareness regarding copyright infringement. Consequently, while factors such as age, gender, education, and income do not affect the quantity of music purchased, they do have notable effects on various aspects of music consumption behaviour.

## 7. CONCLUSION

The music industry has undergone significant transformations over the last two decades. Initially, cassettes dominated the market in India during the 1980s, establishing the country as a major producer and seller of music cassettes by the latter half of the decade. However, cassette dominance waned with the emergence of newer music formats towards the end of the 1990s, particularly with the rise of the MP3 format and MP3 players. These devices offered greater storage capacity and utilized compression technology, leading to the decline of the cassette industry.

The proliferation of mobile phones also played a pivotal role in reshaping music consumption habits. Smartphones, in particular, made it convenient for users to listen to and store large libraries of songs, rendering traditional CD and MP3 players obsolete. This shift towards mobile-based music consumption resulted in mobile ring tones and song sales becoming a primary revenue source for the industry.

Furthermore, the widespread availability of the internet facilitated easier and cheaper access to music online. Peer-to-peer networks and file-sharing platforms revolutionized music streaming and downloading, while online platforms like YouTube provided access to vast repositories of music. This gradual transition from physical to digital music formats has fundamentally altered music consumption patterns, reflecting a paradigm shift in how individuals access and enjoy music in the modern era.

## REFERENCES

[1] Ahmad, N. (2015). Impact of Music on Mood: Empirical Investigation. *Research on Humanities and Social Sciences www.iiste.org.*

[2] Brousseau, E. (2008). The Economics of Music Production. *Communications & Strategies, No. 72, 4th quarter 2008, p. 131.*

[3] Madison, G. and Schiölde, G. (2017). Repeated Listening Increases the Liking for Music Regardless of Its Complexity: Implications for the Appreciation and Aesthetics of Music. *Frontiers in neuroscience, 11*, 147. https://doi.org/10.3389/fnins.2017.00147*2017; 11: 147.*, 2.

[4] Hinduja (2006). S. A critical examination of the digital music phenomenon. Crit Crim 14, 387–409 https://doi.org/10.1007/s10612-006-9006-0

[5] Hougaard, J.L. (2009). Selling Digital Music: Business Models for Public Goods. *Netnomics,* 11(09–19) · April 2009.

[6] Hubbs, G. (2015). Digital Music and Public Goods. *Research paper, Department of Philosophy.*

[7] Kleve, P. (1999). MP3: The End Of Copyright As We Know It? *Proceedings of the IASTED International Conference Law.*

[8] Margounakis Dimitrios, P.D. (2013). The Effect of Networking Revolution on Digital Music. *International Journal of Digital Society (IJDS),* Volume 4, Issue 2, June 2013, 779–788.

[9] Pagnin, A. (2016). Evolution and development of music consumption. *University of Bologna Public and corporate communication.*

[10] Throsby, D. (2008). The concentric circles model of the cultural industries. *Cultural Trends,* 17(3):147–164 · September 2008.

# A Study on College Students' Perception Towards Digital Finance in Bengaluru City

**M.K. Shwetha[1] and Suma Singh[2]**

[1]Research Scholar, Department of Economics,
Bengaluru City University, Bengaluru, India

[2]Associate Professor, Department of Economics,
Mount Carmel College (Autonomous), Bengaluru, India

E-mail: [1]mkshwetha11@gmail.com; [2]sumasingh@mccblr.edu.in

***ABSTRACT:*** *In recent years, there has been a remarkable transition towards digital finance, driven by the rapid advancement of technology and changing consumer preferences. Financial institutions are using the various digital platforms to reach out the needs of the diverse customers. Digital financial transactions are very popular among people particularly with younger generations. Studying digital banking habits among college students is important as it reflects the intersection of financial behaviours, technological trends, and the unique circumstances of this demographic group. This paper attempts to evaluate the familiarity, perception and problems in digital finance among the college students. The financial decisions of college students can have broader economic and social implication. The present study evaluates the association between familiarity, perception and problems in digital finance and socio-economic variables of the students. The convenient sampling technique is used for data collection, and for the analysis of the data SPSS has been used. A standard methodology like Reliability test, Chi-square/ Fisher's Test, Kruskal Wallis H Test, Post Hoc analysis etc. has been used to compare, analyse and interpret the data and draw meaningful conclusions.*

**Keywords**: College Students, Digital Banking, Digital Finance, Transition.

## 1. INTRODUCTION

The world of finance is rapidly evolving, driven by advancements in technology and changing consumer behaviours. As humanity moves further into the digital age, several emerging trends are reshaping the financial services landscape. Today information technology has accelerated the functions of Indian financial institutions. The current era can be rightly said as a digital era and it has become essential for banking and financial institutions to focus on digitalisation for its survival and growth (Kamini Raj, Mamta Sharma 2019).

Digital banking, also known as online banking or e-banking, refers to the use of electronic platforms and technology to conduct various banking activities and services. Digital finance refers to the process of transforming traditional banking and financial services through the use of new technologies. Specifically, using digital products and tools to deliver financial services. It allows individuals to manage their finances, perform transactions, and access banking services through the internet or mobile applications. Digital banking eliminates the need for physical visits to traditional bank branches, providing users with the convenience of conducting financial transactions from the comfort of their homes or on-the-go.

Digital financial services help in delivering basic financial services to the people through mobile phones, electric money models, desktops, cards, and the internet. Payments via mobile phones has become the global standard, especially in developing countries. The increased use of smartphones will drive financial inclusion, enabling even the current unbanked population, estimated by the World Bank at 1.4bn people, to access and participate in the global economy, creating rafts of new opportunities and delivering empowerment to disenfranchised populations.

## 2. RECENT TREND IN DIGITAL FINANCIAL SERVICES IN INDIA

Digital financial Services uprising is a global phenomenon. India's digital payment system is a promising success story in the market. Indian government launched digital India Campaign to reduce dependency of Indian economy on cash and prevent from money laundering. Digital include all financial operations carried out with the help of electronic devices, such as computers, smart phones, or tablets or anything that is connected to the internet and your e-money. As technology is developing, the range of devices and processes to transact electronically continues to increase while the percentage of cash and cheque transactions continues to decrease. Today India is using most common variety of Digital is enormous, from Digital wallets, bank transfers, direct debits to mobile apps, or QR code-based payments (Nila, Tamilselvan and *et al.*, 2023).

In India, a wide variety of digital financial services have been designed and launched and they are being utilized by the customers, thanks to the technology adoption mindset of the customers and the efforts of the Government of India. "Unified Payment Interface" (UPI), "Bharat Interface for Money" (BHIM), Bharat Quick Response (QR) code, National Automated Clearing House, (NACH), Rupay codes, National Electronic Toll collection, and Aadhaar Enabled Payment Services are a few digital financial services that are available in India (Ravikumar, Suresha and *et al.*, 2022)

With its robust stack infrastructure and extensive integration of the Unified Payments Interface (UPI), India currently leads the global charts in real-time digital payments volume, representing more than 40 percent of all such transactions worldwide. The UPI has emerged as a game-changer in digital payments in India, with 2.96 billion digital payment transactions recorded in July 2023. (Amitabh Chaudhry, 2023)

## 3. DIGITAL BANKING AND COLLEGE STUDENTS

Financial institutions have used the country's growing digital penetration to their advantage to further the growth of their financial services. Due to its low prices, rapid speed, and availability of specialized financial services, Digital Financial services is particularly popular with younger generations. Services like savings, payments, insurance, investments and credit are provided through digital infrastructure. This innovation has been fuelled by the quick development of technology, the explosive growth in student behaviour and digital financial services (Amandeep Kaur, Madhvi Gupta, 2023). India has witnessed significant growth in digital infrastructure, with over 692 million internet users as of January 2023. As the financial landscape undergoes a digital transformation it becomes essential for college students to develop financial literacy skills (Navneet Gupta, 2023).

Studying digital banking habits among college students is important for several reasons, reflecting the intersection of financial behaviours, technological trends, and the unique circumstances of this demographic group.

## 4. ITERATURE REVIEW

Sumeet Sharma, Ritu and *et al.*, 2021, are of the opinion that Digital banks represent the future of banking, and today's brick-and -mortar model is set to slowly give way to the click and portal system. Artificial intelligence and machine learning are paving the way toward identifying banking customers pre-and-post buying behaviour. Digital Financial services uprising is a global phenomenon. In India, a wide variety of digital financial services have been designed and launched and they are being utilised by the customers, thanks to the technology adoption mindset of the customers and the efforts of the government of India (Ravikumar, Sreshaa, *et al.* 2022). Financial regulators around the world have realized the tremendous role Digital financial services can play for financial inclusion and seek to unlock their potential by creating enabled environments for Digital financial services (Kamini and Mamta, 2024). Intan Aprilia, Dwiyanjana, 2023 opines that benefiting from technology tends to cause students to behave consumptively. Consumptive behaviour is a person's tendency to consume without restrictions and prioritise wants over needs. Students are one of the group of people who use digital payments to meet their daily needs. Digitalization of banking industry supports the nations development in the era of globalisation and liberalisation. And students are the key enablers for making it sustainable. So, there should be an urge to create awareness and check upon the usage of digital banking by the youths of the country (Fahima and Jihen, 2022). Cat Hollands, 2021 is of the opinion that understanding how college students handle their finances and technology is important for institutions as it helps them cater to the needs and preferences of this demographic. According to their study, a whopping 82% of students prefer using mobile payment apps or contactless payments like Google wallet or Apple pay etc. Financial institutions and intermediaries have started to increase the availability of their digital financial products as a result of their ability to economically reach millions of underserved students (Amandeep Kaur and Madhvi Gupta, 2022).

## 5. OBJECTIVES OF THE STUDY

1. To analyse the association of familiarity, perception towards digital banking services as well as problems in digital banking services with the demographic factors of the respondents.
2. To analyse the association between the Problems in digital banking services and socio-economic variables of the students.
3. To analyse difference in the familiarity towards digital banking services, perception and problems towards digital banking services between various levels of attitude towards money of students.
4. To analyse difference in the familiarity towards digital banking services, perception and problems towards digital banking services between various financial products the students possess.

## 6. HYPOTHESES OF THE STUDY

H1: There is no significant association between the familiarity towards digital banking services and perception towards digital banking services and socio-economic variables of the student.

H2: There is no significant association between the Problems in digital banking services and socio-economic variables of the students.

H3: There is no significant difference in the familiarity towards digital banking services, perception and problems towards digital banking services between various levels of attitude towards money of students

H4: There is no significant difference in the familiarity towards digital banking services, perception and problems towards digital banking services between various financial products the students possess.

## 7. RESEARCH METHODOLOGY

The present study deals with "A study on college students' perception towards Digital Finance in Bengaluru City". The study is based on both primary and secondary data. The primary data is collected from the sample respondents by conducting personal interviews with the help of a structured questionnaire. Secondary data are collected by referring various journals, web sources, previous research reports, and are incorporated whenever necessary to supplement the primary data. A sample of 200 students from various colleges in Bengaluru were chosen as respondents for the study. Convenient sampling technique is followed to select the respondents for the study. Reliability

Test, Fisher's Exact Test value or Chi square test value and Kruskal-Wallis Test are used to examine the relationships, differences and to test the hypothesis.

## 8. RESULTS AND DISCUSSION

### 8.1 Demographic Profile the Respondents

| *Variables* | *Categories of Variable* | *Frequency* | *Percentage (%)* |
|---|---|---|---|
| Gender | Male | 99 | 49.5 |
| | Female | 101 | 50.5 |
| | Total | 200 | 100 |
| Age | 16–18 years | 29 | 14.5 |
| | 19–21 | 140 | 70 |
| | 22–24 | 31 | 15.5 |
| | Total | 200 | 100 |
| Educational qualification | PUC | 10 | 5 |
| | Under graduation | 173 | 86.5 |
| | Post-graduation | 17 | 8.5 |
| | Total | 200 | 100 |
| Discipline of Study | Arts | 4 | 2 |
| | Commerce | 139 | 69.5 |
| | Science | 40 | 20 |
| | Professional | 17 | 8.5 |
| | Total | 200 | 100 |
| Annual Household Income | Less than 5 lakhs | 117 | 58.5 |
| | 5 lakhs–10 lakhs | 51 | 25.5 |
| | Above 10 lakhs | 32 | 16 |
| | Total | 200 | 100 |
| Parental Education | No Formal education | 38 | 19 |
| | PUC | 52 | 26 |
| | Bachelor Degree | 77 | 38.5 |
| | Masters/ Doctoral Degree | 33 | 16.5 |
| | Total | 200 | 100 |
| Residence | Rural | 71 | 35.5 |
| | Urban | 129 | 64.5 |
| | **Total** | **200** | **100** |

## 8.2 Reliability Test

Cronbach's Alpha Reliability Coefficient Value

| *Question Assessed* | *Total Respondents (n=200)* |
|---|---|
| Familiarity towards digital banking services | 0.874 |
| Perception towards digital banking services | 0.864 |
| Problems in digital banking services | 0.836 |
| Overall | 0.867 |

From the above table it is seen that the alpha reliability coefficient is greater than 0.8 for each of the factors and hence the data collected by the researcher is used for different statistical analysis as per the objectives framed for the analysis.

## 8.3 Fisher's Exact Test Value or Chi Square Test Value

1. Fisher's Exact Test and Chi-Square test to analyse the association between socio-economic factors of the total respondents and familiarity, perception towards digital financial services.

H1: There is no significant association between the familiarity towards digital banking services and perception towards digital banking services and socio-economic variables of the student.

2. Table showing Fisher's Exact Test and Chi-Square test to analyse the association between socio-economic factors of the total respondents and familiarity, perception towards digital financial services.

| | *Chi Square Test Value (CSTV); Fisher's Exact Test Value (FETV) and significant value (p value)* | | | |
|---|---|---|---|---|
| | *Familiarity towards digital banking services* | | *Perception towards digital banking services* | |
| Gender | CSTV = 4.135 | P = 0.388> 0.05 (NS) | CSTV = 9.769** | P = 0.000<0.01 (S)) |
| Age | FETV = 26.978** | P = 0.000<0.01 (S) | FETV = 15.565** | P = 0.000<0.01 (S) |
| Qualification | FETV = 12.347 | P = 0.079> 0.05 (NS) | FETV = 14.369** | P = 0.000<0.01 (S) |
| Discipline | FETV = 23.585** | P = 0.000<0.01 (S) | FETV = 15.987 | P = 0.169> 0.05 (NS) |
| Annual Household income | FETV = 19.567** | P = 0.000<0.01 (S) | FETV = 13.308** | P = 0.000<0.01 (S) |
| Parents education | FETV = 19.926** | P = 0.000<0.01 (S) | FETV = 15.237 | P = 0.134> 0.05 (NS) |

| | ***Chi Square Test Value (CSTV); Fisher's Exact Test Value (FETV) and significant value (p value)*** | | | |
|---|---|---|---|---|
| | ***Familiarity towards digital banking services*** | | ***Perception towards digital banking services*** | |
| Location | CSTV = 12.957** | P = 0.000<0.01 (S) | CSTV = 3.158 | P = 0.547> 0.05 (NS) |
| The financial products possessed by students | FETV = 33.483** | P = 0.000<0.01 (S) | FETV = 12.880 | P = 0.967> 0.05 (NS) |

* Significant at 5% l.o.s.
** Significant at 1% l.o.s.

### 8.3.1 *Familiarity Towards Digital Banking Services*

It is observed from the table above that among the demographic factors of the respondents age, discipline, annual household income, parents' education, location and the financial products possessed by the students are significantly associated with familiarity towards digital banking services at 1% level of significance as the p-values are less than 0.01. Hence the null hypothesis is rejected for all the factors considered except for gender and qualification of the students.

Hence most of the personal factors of the respondents have significant impact on the familiarity towards digital banking services which leads to the conclusion that familiarity towards digital banking services is dependent on age, discipline, annual household income, parents' education, location and the financial products possessed by the students.

### 8.3.2 *Perception Towards Digital Banking Services*

It is observed from the table above that among the demographic factors of the respondent's gender, age, qualification and Annual household income are significantly associated with Perception towards digital banking services at 1% level of significance as the p-values are less than 0.01. Hence, the null hypothesis is rejected for the factors gender, age, qualification and annual household income

Hence the personal factors of the respondents such as gender, age, qualification and annual household income have significant impact on the Perception towards digital banking services which leads to the conclusion that Perception towards digital banking services is dependent on gender, age, qualification and annual household income.

Fisher's Exact Test and Chi-Square test to analyse the association between socio-economic factors of the total respondents and problems towards digital financial services.

H2: There is no significant association between the Problems in digital banking services and socio-economic variables of the students.

Table showing Fisher's Exact Test and Chi-Square test to analyse the association between socio-economic factors of the total respondents and problems towards digital financial services.

| | ***Chi Square Test Value (CSTV; Fisher's Exact Test Value (FETV) and significant value (p value)*** | |
|---|---|---|
| | ***Problems in digital banking services*** | |
| Gender | CSTV = 10.239** | P = 0.000<0.01 (S) |
| Age | FETV = 19.299** | P = 0.000<0.01 (S) |
| Qualification | FETV = 8.923 | P = 0.262> 0.05 (NS) |
| Discipline | FETV = 12.178 | P = 0.798> 0.05 (NS) |
| Annual Household income | FETV = 10.664 | P = 0.088> 0.05 (NS) |
| Parents education | FETV = 20.506** | P = 0.000<0.01 (S) |
| Location | CSTV = 5.319 | P = 0.322> 0.05 (NS) |
| The financial products possessed by students | FETV = 22.971 | P = 0.198> 0.05 (NS) |

* Significant at 5% l.o.s.
** Significant at 1% l.o.s.

### 8.3.3 *Problems in Digital Banking Services*

It is observed from the table above (from Fishers Exact/Chi Square Test) that among the demographic factors of the respondent's gender, age and parents' education are significantly associated with perception related to Problems in digital banking services at 1% level of significance as the p-values are less than 0.01. Hence, the null hypothesis is rejected for the factors gender, age and parents' education of the students.

Hence the personal factors of the respondents such gender, age and parents' education have significant impact on the Problems in digital banking services which leads to the conclusion that perception related to Problems in digital banking services is dependent on gender, age and parents' education.

## 8.4 Kruskal-Walli's Test

Kruskal-Walli's test to analyse significant difference in the familiarity towards digital banking services, perception and problems towards digital banking services between various levels of attitude towards money of students.

H3: There is no significant difference in the familiarity towards digital banking services, perception and problems towards digital banking services between various levels of attitude towards money of students.

Table showing Kruskal-Walli's test to analyse significant difference in the familiarity towards digital banking services, perception and problems towards digital banking services between various levels of attitude towards money of students.

**Test Statistics[a,b]**

| | *Familiarity towards digital banking services* | *Perception Towards digital banking services* | *Problems* |
|---|---|---|---|
| Chi-Square | 11.389 | 7.969 | 6.183 |
| df | 3 | 3 | 3 |
| Asymp. Sig. | .010* | .043* | .103 |

a. Kruskal Wallis Test.
b. Grouping Variable: Attitude towards Money.

From Kruskal Walis H Test we can observe that there exists a significant difference in the familiarity and perception towards digital banking services between various levels of attitude towards money by the students at 5% level of significance as p-values are less than 0.05. Hence students' attitude of money has a significant impact on the familiarity and perception towards digital banking services but not on any other considered factors

In order to find whether the perceptions are equal for any two groups of attitudes towards money Post Hoc Analysis was carried out as follows:

## 8.4.2 *Post Hoc Analysis*

Post Hoc Analysis to find whether the perceptions are equal for any two groups of attitudes towards money.

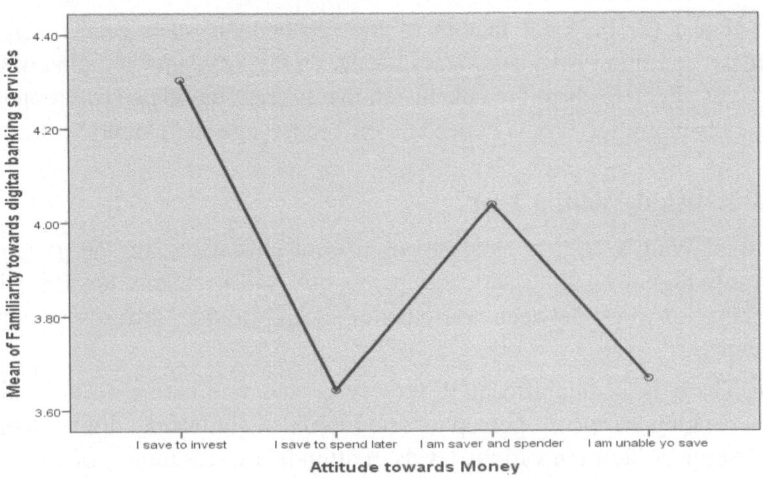

From Post Hoc Analysis there exists two groups. One group consists of students of who save to invest as well as save and spend are at high level of familiarity whereas rest of the students forms second group who are at low level of familiarity with the digital banking services.

Kruskal-Walli's test to analyse significant difference in the familiarity towards digital banking services, perception and problems towards digital banking services between various financial products the students possess.

H4: There is no significant difference in the familiarity towards digital banking services, perception and problems towards digital banking services between various financial products the students possess.

Table showing Kruskal-Walli's test to analyse significant difference in the familiarity towards digital banking services, perception and problems towards digital banking services between various financial products the students possess.

**Test Statistics[a,b]**

| | *Familiarity towards digital banking services* | *Perception Towards digital banking services* | *Problems* |
|---|---|---|---|
| Chi-Square | 15.345 | 3.826 | 5.212 |
| df | 5 | 5 | 5 |
| Asymp. Sig. | .009** | .575 | .391 |

a. Kruskal Wallis Test.

b. Grouping Variable: The financial products possessed by students.

From Kruskal Walis H. Test we can observe that there exists a significant difference in the familiarity towards digital banking services between various financial products the students possess at 1% level of significance as p-value is less than 0.01 Hence financial products possessed by the students has a significant impact on the familiarity towards digital banking services but not on any other considered factors.

In order to find whether the perceptions are equal for any two groups of financial products Post Hoc Analysis was carried out as follows:

### 8.4.4 *Post Hoc Analysis*

Post Hoc Analysis to find whether the perceptions are equal for any two groups of financial products.

From Post Hoc Analysis there exists three groups. One group consists of students of who have credit card and mutual funds are at very high level of familiarity, second group who possess debit card and savings account who are at moderate level of familiarity whereas rest of the students forms third group who are at low level of familiarity with the digital banking services.

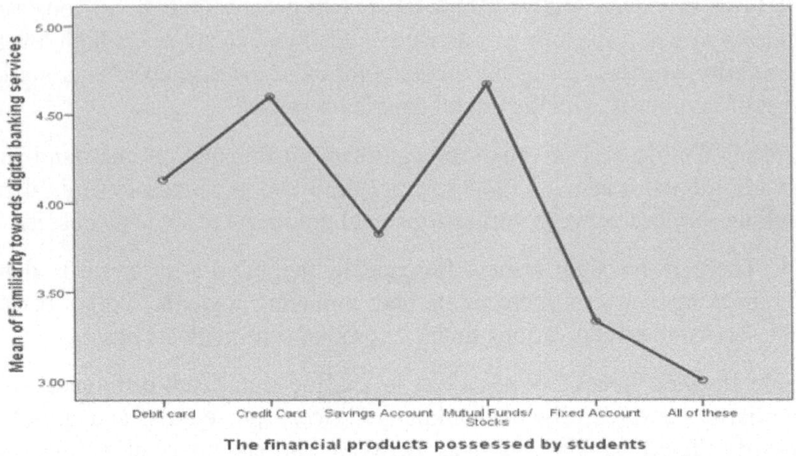


## 9. SUGGESTIONS

1. Since personal factors of the respondents have significant impact of the respondents have significant impact on the familiarity towards digital financial services, banks need to develop a user-friendly, mobile app tailored to college students' preferences. It should be easy to navigate, visually appealing and offers features such as budgeting tools, saving goals, and account insights.
2. The study shows that students' attitude of money has a significant impact on the familiarity and perception towards digital financial services, banks can provide educational resources within the app to help students understand financial concepts like budgeting, saving, investing, and managing debt. Interactive tutorials, videos, and articles can make learning about digital financial services engaging and accessible.
3. Since financial products possessed by the students such as credit card, mutual funds/stocks etc has a significant impact on the familiarity has a significant impact on the familiarity towards banking services, the banks and financial institutions can host virtual workshops on topics relevant to college students' financial products and wellness such as mutual funds, building credit, or preparing for life after graduation.

## 10. CONCLUSION

The increasing reliance on digital technology has transformed various aspects of life, from communication and entertainment to education and, significantly, financial management. As smartphones, high-speed internet, and secure online platforms have become ubiquitous, individuals are embracing digital banking solutions for their efficiency, accessibility, and the array of services they offer. This shift reflects a broader trend of the digitalization of services and the integration of technology into everyday activities, shaping the way people interact with financial institutions and manage their money. The present study has been undertaken to analyse the association of familiarity, perception towards digital banking services as well as problems in digital banking services with the demographic factors of the college students. It is inferred that most of the personal factors of the respondents have significant impact on the familiarity towards digital banking services which leads to the conclusion that familiarity towards digital banking services is dependent on age, discipline, annual household income, parents' education, location and the financial products possessed by the students. Among the demographic factors of the respondent's gender, age, qualification and Annual household income are significantly associated with Perception towards digital banking services at 1% level of significance as the p-values are less than 0.01. Hence the personal factors of the respondents such as gender, age, qualification and annual household income have significant impact on the Perception towards digital banking services which leads to the conclusion that Perception towards digital banking services is dependent on gender, age, qualification and annual household income.

From Kruskal Walis H Test we can observe that there exists a significant difference in the familiarity and perception towards digital banking services between various levels of attitude towards money by the students at 5% level of significance as p-values are less than 0.05. Hence students' attitude of money has a significant impact on the familiarity and perception towards digital banking services.

From Kruskal Walis H Test we can observe that there exists a significant difference in the familiarity towards digital banking services between various financial products the students possess at 1% level of significance as p-value is less than 0.01. Hence financial products possessed by the students has a significant impact on the familiarity towards digital banking services but not on any other considered factors.

College students are often early adopters of new technologies. Understanding their digital banking habits provides insights into emerging trends and preferences in the use of financial technology. Digital financial services can better cater to the needs of college students and empower them to manage their finances more effectively there by contributing to achieve financial inclusion.

Financial technology companies and traditional banks can benefit from understanding the preferences and expectations of college students. This knowledge can guide the development of innovative digital banking solutions and services that cater specifically to this demographic, creating new market opportunities.

In summary, studying digital banking habits among college students offers a comprehensive view of the interplay between technology and finance during a crucial period of individual development. The insights gained can inform financial education initiatives, improve digital banking offerings, and contribute to the broader understanding of the evolving landscape of financial services.

## REFERENCES

[1] Aprilia, Intan and Dwiyanjana, Santyo Nugroho. 'The Influence of Digital Payments and Financial Stressors on Consumptive Behavior of MNC University Students'. *The ES Accounting and Finance* 1, No. 03 (31 July 2023): 143–49. https://doi.org/10.58812/esaf.v1i03.102.

[2] Capture Higher Ed. 'The Financial and Tech Habits of College Students'. Accessed 1 March 2024. https://www.capturehighered.com/client-blog/the-financial-and-tech-habits-of-college-students/

[3] Shankarlal Sundarbai Shasun, R. Fahima Sultana and Jihen Bousrih. 'Digital Banking Penetration: Impact on Students' Usage Frequency and Awareness'. *Review of Economics and Finance* 20 (2022): 562–71. https://doi.org/10.55365/1923.x2022.20.64.

[4] Investopedia. 'Financial Technology (Fintech): Its Uses and Impact on Our Lives'. Accessed 1 March 2024. https://www.investopedia.com/terms/f/fintech.asp.

[5] Kaur, Amandeep and Madhvi Gupta. 'A Study on Students' Perception towards Digital Financial Service'. In *Proceedings of the International Conference on Application of AI and Statistical Decision Making for the Business World, ICASDMBW 2022, 16–17 December 2022, Rukmini Devi Institute of Advanced Studies, Delhi, India*. Delhi, India: EAI, 2023. https://doi.org/10.4108/eai.16-12-2022.2326197.

[6] Khawrin, Mohammad, Dawit Tolossa and Gurudutta Japee. 'Students' Perception of Digital Banking with Special Reference to Higher Education Institutions in Ahmedabad'. *International Journal of Management, Public Policy and Research* 1, no. 4 (30 December 2022): 50–56. https://doi.org/10.55829/ijmpr.v1i4.55.

[7] Nila Chotai, *et al.* (2023). A study on the usage of Digital Payments among the students community, *Journal of Data Acquisition and Processing,* 1368–1380.

[8] Rai, Kamini and Mamta Sharma. 'A Study on Awareness about Digital Financial Services among Students'. *SSRN Electronic Journal*, 2019. https://doi.org/10.2139/ssrn.3308732.

[9] Ravikumar, T., Suresha, B., Prakash, N., Vazirani, Kiran and Krishna, T.A. 'Digital Financial Literacy among Adults in India: Measurement and Validation'. *Cogent Economics & Finance* 10, No. 1 (31 December 2022): 2132631. https://doi.org/10.1080/23322039.2022.2132631.

[10] Razak, Dzuljastri Abdul, Bile Abdisalan Nor, Siti Fatimah Mohamed Noor and Hanudin Amin. 'Factors Influencing Financial Inclusion among University Students in Malaysia: An Empirical Research for International Islamic University Malaysia (IIUM)' 30, No. 2 (2023).

[11] Sharma, Suneet, Ritu Sharma, Ghadeer Kayal, and Jaspreet Kaur. 'Digital Banking: A Meta-Analysis Approach'. *Indian Journal of Marketing* 52 (1 May 2022). https://doi.org/10.17010/ijom/2022/v52/i5/169416.

[12] https://cointelegraph.com/news/5-emerging-digital-finance-trends

[13] https://istart.com.au/opinion-article/trends-in-digital-finance/

[14] https://www.ijrti.org/papers/IJRTI2304144.pdf

[15] https://indoreinstitute.com/blog-post/5-reasons-why-finance-students-should-know-about-digital-banking-solutions/

[16] https://refpress.org/wp-content/uploads/2023/06/Bourish_Fahima_REF.pdf

# A Study of Various Schemes Available for SME's: A Case Study in State Bank of India

**Neha Banu[1] and S. Ranjith Kumar[2]**

[1]Research Scholar, School of Economics and Commerce, CMR University, Bangalore, India

[2]Associate Professor, School of Economics and Commerce, CMR University, Bangalore, India

E-mail: [1]neha@cmr.edu.in; [2]ranjithkumar@cmr.edu.in

***ABSTRACT:*** *Development of SME's sector holds a major share in the sustainable development of the economy. Many of the large enterprises start their businesses as small industries and they need financial assistance to grow up. In such a scenario banks act as intermediaries in order to serve the financial needs of the medium and small scale industries. Banks have started focusing on this segment, since it is found to be more profitable compared to other segments of business as they have greater growth opportunity. SMEs are vital for economic growth and development in both industrialized and developing countries, by playing a key role in creating new jobs. Financing is necessary to help them set up and expand their operations, develop new products. SMEs are also said to be responsible for driving innovation and competition in many economic sectors. Although they create more jobs, there is also a majority of job destruction/contraction. SBI has introduced various schemes for SMEs which will help the economy to grow efficiently and effectively.*

**Keywords:** Developing Countries, Economic Growth, Financing, SBI, SME.

## 1. INTRODUCTION

Small and medium-sized enterprises (SMEs) are the backbone of all economies and are a key source of economic growth, dynamism and flexibility in advanced industrialized countries, as well as in emerging and developing economies. SMEs constitute the dominant form of business organization, accounting for over 95% and up to 99% of enterprises depending on the country. They are responsible for between 60–70% net job creations in Developing countries. Small businesses are particularly important for bringing innovative products or techniques to the market.SMEs are vital for economic growth and development in both industrialized and developing countries, by playing a key role in creating new jobs. Financing is necessary to help them set up and expand their operations, develop new products.

Small and medium-sized enterprises (SMEs) or small and medium-sized businesses (SMBs) are businesses whose personnel numbers fall below certain limits. The abbreviation "SME" is used by international organizations such as the World Bank, the European Union, the United Nations and the World Trade Organization (WTO).

### 1.1 State Bank of India

The State Bank of India (SBI) is an Indian multinational, public sector banking and financial services statutory body. It is a government corporation statutory body headquartered in Mumbai, Maharashtra. SBI is ranked as 236$^{th}$ in the Fortune Global 500 list of the world's biggest corporations of 2019. It is the largest bank in India with a 23% market share in assets, besides a share of one-fourth of the total loan and deposits market.

### 1.2 SME Services Provided by State Bank of India

Majority of the loans to SMEs are been provided by SBI. SBI has introduced various schemes for SMEs. The various schemes are according to the sector in which a particular SME belongs and they are:

1. Asset Backed Loan
2. Asset Backed Loan Commercial Real Estate
3. Cotton Ginning Plus
4. Doctor Plus
5. Export Packing Credit
6. E Dealer Finance Scheme
7. E Vendor Finance Scheme
8. Fleet Finance
9. Lease Rental Discounting
10. Medical Equipment Finance
11. SME Smart Score
12. Stand Up India
13. Prime Minister Employment Generation Programme
14. Pradhan Mantri MUDRA Yojana
15. Credit Guarantee Fund Trust for Micro and Small Enterprises

## 2. STATEMENT OF THE PROBLEM

Despite the significant role played by small and medium-sized enterprises in the Saudi Arabian economy, they face financial constraints that adversely affect their development and limit their potential to boost the economy to the desired target. SMEs create jobs, support innovation and boost the country's exports. Even with the existence of 1.9 million SMEs in the country, they contribute little to Saudi Arabia's GDP compared to advanced economies in the world. The enterprise-level survey by the World Bank indicated that

SMEs experience limited access to credit from financial institutions compared to large corporations in developing countries like Saudi Arabia. Most SMEs lack qualified personnel with skills to provide financial information that has the same quality as those provided by large firms. Therefore, due to lack of audited financial statement, SMEs cannot access credit facilities.

## 3. OBJECTIVE OF THE STUDY

1. To study the various loan schemes available for SME's in SBI.
2. To assess the effectiveness of schemes available.

## 4. METHODOLOGY FOR THE STUDY

Both primary and secondary sources of information are obtained. Primary Data is taken from bank and Secondary data collected from various magazines and internet sources and SBI WEBSITE.

## 5. LITERATURE REVIEW

1. Saravanan (2013) MSME financing is all about allocating funds to the Micro, Small and Medium enterprises. The objectives of this study are to know the lending schemes for MSME and to check the awareness of the customers regarding new schemes introduced. In this study analysis is done on the borrower perceptions and awareness of the schemes and products of SME. Most common obstacles faced by the MSME SECTOR are fluctuations in interest rates. Reduction in the interest rates helps SMEs to opt for the bank loans. Another important finding is through private banks charge high interest and service charges SME's prefer them because of their quality in the services and schemes can widen theirs ME department with more man power and new credit products which increases the quality of services and can easily address customer problems.
2. Srinivas (2014) in his article mentions that MSME sector improvement is noteworthy in industrial sector as its contribution to economy is increasing. The objective of this study is to have a big idea of MSME sector and also financial cooperation of the banks in MSME sector. This study has followed mixed methodology. The major finding of this study is that banks provide better services to MSME sector. In spite of many government policies and schemes banks' traditional method of lending is considered as safe for MSME.
3. Dr. Ram Jass (2013) in his article specifies that major part of the income for banks is through lending loans and earning interests from them. This involves the credit risk, non repayment of the loans given to the borrowers due to many reasons like insolvency, unable to meet their needs etc. Many banks have adopted Credit Risk Assessment Model

which helps in assessing the risk of loan repayment. This study has followed case study analysis and measured the financial risk. One of the major findings of the study is that CGTMSE scheme has been availed on primary securities. Interest rates are charged based on the investor grade of the firm. For, more qualitative services banks are in a need to improvise their Credit Rating Assessment Model.

4. Pallab & Dr. Munish (2013) in his article mention that MSME is the backbone of the Indian economy. The research focuses on the Non-Performing Assets of the bank and its impact in the long run on bank's financial position. Any overdue in the payment of principle and interest amount is considered as a Non Performing Assets. The study is done to elucidate the risk levels from current NPA'S of banks. Some of the macro factors like changes in the market conditions and government policies are also reason for non-payment of loans. In order to avoid NPAs banks should follow pertinent credit appraisal system.
5. Nancy Arora (2013) in her article explains that credit appraisal means valuation of credit done before it is sanctioned to the borrower. The study is done to understand the four parameters like finance, business, industrial and management in CRA model. CRA model is used to assess the borrowers in simpler and regular models. The major finding of the study is that the bank should assess the commercial and financial viability of the project before sanctioning the loan.
6. Dr. Ram Jass (2013) in his article specifies that SME contribution to the national output is increasing day by day. It contributes to 8% of Gross Domestic Product (GDP).This study also finds out the major issues between the borrower and the lender, the bank. The study has followed the mixed methodology. Major findings of his study are that MSMEs prefer bank credit in the case of high financial needs. SME loan hub and SME loan factory can be introduced in banks for further development in SME credit facilities.
7. Akila & Padmavathy (2014) in her article specifies that banks are extending their credit for varied purposes. The study is done to know about the credit appraisal procedure of a bank in Chennai. Credit appraisal system is to appraise the credit facilities to the customers and to ascertain the risk-return. This study helped in identifying the causes for increasing the non- performing assets in the bank. The study is done to find the institutional structure of credit delivery for MSME sector. Significant finding of the study is that banks can follow an abridged application form for all the credit customers which increase the speed of credit proposals. Credit appraisal system is different for different banks. Instead they can follow common simple procedure which is understandable for all credit customers.
8. T. Srinivas (2014) in his study focused on the financial cooperation between banks and MSME sector. An important finding of this study is

that banks provide better services to MSME sector. In spite of many government policies and schemes bank traditional method of lending is considered as safe for MSME.

9. Savalia (2006), in his study on "Role of Small Industries Development Bank in India (SIDBI) industrial development in Gujarat state (with special reference to small scale industries)" made an attempt to study the role of SIDBI in the development of SSI and examine the position of SSI in Gujarat. The study found that SIDBI has sanctioned the maximum amounts to the service industry and followed by infrastructure industry during the study period of 1999–2000 to 2003–04 and the states receiving maximum amounts are Maharashtra followed by Tamil Naidu and Gujarat, it also found that SIDBI has sanctioned and disburse the maximum assistance to the private sector followed by public sector and trust and the maximum amount was towards the establishment of new projects followed by modernization of the existing projects.
10. Vora (2008) did a study on "Impact of selected banking system on small scale industries with special reference to Gujarat" selecting only those banks that satisfy the criteria of nationalized banks, to find the impact or finances of selected banking system on small scale industries and found that the bank credit target and the bank credit achievement in Gujarat for a period of five
11. RoopaKudva (2011) The Mangining Director of CRISIL says it is not easy to attract MSME's to do a credit rating, however it is important to have the credit rating done if the MSME's wants to position itself in the international market as well as there is a rebate from the bankers in the lending terms. Unfortunately the 75% subsidy is available only for the first time/year the MSME gets its rating done subsequently they have to bear the entire cost next year which is a strain on the purse strings. . Producing a new framework for rating SMEs is important, because most would receive low ratings on traditional scales solely because of their small size. The benchmarks used for large corporations have to be abandoned
12. C.B. Bhave (2010) in his opinion the MSME's are a catalyst in most of the economies and constitute a major part of the industrial activity. MSME's generally face financial crisis. He foresees that the SME Stock Exchange will be a great boon to this sector as it will provide a wide pool of capital, increased status and credibility and other benefits.
13. Sangeeta Baksi (2010) TIFAC is of the opinion that, there are few programs which are of utmost importance in the MSME- led technology development efforts, which promote the public private partnership. More so the technological development has never been a straight forwards process. Technological innovations have been the key to the survival of the MSMEs. Four decades of planned development have elevated India to a stage, where the country demonstrates some

remarkable strength in modern technologies for achieving development goals.

14. Y. Srinivas (2005) MSMEs play a very significant role in the economy in terms of balanced and sustainable growth, employment generation, development of entrepreneurial skills and contribution to export earnings. However, despite their importance to the economy, most SMEs are not able to stand up to the challenges of globalization, mainly because of difficulties in the area of financing. With the opening up of the Indian economy, it has become necessary to consider measures for smoothening the flow of credit to this sector. Small and Medium Enterprises (SMEs) play a very significant role in the economy in terms of balanced and sustainable growth, employment generation, development of entrepreneurial skills and contribution to export earnings. However, despite their importance to the economy, most SMEs are not able to stand up to the challenges of globalization, mainly because of difficulties in the area of financing.
15. Keshab DAS (2007) Despite an elaborate and dynamic policy framework, the progress of Indian MSMEs continues to be hindered by some of the basic constraints as poor credit availability, low levels of technology (hence, low product quality and limited exportability) and inadequate or no basic infrastructure, both physical and economic. It is too early to assess the impact and effectiveness of a plethora of new policy measures, announced very recently. He says that much of the potential of small firms to grow and nurture innovativeness is shaped by the kind of infrastructure, both physical and economic, available and can be accessed at reasonable costs. The MSMED ACT attaches importance to networking with stakeholders both upstream and downstream in the entire global value chain, from raw material procurement to processing/manufacturing to marketing to customer services.

## 6. ANALYSIS AND INTERPRETATION

The various loan schemes available for SME's in SBI:

### 6.1 Asset Backed Loan

***Purpose:*** For build-up of current assets and fixed assets needed for business purpose, capacity expansion, modernization, short term working capital (including shoring up of Net Working Capital, etc).

#### 6.1.1 *Features*

- Nature of Facility Dropline Overdraft. Both FB & NFB (LTV: 50% of realizable value)
- *Target Group:* All Business Units who want to avail loan facility for manufacturing and services activities along with self-employed and

professional individuals covered by MSMED Act 2006, wholesale/retail trade.

- Quantum of loan (Min/Max)

  *Minimum loan amount:* >Rs. 10 lacs

  *Maximum loan amount:* Rs. 20 crores
- *Margin (%):* Minimum 25% cash margin for NFB facility
- *Pricing:* Competitive Interest Rate Linked to MCLR
- Repayment Period

  *Dropline OD:* Limits can be sanctioned for periods ranging from 12 months to 180 months with either equated reduction in limit or customized reduction in limit, depending upon the cash accruals. Moratorium under the scheme should not be more than 18 months based on activity. Interest to be serviced monthly during the moratorium period.

  The drawing power shall be reduced monthly so as to have the overdraft liquidated at the end of the period.
- *Processing Fee/Upfront Fee:* 1% of the limits (Upper Cap: Rs. 10 Lacs).

### 6.1.2 *Eligibility Criteria*

- Existing Customer already availing credit facilities from us.
- New units with marketable assets to offer as security.
- Takeover of existing units from other Banks/FIs with satisfactory track record.

  Terms and condition.

### 6.1.3 *Collateral Security*

Immovable property in the form of Equitable/Registered Mortgage of land & building, by way of first charge.

- Industrial property both leased & freehold/land/plot cannot be taken as security for ABL.
- Leasehold property can be taken subject to the conditions mentioned above under the head "Eligible Security".
- No Second Charge or Pari-Passu charge will be extended for other Bank/FI.

## 6.2 Asset Backed Loan Commercial Real Estate

### 6.2.1 *Features*

- *Nature of Facility:* Dropline Overdraft. Both FB & NFB Facility (LTV-Immovable property: 50% of the realizable value)
- ***Purpose:*** Creation/acquisition of real estate such as office buildings, retail space, industrial or warehouse space, multiplex, hotels, restaurants,

gymnasium, amusement parks, cold storage etc. where the prospect for repayment would generally be lease or rental payment or sale of asset.

For both working capital (including pre-operative expenses) and fixed asset.

- *Target Group:* Proprietorship/Partnership/Company
- *Quantum of loan (Min/Max):* Minimum loan amount: >Rs 10 lacs
- Maximum loan amount

  *Tier-II, III Branch:* Rs. 20 Crores

  *Tier-I Branch:* Rs. 50 Crores
- *Margin (%):* 25% both for working capital and fixed assets.
- *Pricing:* Competitive Interest Rate Linked to MCLR
- *Repayment Period Drop-line Overdraft:* Limits can be sanctioned for period of 12 months to 72 months, including moratorium period, with either Equated Reduction in limit or customized reduction in limit depending upon the cash accruals as per projections.

  Interest to be serviced monthly during the period of moratorium also.

  Drawing power shall be reduced so as to have the overdraft liquidated at the end of the period.
- *Processing Fee/Upfront Fee:* 1% of the limits (Upper Cap: Rs. 10 Lacs).

### 6.2.2 *Eligibility Criteria*

- Existing Customer already availing credit facilities from us.
- New units with marketable assets to offer as security
- Takeover of existing units from other Bank/FIs permitted with satisfactory track record (Credit information report to be obtained).

### 6.2.3 *Collateral Security*

Immovable property in the form of Equitable/Registered Mortgage of land and building, by way of first charge.

- Industrial property both leased & freehold/land/plot cannot be taken as security for ABLCRE-CP
- Leasehold property can be taken subject to the conditions mentioned above under the head "Eligible Security".
- No Second Charge or Pari-Passu charge will be extended for other
- Bank/FI.

### 6.2.4 *Other Conditions*

- Cash Flow statement for Builder Finance on Quarterly basis in the month May/Aug/Nov/Feb.

- Drawing power is not linked to quarterly cash flow statement. However, cash flow statement is must to confirm the level of activity/status of the project/end use of the funds.

## 6.3 Export Packing Credit

***Purpose:*** For purchase of raw materials, processing, packing, transportation and warehousing of goods meant for export, It has two essential features, VIZ: Existence of an export order and/or letter of credit and liquidation of the packing credit by submission of export documents within a stipulated perio.

### 6.3.1 *Features*

- Nature of Facility Pre-shipment finance extended as working capital.
- *Target Group:* Manufacturers as well as merchant exporters, are eligible to avail Rupee Packing Credit at concessional rate of interest.
- *Quantum of loan (Min/Max):* Need based Finance
- *Margin (%):* The percentage of margin is determined depending on the nature of order, commodity, capability of exporter, etc. keeping in view the spirit behind RBI guidelines for liberal finance to the export
- *Pricing:* Competitive Pricing
- *Collateral Security:* As applicable in case of Cash Credit/Working capital limits)
- *Repayment Period:* The period for which the Bank gives packing credit depends on the manufacturing/trade cycle or specific requirements of the individual export, normally not exceeding 180 days.
- *Processing Fee/Upfront Fee:* As applicable to cash Credit Facility/ Working Capital Limits.

### 6.3.2 *Eligibility Criteria*

- Existing Customer already availing credit facilities from us.
- New units.
- Takeover of existing units from other Banks/FIs with satisfactory track record. (Credit information report to be obtained)

### 6.3.3 *Other Conditions*

- Since packing credit loans are concessional and purpose oriented, it will be necessary to ensure proper end use of amounts disbursed to the exporters.
- ECGC—Bank's export credit portfolio (pre-shipment or Packing Credit) is insured under Export Credit Insurance for Banks Guarantee Scheme (ECIB WTPC of ECGC Ltd. Premium cost will be borne by bank for those rated 'A' and above.

## 6.4 E-Vendor Finance Scheme

***Purpose:*** Financing receivables of recommended vendors of reputed Corporates/Industry Majors (IMs). Completely web based solution with minimal branch intervention and provides instant credit to vendors account electronically.

### 6.4.1 *Features*

- *Type of Facility:* Cash Credit (Clean)
- *Target Group:* Vendors of reputed Industry Majors/Corporates with whom the Bank has tie-up arrangement
- *Quantum of loan (Min/Max):* Need Based
- *Margin (%):* Nil
- *Pricing:* Competitive Pricing Linked to MCLR
- *Collateral Security:* Nil
- *Repayment Period:* According to tenor of the receivables.
- *Processing Fee/Upfront Fee:* Rs. 10,000 to Rs. 50,000/-.

### 6.4.2 *Eligibility Criteria:*

- Existing borrowers of Bank with continuously making profit for last 3 yr
- *Minimum Turnover Size for IM:* Rs. 500 Cr and above
- *External Rating:* A & above/Internal Rating SB-7 & above (If SBI customer)
- IMs total vendor base at least 50
- Outstanding Sundry Creditors not to exceed three months purchase
- Industry Scenario to be considered/RMD guidelines will be referred.

### 6.4.3 *Other Conditions*

Transactions are done on Internet Banking Platform of the bank (no cheque book required) & which results in easy, convenient & hassle free banking facilities to all stake holders i.e. Bank, IM & Dealer.

- Multiple Channel Repayment Option such as Cash, Cheque, Fund Transfer, NEFT, RTGS etc.
- There are 2 variants under e-VFS:

  *Vendor Exposure:* Financing will be made to the vendors against the supply of goods/services to reputed Corporates/IMs.

  *IM Exposure:* Financing will be made to the reputed corporate/IMs for payment towards the supply received from their vendors.

## 6.5 Fleet Finance

***Purpose:*** To finance new vehicles (Small, Light, Medium, Heavy Commercial Vehicles, Passenger Vehicle).E.g. trucks/tankers/trailers/tippers/buses/luxury buses and passenger vehicles etc.

### 6.5.1 *Features*

- Type of Facility: Term Loan
- Target Group
  Existing Fleet Operators (For Goods or Passenger transport)
  Existing Individuals/firms/companies/trusts/Society/Institutions/Associations
- Quantum of loan (Min/Max)
  *Min:* Rs. 50 lacs
  *Max:* Rs. 10 Cr (higher limit allowed as per Bank's discretion)
- Margin (%)
  *For Cost of Chasis:* 5% (score b/w 35-60%) & 0% (above 60% score)
  *For Cost of Body:* 45% (score b/w 35-60%) & 40% (above 60% score)
  *For fully buile model:* 10% (score b/w 35-60%) & 5% (above 60% score
  *Other expenses:* Min. 50%
- *Pricing:* Competitive Pricing linked to MCLR
- Repayment Period
  Upto 66 months.
  Repayment in EMI basis. Customized repayment is possible depending on cash accruals.
  *Upfront Fee:* 1% of the limit

### 6.5.2 *Eligibility Criteria*

- Existing Fleet Operators (Goods or Passenger) having experience of 2 years or more in the same line.
- Fleet operator having existing fleet of minimum 10 vehicles
- Requirement of minimum 10 new vehicles or minimum loan amount Rs. 50 Lacs
- Transport operators holding national/state route permit and other necessary permits/license/approval.

### 6.5.3 *Collateral Security*

- Up to Rs. 1 Cr: No collateral security. Loans will be covered under CGTMSE.
- Above Rs. 1 Cr: Min 20% tangible.

## *6.6 Lease Rental Discounting*

***Purpose:*** To meet borrower's liquidity mismatch (Proceeds of loan amount not to be used for any speculative purposes, whatsoever, including speculation on real estate and equity shares). A Certificate regarding the end use of funds should be obtained stating that the funds will be utilised for the purposes required in the usual course of business and not utilised for speculative, real estate purposes.

### 6.6.1 *Features*

- *Type of Facility:* Term Loan
- *Target Group:* All MSME Units along with Individuals which are owners of Residential & Commercial Properties let out on Rent
- Quantum of loan (Min/Max)
  *Min:* Rs. 10 lacs
  *Max:* Rs. 50 Cr for NBG; 500 Cr for MCG
- Scale of Finance:
  i. Lowest of:
    a. 95% of Net Present Value (NPV) of net rent receivables as per 1 yr MCLR OR
    b. 70% of realizable value of the property mortgaged OR.
    c. Upto Rs. 50 crore: 70% of net rent receivable for the residual lease period including the period covered under one renewal or loan tenor, whichever is less.

  *Above Rs. 50 crore*: 75% of net rent receivable for the residual lease period including period covered under renewal clause or loan tenor, whichever is less
- *Pricing:* Competitive Pricing Linked to MCLR
- Repayment Period Repayment of loan should be through EMI. An escrow account should invariably be opened with our Bank for credit of rentals against which the loan is sanctioned.
- *Processing Fee/Upfront Fee:* As per extant instructions.

### 6.6.2 Eligibility Criteria

- Owners of residential buildings and commercial properties, which are to be rented or already rented to MNCs/Banks/Large & Medium size Corporates/Government Offices (both Central and State)/reputed Public bodies such as Municipal Corporations etc.
- However, the properties should not be or have been leased to Social Infrastructure projects such as Schools, Colleges, Orphanages, Hospitals, Old age homes, Nursing homes etc.

### 6.6.3 *Collateral Security*

- Equitable Mortgage on building against the rentals of which the loan would be sanctioned or any other acceptable property of similar value. The realizable value of property to be mortgaged should be at least 143% of the loan amount

### 6.6.4 *Other Conditions*

Standing Instructions have to be set up in CBS for transfer of the EMI from the Escrow Account to Term Loan account.

The Loan should be disbursed only after:

- The execution and registration of Lease Deed.
- Noting of EM is mandatory in States where such provision exists. Where creation of EM is not possible Registered Mortgage should be done.
- The occupation of premises by lessee or after the receipt of first lease rent whichever is later.

## 6.7 Medical Equipment Finance

***Purpose:*** For purchase of equipment & funding of ancillary equipment.

### 6.7.1 *Features*

- Type of Facility Term Loan
- *Target Group:* Nursing Homes, Diagnostic Centers and Pathology Laboratories,Eye Centers, ENT Centers, Small and Medium size specialty clients like skin clinics, dental clinics, dialysis centers, endoscopy centers, IVF centers, Medical Practitioners
- Quantum of loan (Min/Max)

  *Minimum:* Above Rs. 10 lacs

  *Maximum:* Upto Rs. 20 crores
- Margin @ 15% uniformly
- *Pricing:* Competitive Pricing Linked to MCLR
- Repayment Period

  *Term Loan:* Loan is repayable in 3–7 years (including moratorium period of 6 months)

  Repayment to commence after 6 months of first disbursement. Repayment can be equated or customized as per the cash accrual of the unit.

  Interest to be serviced on a monthly basis during the moratorium period
- *Processing Fee:* 50% concession on card rates.

### 6.7.2 *Eligibility Criteria*

- Individuals, Partnerships, Corporate, Trust & Societies
- ITR is mandatory in all cases
- Applicant should have minimum 3 years of operations of the diagnostic center, pathological lab, hospital, nursing home, etc. irrespective of constitution.
- Should have required approvals/registrations from the statutory/regulatory authority
- Should have tie-up with/employed qualified doctors

### 6.7.3 *Collateral Security*

- No tangible collateral security for loan amounts upto Rs. 2 crores: They are to be covered under CGTMSE. 50% of CGTMSE fees will be borne by the borrower.
- For loans above Rs. 2 crore and upto Rs. 20 crores: Minimum 25% tangible collateral and personal guarantee of promoters.

### 6.7.4 *Other Conditions*

- It must be ensured that ancillary equipment is only used for purposes connected with the main activity and cost should not be more than 10% of main equipment (for which financing is done).

## 6.8 SME Smart Score

### 6.8.1 *Features*

- *Nature of Facility:* Cash Credit/Term Loan
- *Purpose:* Working Capital needs & Acquisition of fixed assets
- *Target Group:* Individually managed proprietary/partnership firm or closely held public/private limited companies in the Small and medium industrial and trading sector under C&I and SIB segments.
- Quantum of loan (Min/Max)

  *Manufacturing Units:* Rs. 5 lacs to up to Rs. 50 lacs (20% of annual turnover for WC loan and 67% of project cost for TL)

  *Trade & Services:* Rs. 5 lacs to Rs. 25 lacs (15% of annual turnover for WC and 67% of project cost for TL.)
- *Margin (%):* 25% for working capital component and 33% for TL component
- *Pricing:* Competitive Pricing Linked to MCLR
- *Collateral Security:* As per Bank's extant norms for WC and TLs
- *Repayment Period*

WC loan to be renewed every two years with annual review of performance.

TL not more than 5 years excluding moratorium not exceeding 6 months

- *Processing Fee:* As applicable to SSI/SBF/C&I units as per as per Bank's latest Instruction.

### 6.8.2 *Eligibility Criteria*

- The chief promoter/chief executive should be 18 to 65 years of age.

## 6.9 Stand Up India

### 6.9.1 *Features*

- *Nature of Facility:* Composite Loan (Working Capital facilities/Term Loan)
- *Purpose:* To meet all kinds of credit requirement for setting up Greenfield projects under manufacturing, services or the trading sector.
- *Target Group:* SC/ST and Women entrepreneurs
- Quantum of loan (Min/Max)

  *Minimum loan amount:* > Rs. 10 lacs

  *Maximum loan amount:* Rs. 1 crore
- *Margin (%):* Minimum mandatory margin is 10%. Max. Margin money on composite loan would be upto 25% which will be reduced through convergence with Central/State schemes.
- *Pricing:* Competitive Interest rates Linked to MCLR
- *Collateral Security:* No Collateral/Third Party Guarantee to be obtained. All loans to be covered under CGSSI (Credit Guarantee Scheme for Stand-Up India Scheme)
- *Repayment Period:* Maximum of 7 years (including moratorium period upto 18 months)
- *Processing Fee:* 0.20% of loan amount (plus GST as applicable). No other charges are proposed to be recovered.

### 6.9.2 *Eligibility Criteria*

- All loans more than Rs. 10 lakhs and up to Rs. 1 Crore to SC/ST borrowers and women entrepreneurs for Greenfield projects only.

## 6.10 SBI OD Product

***Purpose:*** The scheme proposes to grant National/State level Business Correspondents (BCs) of SBI, overdraft facility for meeting their working capital requirements which will enhance their ability to service more customers in an uninterrupted manner and thereby further the cause of Financial Inclusion.

### 6.10.1 *Features*

- *Nature of Facility:* Running Account OD facility
- *Target Group:* All National/State level Business Correspondents having valid agreement with SBI
- Quantum of loan (Min/Max)

  *Min:* Above Rs. 25 lacs

  *Max:* Less than Rs. 5 Crores. (Loan limit upto maximum 70% of 2 times the average monthly commission )
- *Pricing*

  With collateral security 20% and above: Repo Linked Lending Rate (RLLR) + 2.45%

  Without collateral security: Repo Linked Lending Rate (RLLR) + 2.95%
- *Repayment Period:* Running account facility, to be renewed every year, subject to satisfactory conduct of account.
- *Processing Fee:* 1% of loan amount.

### 6.10.2 *Eligibility Criteria*

- All National/State level Business Correspondents having valid agreement with SBI and having satisfactory business relationship with SBI for at least two years.

### 6.10.3 *Collateral Security*

- Assignment of commission to be received by the BC
- 20% cash collateral, wherever collateral security is offered
- Personal guarantee of the promoter directors.

## 6.11 PM Mudra Yojana

### 6.11.1 *Features*

- *Type of Facility:* Working Capital and Term Loan
- *Purpose:* Business purpose, capacity expansion, modernization
- *Target Group:* Business Enterprises in Manufacturing, Trading and Services sector including allied agricultural activities.
- Quantum of loan (Min/Max)

  *Maximum loan amount:* Upto Rs 10 lacs

  Loans upto Rs. 50,000 are categorised as SHISHU

Loans from Rs. 50,001 to Rs. 500,000 are categorised as KISHORE
Loans from Rs. 500,001/- to Rs. 10,00,000/- are categorised as TARUN

- Margin (%)
  Upto Rs. 50,000/- Nil
  Rs. 50,001 to Rs. 10 lacs: 10%
- *Pricing:* Competitive Pricing Linked to MCLR
- Repayment Period
  *WC/TL:* in 3–5 yrs including a moratorium of upto 6 months depending on the activity/income generation.
  Review of WC/TL to be done annually.
- Processing Fee
  Nil for Shishu and Kishore to MSE Units
  *For Tarun:* 0.50% (plus applicable tax) of Loan amount.

### 6.11.2 *Eligibility Criteria*

- Existing & New units

### 6.11.3 *Collateral Security*

- Nil. To be covered under CGFMU.
- However, as Primary Security, Hyp. Of P&M for TL and Hyp. of Stocks & Receivables for CC to be done.

### 6.11.4 *Other Conditions*

- The loans under Mudra Scheme are guaranteed by Credit Guarantee for Micro Units (CGFMU) and the same is provided through National Credit Guarantee Trustee Company (NCGTC).
- The guarantee cover is available for five years and hence for advances granted under Mudra Scheme the maximum period is 60 months.
- Leads are now available in UdyamiMitra Portal (www.udyamimitra.in). Site can be accessed by Branches with Username and Password
- All Branches to issue MUDRA RuPay Card for all the eligible CC accounts.

## 7. FINDINGS

### 7.1 SME Lending Operations

- ***Information Centre:*** Entrepreneurs expect that all data/information required for preparation of project proposal should made available at one place.

- **Preparation of Project Proposal:** Entrepreneurs experience many difficulties in formulating the project proposal which is required for raising assistance from the banks/the government. Data/information requirements are too many and the same are not available at one place. It is a time taking process, hence, entrepreneurs look for certain arrangements to get the required data/information conveniently and at low cost.
- ***Quantum of Loan Sanctioned:*** Both borrowers and bankers agree that the quantum of loan sanctioned is found to be inadequate in terms of the requirements of the SMEs. This issue is also confirmed from the analysis of the secondary data analysis. Hence, it calls for the review of the existing system of assessment of working capital. Further, an element of fear in the minds of the field personnel has to be taken out when the senior officers from the controlling office extend a moral support to them.
- ***End Use of Borrowed Funds:*** One of the main reasons for the units to become non-performing is the diversion of funds, calling for the present system of follow up and supervision to be strengthened. This suggests a need to introduce the concept of credit monitoring.
- ***Annual Review:*** The working capital limits are expected to be renewed on yearly basis. As part of the annual review, the performance of the unit is reviewed. But in the absence of proper review, the problems of 11 the SMEs are not understood. This leads to under-assessment of credit needs. This also gives a rise to develop an effective annual review format.
- ***Rehabilitation of Sick Units:*** From the survey of sick units, it is observed that success rate in rehabilitation is unsatisfactory. Involvement of banks can be enhanced when their role is specified. Procedures to be followed in banks should be spelt out. There is a need to develop a check list of DOs and D'NOTs in compliance of bank procedures.
- ***Loan Recovery:*** Branch Mangers look for a check-list of recovery measures which are many in number. Such measures relate to non-legal and legal categories. Such check list helps branch managers to choose an appropriate measure for a given case.
- ***Delays in Credit Sanctions:*** Delays are seen at every level lending operations. Such levels include: submission of the loan application form, project formulation, project implementation, annual review and renewal of limits and rehabilitation of sick units.
- ***Limited Bank Products:*** While SME units are operating in the global environment, bank products are found to be limited. The time has come for banks to devise schemes well suited to the changing needs of the units. Cluster based bank products have to be offered. All these products have to provide on line basis. There is also a need to set up a cell to develop credit related products especially for SME units.

## 8. SUGGESTIONS

Regarding 'SMEs Lending Schemes the study has worked out details, as discussed in the earlier chapter For instance.

- It is suggested to Information Centres in the private sector to provide data/information for project formulation.
- Further, the study suggests the banks to introduce "Cash Flow Based Lending" which would ensure the need based finance to the units. And, Credit Monitoring is expected to identify early warning signals of any account to become non-performing and preventive steps are needed to arrest slippage in standard assets.
- Similarly, Annual Review of a borrowable account can be conducted more effectively when banks will use the suggested format for the same. In the same way, the banks look for guidelines on rehabilitation of sick units. In this regard, it is attempted to prepare a checklist comprising DOs and D'NOTs. This check-list is prepared in consultation with the bankers.
- Lastly, the suggested check list of recovery measures is useful for branch managers to know about all recovery measures at one place. This check list is also developed in consultation with branch managers covered under the study, recommendations are made in this chapter which relates to: 1) Organization Structure for SME Lending in banks 2) Systems, Procedures and Technology for SME Lending and 3) People concerned with SME Lending in banks all these recommendations are expected to overcome issues.

## 9. CONCLUSION

The SSI sector is now called as SME sector. This sector deserves liberal institutional credit due to its unique contribution in terms of creation of employment, foreign exchange earnings, reduction in regional disparities, etc. But in reality, such supply of institutional credit is too less and often delayed. In addition, the sector has many other expectations from banks. There are many factors, internal and external, responsible for the inadequate and delayed supply of credit. The second phase of reform focuses on organizational aspects of banking business. In particular, efforts of banks in providing finance to the SSI sector need to be strengthened. Towards this end, they have to spell out their policies in financing of SSI in the changing context. The existing credit schemes also need a review in the context of the growing expectations of SMEs. To conclude, banks have a long way to go to double the credit flow to the SME sector during the next five year. Hence, they have many tasks on hand and hurdle to overcome during the second phase of reforms to make bank lending organizationally effective. These tasks, when completed and constraints overcome will certainly strengthen the banker-borrower relationship.

## BIBLIOGRAPHY


[1] Adrian, Wilkinson (1999). "Employment relations in SMEs", *Employee Relations*, Vol. 21, Iss. 3 pp. 206–217.

[2] Andy, Neely; Mike, Gregory and Ken, Platts (1995). Performance measurement system design; A literature review and research agenda, *International Journal of Operations& Production Management*, Vol. 15, No. 4, 1995, pp. 80–116.

[3] Das, K. (2008). SMEs in India: Issues and Possibilities in Times of Globalisation', inLim, H. (ed.), SME in Asia and Globalization, ERIA Research Project Report 2007–5, pp. 69–97.

[4] Fridah Muriungi Mwobobia (2012). The Challenges Facing Small-Scale Women Entrepreneurs: A Case of Kenya, *International journal of business administration*, Vol. 3, Issue 2, pp. 112–121.

[5] Gisha, P. Mathai (2015). Challenges and Issues in Micro, Small and MediumEnterprises (MSMEs) in India: *A Current Scenario of Economic Growth,* Vol. 4, Issue 7, pp. 162–163.

[6] Hooi, L.W. (2006). Implementing e-hrm: the readiness of sme manufacturing companyin Malaysia, *Asia pacific business review*, Vol. 12, No. 4, pp. 465–485.

[7] Ishu, Garg and Suraj, Walia (2012). Micro, Small & Medium Enterprises (MSMEs) Post Reform India: Status & Performance, Vol. 1, No. 3, pp 134–141.

[8] McEvoy, G. (1984). "Small business personnel practices", *Journal of Small Business,* October, pp. 1–8.

[9] Mishu, Tripathi; Saurabh, Tripathi and Rikin, Dedhia (2016). Challenges faced by of Science technology and management, Vol. 5, Issue 3, pp. 69–77. *Micro, Small and Medium Enterprise (MSME) Sector in India, International Journal.*

[10] Mukund, Chandra Mehta (2013). Challenges and Opportunities in Micro, Small and Humanity and Economics (ICMHE'2013) May 6–7, 2013 Kuala Lumpur (Malaysia), pp. 134–136 Medium Enterprises in India, 2$^{nd}$ *International Conference on Management*,

[11] Neeru Garg (2014). Micro, Small and Medium Enterprises in India: Current Scenario and Challenges, *Paripex - Indian Journal of Research,* Vol. 3, Issue 9, pp. 11–13.

[12] Nirmal, Ganguly (1988). Small scale sector: Problems and prospects, Yojana, March 1–15, pp. 10–24.

[13] Aruna, N. (2015). Problems Faced By Micro, Small and Medium Enterprises—A business and management, Vol. 14, Issue 4, pp. 43–49, *Special Reference to Small Entrepreneurs in Visakhapatnam, IOSR Journal of.*

[14] Kumar, N.V.R. Jyoti and Lalhunthara (2015). Challenges the operational constraints Management & Extension Journal, Vol 42, Issue 2, pp 47–64, *Faced by micro entrepreneurs in Mizoram, Small Enterprises Development.*

[15] Rajesh, K. Pillania (2008). "Creation and categorization of knowledge in automotive components SMEs in India", *Management Decision*, Vol. 46, Iss 10, pp. 1452–1464.

# Finance

# Socio-Economic Impact of MGNREGA: A Paradigm Shift with Special Reference to Women Senior Citizens

**I.B. Cirappa[1] and J. Shivanna[2]**

[1]Associate Professor, Department of Studies and Research in Commerce, Davangere University Shivagangothri, Davangere, India

[2]Research Scholar, Department of Studies and Research in Commerce, Davangere University Shivagangothri, Davangere, India

E-mail: [2]shivmelukunte@gmail.com

***ABSTRACT:*** *Rural development has emerged as a significant concern for governments characterized by a substantial rural populace, prompting the implementation of diverse initiatives aimed at fostering the advancement of impoverished and marginalized individuals residing in rural regions. The significance of rural regions in the development of countries such as India requires little substantiation, as it is apparent from the strategic focus of government programmes that rural areas serve as catalysts for the nation's progress. These initiatives have been designed to harness the available resources for the purpose of improving the living conditions and overall well-being of the rural population. A considerable proportion of those experiencing poverty in India are mostly located in rural regions and heavily rely on wage labour as their primary means of sustenance. The government has consistently implemented various public works projects and social security measures in order to alleviate the hardships faced by individuals and improve their circumstances. The Act has been implemented nationwide to ensure the provision of job opportunities for rural communities, hence promoting sustainable livelihood support at the community level. The Mahatma Gandhi National Rural Employment Guarantee Act (MGNREGA), which was passed in 2005, is a ground-breaking piece of legislation aimed at providing a legal assurance of 100 days of employment to individuals living in rural areas who face limited capacity to bear risks, have poor creditworthiness to engage in self-employment endeavors, and exhibit a strong inclination towards wage labour. A random selection approach was used to choose a sample of 200 women senior citizen for inclusion in the research, so ensuring the attainment of representative findings.*

**Keywords:** Awareness, Economic Security, MGNREGA, Social Inclusion, Women Senior Citizens.

## 1. INTRODUCTION

The MGNREGA is an all-encompassing public works plan that ensures rural families will have paid employment for a total of one hundred days each year. The goal of this statewide public works plan is to provide families in rural areas paid employment for a total of one hundred days each year. The purpose of this research is to assess the degree to which the project contributes to the realization of "genuine transformative social protection" [7]. The MGNREGA is an extensive public works initiative that has as its primary objective the provision of 100 days of paid employment to rural families on a yearly basis. The purpose of this research is to assess the degree to which the project contributes to the realization of "genuine transformative social protection [1]." By undertaking an investigation of the Mahatma Gandhi National Rural Employment Guarantee Act (MGNREGA) in India, this paper makes an important intellectual addition to the continuing debate over social protection programmes. The MGNREGA is an all-encompassing public works plan that ensures rural families will have paid employment for a total of one hundred days each year. The study is based on empirical facts, which enables a full understanding of the nature of this programme as well as its effects. The purpose of this research is to assess the degree to which the project contributes to the realization of "genuine transformative social protection." It is the purpose of this project to investigate, by means of a stringent econometric analysis, if the passing of this law has led to a decrease in the amount of debt that is carried by people of rural areas. This paper makes a novel effort to carry out a complete analysis at the national level using data that is available to the general public in order to evaluate the impact of the (MGNREGA) on the amount of debt held by rural families. The burden of debt carried by rural families is one of the most important contributors to the financial difficulties experienced by agriculturally active households. Due to what they believe to be a lack of potential for profit in the agricultural sector, a number of small-scale farmers have left the business as a result of the extent and intensity of rural indebtedness [5]. The results of this research demonstrate that the law described above is effective in reducing the total amount of outstanding debt, which is a very positive conclusion. On the other hand, it is essential to point out that the accomplishments of the law have been tainted by instances of corruption and irregularities, in addition to the fact that the assets that are being produced do not have a sustainable future [9].

## 2. THE RESEARCH BACKGROUND

The focus, methods, tactics, and initiatives pertaining to rural development in India have seen significant transformations over the years [5]. As a result, it has acquired new dimensions and viewpoints. The active involvement of development stakeholders is crucial for enhancing the quality and significance of rural development initiatives. Similar to how implementation serves as the benchmark for planning, the active involvement of individuals is of utmost importance in the context of rural development [3]. The involvement of individuals is a fundamental need for the development process, as seen from both procedural and philosophical standpoints. In order to ensure the participatory nature of development plans, it is essential for development planners and administrators to actively seek the involvement of diverse rural populations [11]. Several poverty reduction and job generating initiatives were developed with the aim of enabling individuals to generate additional income outside the agricultural sector. None of the aforementioned projects provided complete coverage over the whole nation. However, in some regions, a subset of these seven programmes were implemented concurrently, targeting the same categories of individuals. The issues pertaining to this region revolve on the fact that although the project is intended to primarily benefit small and marginalized farmers, it has mostly served the interests of medium and large-scale farmers due to their convenient access to government financial institutions. One significant drawback of these schemes was their transformation into simply subsidy-giving initiatives, devoid of any strategic framework to assist the rural impoverished in attaining increased income levels. The advent of the Mahatma Gandhi National Rural Employment Guarantee Act is a significant milestone in the realm of rural development within the context of India's history. Among the various wage employment initiatives devised and executed thus far to ensure the economic stability of the rural workforce in

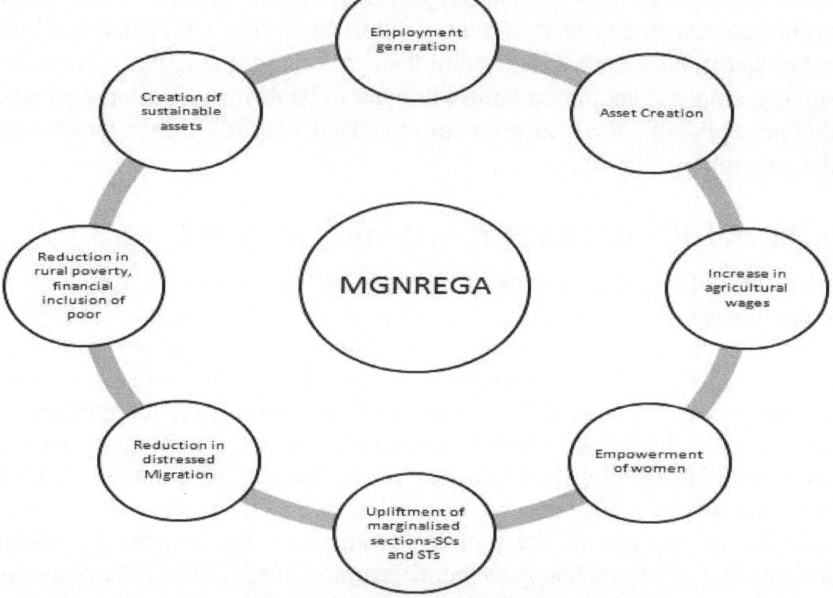


**Figure 1**

*Source:* https://blog.forumias.com/wp-content/uploads/2018/05/man.jpg

post-independence India, (MGNREGA) stands out as distinctive. This programme is characterized by its community-oriented approach and responsive nature, as it grants legal entitlement and the right to a minimum of 100 days of assured wage employment per fiscal year to eligible households [9].

The ramifications of unemployment among those with higher education levels have significant societal implications. It may be seen that individuals with higher levels of credentials are often employed in positions that might be performed by those with lower levels of qualifications. This phenomenon leads to the underutilization of an individual's potential. Graduate engineers are often employed in positions that may feasibly be fulfilled by those with diplomas. In a similar vein, it is plausible to encounter individuals with postgraduate credentials employed as clerks and typists, despite the possibility of such tasks being adequately performed by those with matriculation-level education. This phenomenon occurs because to the limited employment opportunities available to those with lower credentials, prompting them to pursue more education in the expectation that it would enhance their eligibility for the same work positions. Numerous individuals engaging in illicit activities such as theft, pickpocketing, smuggling, and drug trafficking often resort to these pursuits due to their inability to get legal means of employment. The potential connection between the difficulties experienced by jobless youth and the emergence of terrorism should be acknowledged. The segment of the population with advanced levels of education who are now without employment harbor feelings of resentment against society due to their current circumstances. The individuals hold the belief that if this system fails to fulfil their expectations in terms of providing suitable employment opportunities, it ought to be dismantled. Consequently, this prompts individuals to resort to organized acts of violence directed on the governing authority.

## 3. PREVIOUS RESEARCH NOTABLE STUDIES

Bhattarai (2018) [3] conceptualized and put into action by the government of India, covers all of the rural regions located inside the country. Almost 10 years after the program's inception, the purpose of this research study is to conduct an exhaustive investigation of the initiative by concentrating on micro-level evaluations and the myriad of different effects the programme has at many dimensions. This programme is designed to bring together a number of different welfare and rural development programmes that are currently being carried out at the national as well as the state level. The book includes an analysis of the program's outcomes and delivers significant insights on the information gathered. Kumar and Singh (2018) [9] categorized the programmes that aim to alleviate poverty in India according to whether or not they concentrate on urban or rural areas. Since it is common knowledge that the incidence of poverty is disproportionately high in rural areas, the bulk of programmes are geared primarily towards finding solutions to the problem of rural poverty. The fight against poverty in rural areas presents a number of important problems as a result of the myriad of topographical and infrastructural barriers that exist there. The programmes may essentially be broken down into a few different categories, including wage employment programmes, self-employment programmes, food security programmes, social security programmes, and urban poverty reduction initiatives. The implementation of sector-specific policies was the primary focus of the post-independence five-year plans, which had as their primary objective the reduction of poverty. Santoshsingh and Negi (2017) [17], discussed that India is primarily an agricultural nation, and rural unskilled labour has a significant impact on the country's economy. The majority of people who live in rural regions, especially those who are living in poverty, depend primarily on the wages that they obtain from unskilled, informal, and physical jobs. Through the creation of new employment possibilities, the Mahatma Gandhi National Rural Employment Guarantee Act (MGNREGA) would have the main effect of improving the socioeconomic conditions of rural communities who are already in a disadvantaged position. The Act provides a mechanism for people to participate in employment during times of economic difficulty, so helping rural communities living in poverty to maintain their level of consumption and expand their livelihood resources during this critical interval by providing them with the opportunity to work. To achieve social justice and balanced development is not solely reliant on economic growth; rather, it requires a parallel emphasis on alleviating poverty and providing work opportunities for disadvantaged and marginalized elements of society. This is because economic growth alone is not enough to bring about social justice and balanced development. Dhawan and Ajaykumar (2017), [4] argued that the plan that was chosen to be implemented in India is largely viewed as a very significant step forward in terms of both rural development and job opportunities. This specific project, in contrast to other rural development and employment programmes that came before it, provides a guarantee of a minimum of one hundred and twenty days of unskilled physical labour per year. Individuals who are unable to work the minimum number of days necessary to qualify for unemployment benefits may still be eligible for benefits under certain circumstances. The general belief is that the execution of this plan will have a revolutionary effect on the socioeconomic landscape of rural India. This view is supported by a growing body of research. The rural population's overall social and economic well-being has been considerably impacted by this plan in the state of Himachal Pradesh, where it has been effectively implemented. The use of this technique has made it easier for many different subsets of the rural people to gain their independence. Because of the adoption of the system, there has been a significant increase in the purchasing power of women, which has led to demonstrable improvements in the expansion of the regional economy.

## 4. SOCIAL AND ECONOMIC DEVELOPMENT OF RURAL PEOPLE

The major goal of rural development is to improve people's social and economic conditions who live in rural regions. Most of the time, this is done by improving their income and giving them easier access to other crucial social resources in order to bring about lasting improvements in their quality of life. Women's rights, roles, and economic possibilities all contribute to their economic status, which in turn affects their overall status. Women's economic empowerment has emerged as a proxy for societal well-being. However, not all kinds of growth result in women's economic opportunities improving. Women's behaviours are connected to economic status and impacted by the prevalent social ideology. Numerous government programmes are in place to promote economic and social progress in India's rural areas. Optimal economic development may benefit from several factors, and many countries are beginning to see that better rural management is one of them. The rural sector is essential to society since it encourages the progress of civilizations and makes it possible for people to work towards their goals of bettering their standard of living. There exists a considerable relationship between economic advancement and rural society, as the bulk of resources required for development come from rural communities. India's rural areas have always played an important role in the country's economic and social stability. Agriculture, livestock, forestry, fisheries, mining, and rural tourism are just few of the few industries that dominate rural areas' economies. These enterprises would not be able to expand without the region's abundant natural resources. Significant levels of underdevelopment are evident in India's rural communities, which may be related to a wide range of societal problems.

## 5. NEED FOR THE STUDY AND SIGNIFICANCE

The study reveals that women have experienced enhanced empowerment and enrichment as a consequence of the programme. The plan's principal impact is on its potential to bring in money, increase participation in society, and give women a voice in policymaking. The need for rural women in low-income positions to have access to economic opportunities and to be given the tools to improve their own situations has prompted this study. After much struggle, the legislation for job guarantee was passed, and it represents a major step forward in realizing the full right to work in the context of developing nations. This legislation stands apart from similar public service delivery plans since it has been formally adopted by the Parliament of India. This statute has been the catalyst for a quiet revolution in America's rural areas. This initiative is unique in comparison to other job creation initiatives because of how it was conceived. There must be separate strategies for enforcing the right to work for people and implementing programmes to create new jobs. The objective now is to make sure that everyone in rural areas, but notably women, understands how the Scheme works in its entirety. This study is an effort to investigate the implementation of (MGNREGA) in selected blocks in Madurai District, Tamil Nadu. The major aim is to analyses the level of empowerment of rural women via the MGNREGA project and to examine the demographic features of the sample group.

## 6. STATEMENT OF THE PROBLEM

The Mahatma Gandhi National Rural Employment Guarantee Act (MGNREGA) in India, introduced with the aim of enhancing rural livelihoods, raises critical questions regarding its socio-economic impact. Firstly, there is a need to comprehensively assess the extent to which MGNREGA has achieved its primary objective of employment generation in rural areas. Understanding the quality and sustainability of the employment created, including factors such as wages, job duration, and the overall impact on the livelihoods of the beneficiaries, is essential. Secondly, the socio-economic implications of MGNREGA on income and poverty levels demand rigorous examination. Evaluating whether the program has effectively contributed to household incomes and acted as a catalyst for poverty alleviation is crucial for determining its overall success. Thirdly, the program's role in skill development and capacity building needs thorough exploration. Beyond providing immediate employment, understanding whether MGNREGA has equipped the rural workforce with transferable skills for broader economic opportunities is pivotal for long-term socio-economic development. Additionally, the gender dynamics of MGNREGA warrant in-depth scrutiny. Analyzing the impact on women's participation in the workforce, economic empowerment, and improvements in gender-related indicators is necessary for a nuanced understanding of the program's socio-economic effects. Furthermore, the relationship between MGNREGA and agricultural productivity poses important questions. Examining how the program influences farm labor availability, cropping patterns, and modern agricultural practices is crucial for determining its impact on the agricultural sector. The study must also investigate the contribution of MGNREGA to rural infrastructure development. Assessing the effectiveness of the program in creating assets such as roads, water conservation structures, and community facilities is essential for understanding its role in improving overall living standards. Moreover, considering the environmental sustainability of MGNREGA projects is imperative. Evaluating their impact on natural resources, biodiversity, and ecological balance is essential to ensure that the program aligns with broader sustainable development goals. Finally, a comprehensive analysis of the challenges in MGNREGA's implementation and its overall effectiveness is crucial for informing policy decisions. Addressing these multifaceted issues will contribute to a nuanced understanding of the socio-economic impact of MGNREGA and inform future policy directions.

## 7. RESEARCH OBJECTIVES

In order to assess the demographic characteristics of the selected participants and evaluate the impact of the (MGREGA) on the empowerment of women living in rural areas of Davangere district.

## 8. RESEARCH METHODOLOGY

The research is characterized by its empirical nature, since it incorporates a comprehensive range of primary and secondary sources in order to provide a holistic understanding of the subject matter. The collection of primary data was conducted via the use of a structured questionnaire and a series of face-to-face interviews [4]. The study's representative sample comprises farmers who are on the verge of subsistence and agricultural workers. A random selection approach was used to choose a sample of 50 senior citizen are included for inclusion in the research, so ensuring the attainment of representative findings. The study revealed that individuals who consistently participated in the programme demonstrated noteworthy enhancements across various socioeconomic measures [15]. The primary method used for data collection was accessing many government offices and thoroughly studying numerous official publications and websites. The secondary data used in this research was obtained from the Ministry of Agriculture and Rural Development.

## 9. ANALYSIS, FINDINGS, AND RESULTS—SOCIO-ECONOMIC IMPACT OF MGNREGA

The aforementioned issues hindered the rural women's ability to fully access and use the resources available to them. In order to enhance the quality of life for women living in rural areas, it is essential to provide a well-structured pathway that facilitates the attainment of a wide range of advantages. It offers supplementary sources of income that contribute to the livelihood security, as well as the enhancement of child education and health outcomes within rural households. Additionally, it facilitates the development of essential infrastructure at the village level, while simultaneously promoting the protection of natural resources and the environment. The level of importance is measured using the five point Likert scale and the significant difference in the rank is tested with the help of Friedman test as below.

**Table 1:** Results of Friedman Test

| *Factors* | *Mean* | *SD* | *Mean Rank* | *Rank* |
|---|---|---|---|---|
| Employment Generation | 4.62 | 0.786 | 5.68 | III |
| Poverty Alleviation | 3.98 | 0.735 | 5.71 | II |

| *Factors* | *Mean* | *SD* | *Mean Rank* | *Rank* |
|---|---|---|---|---|
| Women Empowerment | 3.61 | 0.620 | 5.54 | IV |
| Asset Creation | 4.01 | 0.741 | 5.32 | VII |
| Skill Development | 4.24 | 0.756 | 5.96 | I |
| Agricultural Productivity | 4.56 | 0.639 | 5.31 | VIII |
| Rural Infrastructure Development | 4.81 | 0.782 | 5.35 | VI |
| Social security | 4.33 | 0.711 | 5.47 | V |
| Awareness and Social Inclusion | 4.54 | 0.757 | 5.07 | X |
| Reduced Distress Migration | 4.23 | 0.785 | 5.19 | IX |
| Chi-Square | 64.087 | | | |
| df | 9 | | | |
| p-value | <0.001 | | | |

Table 1 describes the results of the Friedman test for Essentials of Emotional Intelligence among the employees working in information technology companies in the study area. The study's outcome describes the chi-square and p-value is 64.087& <0.001. The p-value is <0.01. Employment Generation: MGNREGA has been successful in providing employment opportunities in rural areas, especially during the agricultural off-season. This has helped in reducing seasonal unemployment and distress migration. Poverty Alleviation: By providing wage employment, MGNREGA contributes to poverty reduction by putting money directly in the hands of rural households. This income, in turn, can be used for consumption and basic needs. Women Empowerment: The participation of women in the workforce has increased, leading to greater financial independence and decision-making power. Asset Creation: The program focuses on creating durable assets for sustainable development, such as water conservation structures, rural infrastructure, and irrigation facilities. This contributes to the overall improvement of rural livelihoods. Skill Development: The work carried out under MGNREGA often involves unskilled manual labor. However, over time, it can contribute to skill development and capacity building among the rural workforce. Agricultural Productivity: By addressing the issue of seasonal unemployment, MGNREGA indirectly supports agricultural productivity. Farmers can access a stable labor force during peak agricultural seasons, contributing to increased crop yields. Rural Infrastructure Development: MGNREGA investments in rural infrastructure, such as roads, ponds, and check dams, lead to improved connectivity and accessibility. This, in turn, supports economic activities and market linkages. Social Security: MGNREGA acts as a social safety net by providing a source of employment and income during times of economic distress, particularly in drought or flood-affected regions. Reduced Distress Migration: The availability of employment opportunities in rural areas through MGNREGA has the potential to reduce distress migration to urban areas in search of livelihoods. Awareness and Social Inclusion: The program has increased awareness among rural communities about their rights and entitlements. Continuous evaluation and refinement of the program are necessary to address these challenges and enhance its effectiveness.

## 10. FACTORS INFLUENCING MGNREGA

The Mahatma Gandhi National Rural Employment Guarantee Act (MGNREGA) is a social welfare program in India aimed at providing employment opportunities to rural households, thereby enhancing livelihood security in rural areas. Several factors influence the implementation and success of MGNREGA. Garret ranking technique is applied. The result is given in the Table 2.

**Table 2**

| *Factors* | *Rank* | *1* | *2* | *3* | *4* | *5* | *6* | *7* | *Score* | *Rank* |
|---|---|---|---|---|---|---|---|---|---|---|
| | *GV* | *79* | *66* | *58* | *50* | *43* | *35* | *22* | | |
| Demand for Employment | f | 41 | 22 | 12 | 20 | 42 | 11 | 52 | 9722 | V |
| | fx | 3239 | 1452 | 696 | 1000 | 1806 | 385 | 1144 | | |
| Economic security | f | 37 | 45 | 14 | 26 | 28 | 18 | 32 | 10543 | II |
| | fx | 2923 | 2970 | 812 | 1300 | 1204 | 630 | 704 | | |
| Social Awareness and Participation | f | 36 | 21 | 38 | 22 | 28 | 39 | 16 | 10455 | III |
| | fx | 2844 | 1386 | 2204 | 1100 | 1204 | 1365 | 352 | | |
| Agricultural development | f | 32 | 15 | 35 | 72 | 20 | 7 | 19 | 10671 | I |
| | fx | 2528 | 990 | 2030 | 3600 | 860 | 245 | 418 | | |
| Environmental Considerations | f | 35 | 22 | 25 | 31 | 32 | 30 | 25 | 10193 | IV |
| | fx | 2765 | 1452 | 1450 | 1550 | 1376 | 1050 | 550 | | |
| Budgetary Allocations | f | 26 | 28 | 11 | 19 | 22 | 58 | 36 | 9258 | VII |
| | fx | 2054 | 1848 | 638 | 950 | 946 | 2030 | 792 | | |
| Self-interaction | f | 21 | 32 | 26 | 19 | 35 | 33 | 34 | 9637 | VI |
| | fx | 1659 | 2112 | 1508 | 950 | 1505 | 1155 | 748 | | |

Agricultural development (10671) is ranked first by the sample respondents. The Mahatma Gandhi National Rural Employment Guarantee Act (MGNREGA) has had a notable impact on agricultural development in

India, marking a significant intersection between rural employment and the agricultural sector. One of the key ways in which MGNREGA has influenced agricultural development is through the provision of a reliable source of labor for rural farming activities. By guaranteeing employment opportunities, especially during lean agricultural seasons, MGNREGA ensures a more stable and available workforce for farmers. Moreover, MGNREGA projects often include activities related to water conservation, land development, and afforestation, directly contributing to improved agricultural infrastructure. The creation of water conservation structures, such as check dams and farm ponds, enhances the availability of water for irrigation, positively impacting crop yields and fostering sustainable agricultural practices. The program's emphasis on asset creation aligns with the broader goal of enhancing rural livelihoods, as the infrastructure developed under MGNREGA contributes to the overall improvement of the rural landscape. Improved connectivity through the construction of roads, for example, facilitates the transportation of agricultural produce to markets, reducing post-harvest losses and increasing farmers' access to markets. Furthermore, the increased income in rural households resulting from MGNREGA employment opportunities can translate into higher investment capacity for farmers. This, in turn, can lead to the adoption of modern agricultural techniques, purchase of better seeds and fertilizers, and overall improvement in farming practices. While MGNREGA has a positive impact on agricultural development, challenges exist, such as the need for effective coordination between MGNREGA and existing agricultural schemes to ensure synergy and maximize benefits. Additionally, addressing the seasonal nature of MGNREGA employment and aligning it with agricultural cycles could further enhance its impact on the sector. In summary, MGNREGA plays a crucial role in promoting agricultural development by providing a stable labor force, contributing to infrastructure development, and fostering economic conditions conducive to improved farming practices. Integrating MGNREGA with agricultural policies and addressing implementation challenges can enhance its effectiveness in promoting sustainable agricultural development in rural India. Economic security (10543) is ranked second by the respondents. The Mahatma Gandhi National Rural Employment Guarantee Act (MGNREGA) has had a substantial impact on economic security, particularly in rural areas of India. The program, by guaranteeing 100 days of employment to every rural household, acts as a powerful social safety net, providing a source of income during times of economic uncertainty. This has a direct and positive influence on the economic security of vulnerable populations in rural communities. MGNREGA's impact on economic security is evident in its role in mitigating poverty. By offering employment opportunities and a steady income stream, the program contributes to lifting households out of poverty and preventing them from falling deeper into financial distress. The wages earned through MGNREGA empower rural families to meet their basic needs, including food, healthcare, and education, thereby enhancing their overall economic well-being. Furthermore, MGNREGA promotes financial inclusion by injecting money directly into the hands of rural laborers. The timely payment of wages ensures that the economic benefits of the program are realized promptly, contributing to increased liquidity in local economies. This, in turn, stimulates demand for goods and services at the grassroots level, fostering economic activity in rural areas. The economic security impact of MGNREGA extends beyond immediate income to long- term implications. By creating durable assets through various projects, such as roads, water conservation structures, and rural infrastructure, the program lays the foundation for sustained economic development. These assets not only contribute to improved living standards but also enhance the overall economic resilience of rural communities. While MGNREGA undeniably plays a pivotal role in enhancing economic security, challenges persist, including delays in wage payments and variations in the demand for employment across seasons. Addressing these issues and ensuring the program's effective implementation are crucial for maximizing its impact on economic security and ensuring the well-being of India's rural population. In essence, MGNREGA stands as a cornerstone in promoting economic security by providing a safety net, empowering rural households, and fostering sustainable economic development in the country's rural hinterlands.

## 11. DISCUSSION

**Demand for Employment:** The success of MGNREGA is closely linked to the demand for employment in rural areas. Factors such as agricultural seasons, availability of alternative employment opportunities, and economic conditions influence the demand for MGNREGA jobs. Implementation at the Grassroots Level: Effective implementation of MGNREGA relies on the efficiency and transparency of the administrative machinery at the grassroots level. Timely payment of wages, proper record-keeping, and monitoring mechanisms are crucial for the program's success. Social Awareness and Participation: Public awareness and participation play a vital role in the success of MGNREGA. Communities need to be informed about their rights under the program, the processes involved, and how to access employment opportunities. Infrastructure Development: MGNREGA is not only a source of employment but also a means for rural infrastructure development. The availability of projects that contribute to local infrastructure, such as water conservation, road construction, and afforestation, can enhance the program's impact. Budgetary Allocations: Adequate budgetary allocations are essential to meet the demand for employment and ensure the timely payment of wages. Insufficient funds can lead to delays in implementing projects and paying workers, affecting the program's credibility. Technology

Integration: The use of technology in the form of digital platforms for job registration, fund disbursement, and monitoring can improve the efficiency and transparency of MGNREGA operations. This includes the use of mobile applications, biometric authentication, and online record-keeping. Coordination with **Other Schemes:** MGNREGA's success is also influenced by its coordination with other rural development schemes. Synergy with programs related to agriculture, health, and education can create a holistic approach to addressing rural poverty and development. Environmental Considerations: Projects under MGNREGA often involve natural resource management and environmental conservation. Incorporating sustainable practices and ensuring that projects adhere to environmental regulations contribute to the long-term success of the program. Political Will and Stability: Political commitment and stability at both the central and state levels are crucial for the sustained implementation of MGNREGA. Changes in political leadership or policy direction can impact the program's continuity and effectiveness. Considering and addressing these factors collectively can contribute to the success of MGNREGA in achieving its objectives of providing livelihood security and fostering rural development in India.

## 12. CONCLUSION

The Mahatma Gandhi National Rural Employment Guarantee Act (MGNREGA) functions as an effective tool for alleviating poverty and improving socio-economic conditions, particularly targeting rural women [13]. The intervention has been essential in producing transformative outcomes in the lives of women living in rural regions. There is evidence to suggest that women who participate in the (MGNREGA) programme have experienced enhanced security and the ability to start savings in financial institutions [9]. The acknowledgement of rural women has seen a notable rise, resulting in their heightened engagement in addressing both the collective challenges faced by the community as a whole, and the specific issues encountered by women individually. MGNREGA has had a profound impact among its beneficiaries, the rural households who avail themselves of the program. The program's focus on unskilled manual labor ensures that even the most marginalized individuals in rural communities have the opportunity to contribute to and benefit from their local economies [14]. One notable outcome is the positive shift in the socio-economic status of women within these households. The mandated inclusion of women in the workforce, comprising at least one-third of participants, has not only increased their financial independence but has also fostered a sense of empowerment and agency [12]. Women are now active contributors to their family's income, leading to a more equitable distribution of resources and decision-making power. Furthermore, MGNREGA's emphasis on creating durable assets has resulted in tangible improvements in rural infrastructure. From the construction of water conservation structures to the development of essential facilities, the program has not only provided employment but has also left a lasting impact on the overall quality of life in rural areas [16]. This has translated into improved connectivity, better agricultural practices, and enhanced access to essential services. In essence, MGNREGA has not only addressed immediate economic challenges for rural households but has also contributed to their long-term development. The program's multi-faceted approach, encompassing employment generation, women's empowerment, and asset creation, highlights its significance in promoting sustainable and inclusive growth in rural India [11]. As of my last knowledge update in January 2022, the Mahatma Gandhi National Rural Employment Guarantee Act (MGNREGA) is a social security and employment generation scheme in India. It guarantees the right to work and aims to enhance livelihood security in rural areas by providing at least 100 days of wage employment in a financial year to every household whose adult members volunteer to do unskilled manual work. A paradigm shift in the context of MGNREGA could refer to a fundamental change in the way the program is conceptualized, implemented, or perceived. This shift might involve changes in policies, strategies, or the overall approach to address the evolving challenges and needs of rural employment and development. The researcher concluded that The Mahatma Gandhi National Rural Employment Guarantee Act (MGNREGA) has had a notable impact on agricultural development in India, marking a significant intersection between rural employment and the agricultural sector and The Mahatma Gandhi National Rural Employment Guarantee Act (MGNREGA) has had a substantial impact on economic security, particularly in rural areas of India. The program, by guaranteeing 100 days of employment to every rural household, acts as a powerful social safety net, providing a source of income during times of economic uncertainty.

## REFERENCES


[1] Ahuja, U.R., Tyagi, D., Chauhan, S. and Chaudhary, K.R. (2011). "Impact of MGNREGA on Rural Employment and Migration: A Study in Agriculturally-backward and Agriculturally-advanced Districts of Haryana." *Agricultural Economics Research Review,* 24: 495–502.

[2] Bhatia, R., Chinoy, C.L., Kaushish, B., Puri, J., Chaher, V.S. and Waddington, H.. (2016). "Examining the Evidence on the Effectiveness of India's Rural Employment Guarantee Act." *International Initiative for Impact Evaluation,* Working Paper No. 27.

[3] Bhattarai (2018). Employment Guarantee Programme and Dynamics of Rural Transformation in India: Challenges and Opportunities—Springer Publications, New Delhi.

[4] Dhawan and Ajay Kumar (2017). -Socio-economic impact of Mahatma Gandhi national rural employment guarantee scheme (MGNREGS) in Himachal Pradesh - *International Journal of Commerce and Management Research,* Volume 3; Issue 11; pp. 01–08.

[5] Dinesh, Kumar and Singh, Prem (2018). A study of poverty alleviation programmes in India, *International Journal of Applied Research*; Vol. 4 (10), pp. 171–174.

[6] Kanungo, M. (2012). Rural Development through Microfinance, MGNREGA and Women Empowerment, Odisha Review.

[7] Kaushil, S., Yadav, S.M.S. and Durgaprasad, P. (2010). Planning and Implementation of National Rural Employment Guarantee Scheme in Haryana, *National Institute of Rural Development*, Hyderabad.

[8] Khan, A.U. and Saiuja, M.R. (2007). Impact of MENREGA on Rural Livelihoods, Paper Presented in 10th Sustainable Development Conference on Sustainable Solutions: A Spotlight on South Asian Research, ut Islanmbad, Pakistan, December 10–12.

[9] Kumar, D. (2010). MNREGA Good but has Milesto Go, Says Plan Panel, The Economic Times, Quoting a Planning Commission Report, New Delhi.

[10] Mahapatra, R., Sakhuja, N., Das, S. and Singh, S. (2008). National Rural Employment Gurantee Act: Opportunities and Challenges, Centre for Science and Environment, New Delhi.

[11] Mathur, L. (2007). Employment Guarantee: Progress So Far. Economic and Political Weekly, December 2007.

[12] Mehta, P.K., Bhawana, Mangala and Niti, Saxena (2012), Transforming Lives through MGNREGA: A case of Mewat, Institute of Rural Research and Development, Gurgaon.

[13] Ministry of Rural Development (2012). Report of the Committee for Revision of MGNREGA Operational Guidelines, Government of India.

[14] NCAER and PIF (2009). Evaluating Performance of NREGA. New Delhi. National Council of Applied Economic Research & Public Interest Foundation.

[15] Pankaj, A. and Rukmini, Tankha (2010). Empowerment Effects of the NREGS on Women Workers: Study in four States', Economic & Political Weekly, Vol. XLV, No. 30.

[16] Roul, S. (2010). Greeting India through MGNREGA-Convergent Action for Benefits beyond Employment Generation, State of India Livelihoods Report, Sage Publication.

[17] Santosh, Singh and Negi, R.S. (2017). Impact of MGNREGA on Poverty and Ameliorate Socio-economic Status: A Study in Pauri Garhwal District of Uttarakhand, *Asian Journal of Agricultural Extension, Economics & Sociology*, Vol. 20 (4).

[18] Muthumari, M., Meenakumari, S. and Nagarajan, I. (2022). Empowerment of Rural Women Through Mgnrega—A Study With Special Reference to Virudhunagar District, *Business, Management and Economics Engineering,* ISSN: 2669-2481/eISSN: 2669-249X2022, Volume 20, Issue 2, pp. 2465–2467.

# The Green Imperative: Financing a Sustainable Future

**Manisha Vikas Jagtap**
Department of Management Studies (MBA), Rajarambapu Institute of Technology, Shivaji University, Kolhapur, Sangli, Maharashtra, India

***ABSTRACT:*** *Green finance refers to the introduction of novel instruments, methods, and policies that are intended to incentivize the financial industry to appropriately take climate and environmental aspects into account when managing financial risk and making investment decisions. The growing impact of global warming is illustrated in the Sustainable Goal Report 2022, which details increasing challenges such as depletion of the ozone layer, global warming, rising pollution levels, intense competition for limited non-renewable energy sources, and other environmental issues. This emphasizes the necessity of making the green transition away from fossil fuels, which are vulnerable to supply outages and volatility, and towards renewable sources of energy like wind and solar. As a result, every stakeholder are becoming more aware of the need to safeguard the environment and preserve natural resources. Green finance seeks to strike a balance between human behavior and the environment. No single definition of green financing applies to all nations and regions because the shift to a lower-carbon economy requires various and extensive transformations. Nonetheless, the common theme of green finance is investment that fosters a low-carbon, climate-resilient economy. This means that green finance is any structured financial activity—a product or service—designed to have a positive impact on the environment. It is a collection of loans, debt instruments, and investments used to support the development of green projects, reduce the environmental impact of more conventional enterprises, or a mix of the two. As the risks associated with environmentally harmful goods and services increase, green finance is starting to gain traction.*

**Keywords**: Environment, Finance, Government, Green, Investment, Organizations, Sustainable.

## 1. INTRODUCTION

The increasing severity of global warming highlights the pressing need for a transition towards environmentally sustainable practices. Moving away from volatile fossil fuels prone to supply disruptions and embracing renewable energy sources like wind and solar is not only an environmental necessity but also an economic imperative.[1] Concerns regarding environmental degradation, including ozone depletion, pollution, resource depletion, and competition for non-renewable energy sources, are compelling stakeholders across various sectors to prioritize sustainability.[2]

The International Finance Corporation (IFC) defines green finance as funding of projects that have positive environmental effects.[3] The United Nations Framework Convention on Climate Change (UNFCCC) proposes a broader definition encompassing financing from various sources to support mitigation and adaptation actions against climate change. However, the overarching goal of green finance is consistent to invest in projects that promote a sustainable, lower-carbon, and climate-resilient economy.[4] According to the World Economic Forum, green finance refers to any kind of organized financial service, product, or activity intended to enhance environmental results. This includes debt instruments, investments, and loans intended to promote the growth of environmentally friendly projects, lessen the environmental impact of traditional projects, or both. As the risks associated with environmentally damaging practices escalate, green finance is increasingly becoming mainstream.[5] The 2015 Paris Agreement has identified financial considerations as one of its three long-term objectives, alongside limiting the increase in global average temperature and enhancing adaptation to the impacts of climate change. The significance of finance in facilitating the green transition and its crucial role in climate action are acknowledged in Article 2.1c of the Agreement, which emphasizes the need to align financial flows with a trajectory towards reduced greenhouse gas emissions and resilient development (UNFCCC, 2015).[6]

## *Beyond Definition: The Diverse Functions of Green Finance*

Green finance serves as a cornerstone in funding a wide spectrum of both public and private green investments. Its pivotal functions encompass:

1. ***Financing Environmental Goods and Services:*** Green finance plays a crucial role in supporting initiatives aimed at the provision of environmental goods and services.[7] This includes funding projects related to water management, biodiversity protection, and landscape conservation. By allocating resources to these endeavors, green finance contributes to the preservation and sustainable management of natural resources and ecosystems.[8]
2. ***Mitigating and Compensating Environmental Damage:*** One of the key roles of green finance is to facilitate efforts aimed at mitigating and compensating for environmental damage.[9] This involves allocating funds towards initiatives designed to minimize harm caused to the environment and climate. By financing activities such as pollution control measures, habitat restoration, and emission reduction projects, green finance helps mitigate the adverse impacts of human activities on the environment.[10]
3. ***Funding Public Policies:*** Green finance helps in enabling the implementation of environmental policies and projects at the public level. This includes financing initiatives focused on mitigation, adaptation, and damage reduction in response to environmental

challenges. By providing the necessary financial resources, green finance supports governments and public entities in achieving their environmental objectives and promoting sustainable development.[11]

Thus it can be said that, green finance serves as a vital mechanism for mobilizing capital towards environmentally beneficial endeavors, ranging from the provision of essential environmental goods and services to the mitigation of environmental damage and the implementation of public policies aimed at addressing environmental challenges. By fulfilling these critical functions, green finance plays a central role in advancing sustainability goals and fostering the transition towards a greener and more resilient economy.

## 2. IMPORTANCE OF GREEN FINANCING

Green finance provides both economic and environmental benefits to all stakeholders. By expanding access to environmental friendly products and services for individuals and businesses. It promotes a more equitable transition to a low-carbon society and supports socially inclusive growth by increasing access to environmentally friendly products and services for individuals and businesses. Green finance attempts to boost the flow of funds towards pressing issues of sustainable development from the public, commercial, and nonprofit sectors. A central aspect of this is securing opportunities that provide a respectable rate of return along with environmental benefits, improving accountability, and effectively managing environmental and social risks.[12] According to Fact Sheet on Green finance published by ESCAP highlighted some of the key benefits and the challenges associated with Green Finance:[13]

1. ***Promotes technology diffusion and eco-efficient infrastructure:*** By investing in environmentally friendly technologies like clean energy, Green Finance facilitates the diffusion of these technologies. This not only helps in reducing costs but also accelerates their adoption, thereby promoting the development of eco-efficient infrastructure.
2. ***Creates a comparative advantage:*** With the increasing demand for low-carbon solutions due to climate change and other environmental challenges, countries and businesses that invest in Green Finance gain a competitive edge. They are better positioned to comply with future environmental regulations and meet consumer preferences for sustainability.
3. ***Adds business value:*** Companies and organizations involved in Green Finance enhance their portfolios and reputations. This can attract environmentally conscious investors and customers, ultimately driving business growth and profitability.
4. ***Enhances economic prospects:*** Governments supporting Green Finance initiatives can bolster their economies in various ways. By

promoting domestic markets for alternative resources and technologies, they reduce dependence on finite resources and foster innovation. Moreover, investing in green projects creates job opportunities and stimulates economic growth in emerging sectors.

Overall, Green Finance not only addresses environmental challenges but also offers significant economic and social benefits, making it a compelling strategy for sustainable development.[14]

Following are the challenges that indeed present significant hurdles to the widespread adoption and effectiveness of Green Finance:

1. ***Mispricing and lack of pricing of risks:*** Inaccurate assessment of risks associated with green investments can deter private investors. This may arise from uncertainties in policy frameworks, technological innovations, or market dynamics, making it difficult to evaluate the potential returns and risks involved in green projects.[15]
2. ***Market distortions and deficiencies:*** Existing market structures often favor traditional energy sources due to subsidies and failure to internalize environmental costs. This distorts the true cost of energy and makes investments in green alternatives comparatively less attractive. Moreover, the lack of diverse and accessible green finance products limits investment opportunities in sustainable projects.
3. ***Competing objectives:*** Balancing the financial objectives of private investors with the environmental and developmental goals of public green finance providers and policymakers can be challenging. Investors can select short-term returns over long-term environmental benefits, creating tension between profit motives and sustainability objectives.
4. Limited capital and awareness: Small and medium-sized businesses, in particular, face difficulties accessing green financing due to constraints in liquidity and capital. Additionally, a lack of awareness about the long-term benefits of green investments and a shortage of expertise in integrating environmental considerations into financial decision-making further hinder the expansion of green finance.[16]
5. ***Inadequate regulatory frameworks:*** Regulatory frameworks play a key role in influencing the direction of financial markets. However, in the realm of green finance, there are often gaps in regulation that fail to adequately incentivize or mandate sustainable investment practices. This can include lax enforcement of environmental standards, absence of clear guidelines for green investments, and insufficient penalties for unsustainable practices.[17] Without robust regulations, investors may lack the confidence and motivation to prioritize green investments.
6. ***Technical Infrastructure:*** The technical infrastructure required to support green finance initiatives is still evolving. This encompasses everything from data collection and analysis tools to digital platforms for trading and monitoring green investments. Insufficient technical infrastructure can hinder the efficient allocation of capital to

environmentally sustainable projects, as investors may struggle to assess the environmental impact of their investments or lack access to relevant market information.

7. ***Standardized Metrics:*** The absence of standardized metrics for evaluating environmental performance is a significant barrier to the growth of green finance. Without universally accepted metrics, investors may struggle to compare the environmental credentials of different investment opportunities accurately. This lack of clarity can lead to confusion and uncertainty, ultimately deterring investors from engaging in green finance.
8. ***Lack of Regulatory Incentives:*** Regulatory incentives are crucial for encouraging investors to allocate capital towards sustainable projects.[18] However, in many jurisdictions; there is a dearth of regulatory incentives for green investments.
9. ***Lack of reliable data, climate disclosure requirements and taxonomies:*** Many countries are facing a critical challenge i.e. the lack of high quality, reliable data regarding climate-related issues. Additionally, there is a lack of standardized climate disclosure requirements and taxonomies, which complicates ensuring that investments align with climate objectives. [19]

## 3. GREEN FINANCE: MANAGING RISKS AND SEIZING OPPORTUNITIES

Transitioning to a low-carbon economy demands substantial investments, which rely heavily on robust engagement from the private sector.[20] Integrating Environmental, Social, and Governance (ESG) factors into private investments not only enhances risk management but also serves as a catalyst for innovation and new opportunities, generating long-term return for both companies and society.[21]

These strategies are essential for overcoming obstacles in Green Finance:

1. ***Addressing Microeconomic Obstacles:*** Managing the disconnect between long-term green investments and short-term investor requires innovative financial instruments and mechanisms. Governments can incentivize long-term investment through policies such as tax incentives, subsidies, and green bonds. Integrating financial and environmental policies ensures coherence and effectiveness in green investment strategies.[22]
2. ***Standardizing Definitions and Creating Taxonomies***: Establishing clear definitions of what qualifies as 'green' and developing a taxonomy of green activities provides clarity for investors and financial institutions.[23] Standardization enables comparability, facilitates the assessment of environmental impacts, and guides investment decisions towards truly sustainable projects.

3. ***Implementing Basic Green Finance Criteria:*** Adopting uniform green finance criteria guides investment decisions and ensures alignment with environmental objectives.[24] These criteria serve as benchmarks for directing capital flows towards environmentally sustainable initiatives, while also facilitating effective market monitoring and risk management.
4. ***Enhancing Disclosure Standards:*** Standardized disclosure standards enhance transparency and accountability in green finance. Investors need reliable information on the environmental performance of investments to make informed decisions.[25] Clear disclosure requirements provide this information, building trust and confidence in green financial products.
5. ***Promoting Voluntary Standards and Legislative Incentives:*** Encouraging voluntary adoption of green finance standards by market participants can drive sustainability efforts. Legislative incentives, such as tax breaks or subsidies for green investments, provide additional motivation. This dual approach fosters a culture of sustainability while providing a regulatory framework to support and reinforce environmental goals.

## 4. DIVERSE RANGE OF GREEN FINANCING INSTRUMENTS

Green financing has been witnessing a swift expansion facilitated by a varied array of financial instruments accessible to both issuers and investors. These instruments comprise a wide spectrum, including green bonds, green loans, sustainable bonds, sustainability-linked bonds and loans, blue bonds, and social bonds. Social bonds have beneficial spillover effects on the environment even though they are not directly in line with the goals of green financing. Overall, the availability of diverse financial instruments underscores the growing interest and commitment towards sustainable finance across various sectors. By leveraging these instruments effectively, issuers and investors can drive positive environmental and social impact while also generating financial returns.

**Green Bonds:** Green bonds represent a notable avenue for financing environmentally beneficial projects. These financial instruments are specifically designed to finance environmental or climate projects, spanning various sectors such as renewable energy, energy efficiency, pollution control, biodiversity conservation, and sustainable transportation. The green bond market has witnessed remarkable growth since its inception, with issuance doubling between 2020 and 2021, reaching a total value exceeding $620 billion.

**Sustainability Bonds:** Sustainable bonds broaden the scope by encompassing a broader range of sustainability initiatives beyond just environmental considerations. Committed to financing a diverse array of projects that align with both environmental and social objectives outlined in the United Nations Sustainable Development Goals (SDGs). Such projects may embrace corporate, bank, asset-backed, project, sovereign, and municipal bonds, contributing to broader sustainability initiatives.

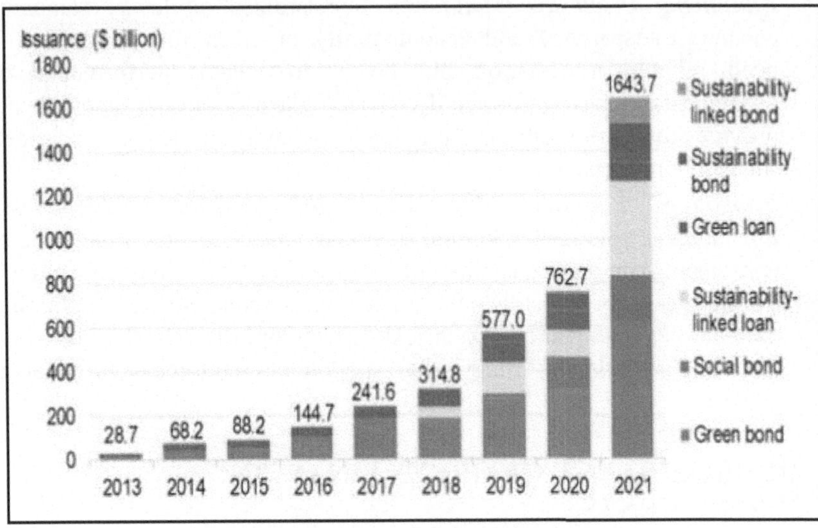


**Figure 1:** Sustainable Debt Annual Issuance

*Source:* BloombergNEF, Bloomberg LP.

**Sustainability-Linked Bonds:** Sustainability-linked bonds and loans tie financial incentives to the achievement of predefined sustainability targets, encouraging issuers to actively pursue sustainable practices. These bonds feature financial characteristics that fluctuate based on predefined sustainability targets set by the issuer. By linking financial incentives to sustainability performance, these bonds aim to encourage issuers to actively pursue and achieve environmental and social goals. Notably, they became eligible for inclusion in asset-purchase programs by the European Central Bank in 2021, signifying their increasing recognition and importance in the financial market.

**Green Loans:** Green loans offer similar opportunities for businesses seeking sustainable financing solutions. Funds from these loans are exclusively allocated to support environmentally beneficial projects aimed at addressing growing impact of global warming. Borrowers are required to provide periodic reports on the usage of funds and the performance of the projects funded by these loans, ensuring transparency and accountability.

**Sustainability-Linked Loans:** These loans offer variable interest rates contingent upon the sustainability performance of the borrower. By tying financial incentives to the achievement of sustainability targets, these loans incentivize borrowers to adopt and maintain sustainable practices, driving positive environmental and social impact.

**Blue Bonds:** Blue bonds specifically target marine and aquatic conservation projects, contributing to the preservation of marine ecosystems and biodiversity. Issued to finance projects related to marine and ocean conservation, including initiatives such as marine conservation, sustainable fisheries management, and ocean ecosystem preservation. The Seychelles Blue Bond, launched in 2018, was among the pioneering initiatives in this domain, demonstrating the potential for leveraging financial instruments to address pressing environmental challenges in marine ecosystems.

**Social Bonds:** Social bonds, though primarily focused on addressing social issues such as healthcare, education, or affordable housing, can indirectly support environmental goals. For instance, investments in sustainable food systems or projects aligned with green transformation efforts can be financed through social bonds, leading to positive outcomes for the environment. While distinct from green initiatives, social bonds complement efforts to promote sustainability by addressing social equity and well-being concerns.

## 5. GREEN FINANCE AND STAKEHOLDER ROLES

1. **Governments:** Many governments around the world need to develop infrastructure that would not only facilitate the development of capital markets but also enable better financing for climate-related projects.[26] Governments must prioritize the development of infrastructure conducive to long-term resource management. This strategic investment not only enhances a country's competitiveness but also serves as a catalyst for attracting private-sector capital into domestic green markets.[27] Innovative-financing mechanisms can play a pivotal role in supporting technical assistance programs and fostering the growth of new climate finance markets. By devising guidelines, conducting training programs for local stakeholders, and advocating for the adoption of international best practices, these financing structures can effectively promote climate-friendly investments in emerging markets.[28]
2. **Investors:** Despite constraints like high upfront costs and illiquid markets, investors are increasingly recognizing growing array of green investment opportunities and the potential to access new markets and consumer bases. Institutional investors, asset managers, and financial institutions are increasingly integrating climate considerations into their investment decisions.[29] It includes divesting from fossil fuels, investing in renewable energy projects, and incorporating Environmental, Social, and Governance (ESG) criteria into their portfolios. Furthermore, impact investing—in which investors aim to achieve both financial returns and favourable environmental outcomes—is gaining popularity. Notably, the international investment firm BlackRock highlighted

climate risk disclosure as one of their primary engagement themes in their list of investment priorities in March 2017. Companies must now specifically describe how climate risks could affect their business operations and explain how they plan to adapt to and mitigate these risks. This shift made it very evident that people now view climate change as a serious financial risk that cannot be disregarded.

3. **Regulators:** Initiatives like disclosure requirements by regulatory bodies facilitate the development of green finance markets. In September 2016, the Luxembourg Green Exchange took a significant step towards fostering the growth of green finance by introducing a dedicated segment for Sustainable and Social (S&S) project bonds. This sector, valued at over US$23 trillion, encompasses initiatives aimed at promoting sustainability and addressing social challenges. The establishment of this segment served to enhance the visibility of S&S projects and streamline their financing processes, thereby catalyzing their implementation. Around the same time, in June 2017, the Securities and Exchange Board of India (SEBI) finalized disclosure requirements for the issuance and listing of green debt securities. By establishing clear guidelines for green debt issuance, SEBI aims to promote transparency and accountability in sustainable financing initiatives, thereby encouraging greater participation from investors and facilitating the flow of capital into environmentally beneficial projects.
4. **Policy Makers:** Legislative measures, such as mandatory climate risk reporting and pilot programs for green financing, promote the integration of climate considerations into investment decisions. In January 2016, France took a significant step towards promoting green finance with the enactment of the Energy Transition for Green Growth Act. This legislation mandated that institutional investors and fund managers include disclosures in their annual reports regarding integration of climate change deliberations into their investment and risk management strategies. By requiring transparency on climate-related factors, this act aimed to encourage greater accountability and alignment of investment practices with sustainability goals. Similarly, China has demonstrated ambitious efforts to advance green finance through the establishment of pilot zones in several provinces, including Guangdong, Guizhou, Jiangxi, Zhejiang, and Xinjiang. These pilot zones serve as testing grounds for various aspects of green financing initiatives. Within these programs, banks are encouraged to explore innovative financing mechanisms aimed at supporting environmentally sustainable projects. Additionally, the initiative incentivizes the financial sector to hasten the development of green insurance and credit enhancement instruments within these regions. By fostering experimentation and incentivizing progress in green finance, China aims to strengthen its capacity for sustainable development and mitigate the impacts of climate change.

## 6. CONCLUSION

The concept of "greening finance" encapsulates the broader notion of "greening the financial system." It entails the dissemination of new tools, techniques, and guidelines aimed at encouraging the financial sector to adequately consider climate and environmental factors in both financial risk management and investment decision-making processes. Promoting green financing involves a multifaceted approach that can be facilitated through various means. This includes implementing changes in regulatory frameworks at the national level to incentivize environmentally sustainable practices. Additionally, harmonizing public financial incentives can encourage the adoption of green investment strategies across different sectors of the economy.

Furthermore, increasing the availability of green financing from diverse sources is essential for driving investment in environmentally beneficial projects. Aligning public sector financing decisions with the environmental aspects of the Sustainable Development Goals (SDGs) can provide a crucial framework for directing capital towards sustainable development initiatives.. The issuance and utilization of green bonds represent another avenue for promoting green financing. These financial instruments are specifically earmarked for funding projects with positive environmental impacts, thereby channeling capital towards initiatives that contribute to sustainability. Overall, promoting green financing requires a comprehensive approach that involves regulatory, financial, and institutional interventions to incentivize investments that align with environmental objectives and contribute to long-term sustainable development.

## REFERENCES

[1] Scaling up Climate Finance for Emerging Markets and Developing Economies Speech by Deputy Managing Director Bo Li at EIB Group Forum 2023 published on February 27, 2023. https://www.imf.org/en/News/Articles/2023/02/28/sp022823-scaling-up-climate-finance-for-emerging-markets-and-developing-economies.

[2] Sushma, B.S. (2021). Green Finance -An Effective Tool to Sustainability. International Journal of Creative Research Thought (IJCRT), 9 (1), pp. 4256–4263.

[3] Gafoor, A., Perumbalath, S., Daimari, P. and Naheem, K. (2024). Trends and patterns in green finance research: A bibliometric study. Innovation and Green Development, 3(2024). https://www.sciencedirect.com/science/article/pii/S2949753123000875.

[4] Zhang, D., Zhang, Z. and Managi, S. (2019). A bibliometric analysis on green finance: Current status, development, and future directions. Finance Research Letters, 29, pp. 425–430.

[5] Fleming, S. World Economic Forum (2020). What is Green Finance and Why is it Important [blog post]. Retrieved from https://www.weforum.org/

agenda/2020/11/what-is-green-finance/#:~:text=Green%20finance%20is%20any%20structured,could%20soon% 20hit%20%242.36%20trillion.

[6] https://unfccc.int/most-requested/key-aspects-of-the-paris-agreement

[7] https://emeritus.org/blog/finance-what-is-green-finance/#:~:text=Green%20finance%20delivers%20economic%20and,in%20more%20socially%20inclusive%20growth.

[8] China Council for International Cooperation on Environment and Development (CCICED) Secretariat (2023). Green Finance. In: Green Recovery with Resilience and High Quality Development. Springer, Singapore. https://doi.org/10.1007/978-981-19-9470-8_9.

[9] Fu, C., Lu, L. and Pirabi, M. (2023). Advancing green finance: a review of sustainable development. Digital Economy and Sustainable Development, 1(20). https://doi.org/10.1007/s44265-023-00020-3.

[10] China Council for International Cooperation on Environment and Development (CCICED) Secretariat. (2022). Green Finance. In: Green Consensus and High Quality Development. Springer, Singapore. https://doi.org/10.1007/978-981-16-4799-4_10

[11] Zhang KQ, Chen HH, Tang LZ and Qiao S (2022) Green Finance, Innovation and the Energy-Environment-Climate Nexus. Front. Environ. Sci. 10:879681. doi: 10.3389/fenvs.2022.879681

[12] https://www.unep.org/regions/asia-and-pacific/regional-initiatives/supporting-resource-efficiency/green-financing

[13] https://www.unescap.org/sites/default/files/28.%20FS-Green-Finance.pdf

[14] Low Carbon Green Growth Roadmap for Asia and the Pacific: Fact Sheet—Green finance retrieved from: https://www.unescap.org/sites/default/files/28.%20FS-Green-Finance.pdf

[15] Boffo, R. and R. Patalano (2020). "ESG Investing: Practices, Progress and Challenges", OECD Paris, www.oecd.org/finance/ESG-Investing-Practices-Progress-and-Challenges.pdf

[16] Kochhar. K. (2022). Green Finance: An approach toward Sustainable Development Goals (SDGs). Asian Journal of Management. 13(1):17-20.

[17] Park, H., Kim, J.D. Transition towards green banking: role of financial regulators and financial institutions. AJSSR 5, 5 (2020). https://doi.rg/10.1186/s41180-020-00034-3

[18] Nicholls A. Policies, Initiatives, And Regulations Related to Sustainable Finance, https://www.adb.org/sites/default/files/institutional-document/691951/ado2021bp-policies-initiatives-regulations.pdf.

[19] OECD (2021), Financial Markets and Climate Transition: Opportunities, Challenges and Policy Implications, https://www.oecd.org/finance/Financial-Markets-and-ClimateTransition-Opportunities-challenges-and-policy-implications.htm

[20] OECD (2015), Monitoring The Transition to a Low carbon Economy a strategic approach to local development, https://www.oecd.org/cfe/leed/Monitoring-Green-Transition-Final2.pdf

[21] Mohammad, W. Wasiuzzaman, S. (2021). Environmental, Social and Governance (ESG) disclosure, competitive advantage and performance of firms in Malaysia. Cleaner Environmental Systems, 2, Retrieved from: https://www.sciencedirect.com/science/article/pii/S2666789421000076

[22] Clarka, R. Reeda, J. Sunderland, T. (2018). Bridging funding gaps for climate and sustainable development: Pitfalls, progress and potential of private finance. Land Use Policy, 71, 335-346. Retrieved from: https://www.sciencedirect.com/science/article/pii/S0264837717310049?via%3Dihub

[23] OECD report Developing Sustainable Finance Definitions and Taxonomies, OECD Publishing, Paris, https://doi.org/10.1787/134a2dbe-en.

[24] Boffo, R., Marshall C. and Patalano R. (2020), "ESG Investing: Environmental Pillar Scoring and Reporting", OECD Paris, www.oecd.org/finance/esg-investing-environmental-pillar-scoring-and-reporting.pdf.

[25] Poole, V. Sullivan, K. (2021) Tectonic shifts: How ESG is changing business, moving markets, and driving regulation. https://www2.deloitte.com/us/en/insights/topics/strategy/esg-disclosure-regulation.html

[26] OECD Environment Policy Paper No. 14. Climate-Resilient Infrastructure Policy Perspectives. https://www.oecd.org/environment/cc/policy-perspectives-climate-resilient-infrastructure.pdf

[27] OECD(2020), Strengthening the Role of Private Finance in Infrastructure Development in Eastern Partner Countries, OECD Publishing, Paris, www.oecd.org/eurasia/competitivenessprogramme/eastern-partners/Strengthening-the-Role-of-Private-Finance-in-InfrastructureDevelopment-in-Eastern-Partner-Countries-EN.pdf.

[28] Panayotou T. Innovative Financial Mechanisms for Sustainable Sector Financing. https://sustainabledevelopment.un.org/content/dsd/resources/res_pdfs/publications/sdt_fin/nairobi_meeting_part4.pdf

[29] OECD (2018). https://www.oecd.org/sd-roundtable/papersandpublications/Integrating%20Climate%20Change-related%20Factors%20in%20Institutional%20Investment.pdf

# Beyond The Hype: A Critical Examination of the Dual Nature of Social Media's Influence on Financial Literacy

**Diksha[1], Sania Bassi[2] and Abheeti[3]**
Research Scholar, School of Business Studies,
Punjab Agricultural University, Ludhiana, Punjab, India
E-mail: [1]diksha-2158004@pau.edu; [2]sania-2158010@pau.edu;
[3]abheeti-2158001@pau.edu

***ABSTRACT:*** *This paper explores the complex relationship between social media and financial literacy, attempting to elucidate the multifaceted dynamics within this evolving domain. Through an examination of the diverse social media components and the emergence of finfluencers, it seeks to understand the evolving landscape of financial literacy facilitated by digital platforms. The paper investigates both the positive and negative aspects of social media's role in shaping financial literacy, providing insights into broader implications and complexities involved. By analysing the nuances of social media's influence on financial knowledge and decision-making, this paper contributes to a better understanding of the digital era's impact on financial literacy. It emphasizes the significance of responsible participation in navigating the digital financial landscape, highlighting the need for individuals to critically evaluate information and make informed financial decisions in an increasingly interconnected and dynamic online environment.*

**Keywords:** Financial Literacy, Finfluencers, Finfluencing, Social Media.

## 1. INTRODUCTION

Undoubtedly, social networking sites had smaller predecessors, Six Degrees appeared as the first widely recognised social media site as we know it today. This platform, which was founded in 1997 and enabled users to communicate with others by creating profiles, was a major advancement in the development of social networking websites (Ortiz-Ospina, 2023). But social media's constant evolution till date, has kept it buzzing with fresh trends. The platforms consistently come up with new features, content formats, and algorithmic changes to make sure that users always have something fresh to interact with and explore, keeping the platforms permanently trendy and relevant.

Social media applications are becoming more and more important to people in their daily lives. They are more likely to move their interactions to social media sites like Twitter, Facebook, Instagram, and LinkedIn. As a result, this change has a favourable effect on their beliefs and actions about different social networking platforms (Alalwan *et al.*, 2017). Due to social media's dominance over people's free time, internet users between the ages of 16–64 years spend 2 hours and 23 minutes each day on social media (Kemp, 2024). From communicating personal updates to keeping up with current events and news, from being a source of entertainment to trading educational content, social media accommodates a diverse array of information types, fostering a dynamic and continually evolving digital landscape. Therefore, in addition to being used for social interaction, entertainment and communication, social media has quickly replaced traditional media channels as a versatile instrument for dissemination of information.

As the saying goes, curious minds never stop learning, so it seems crucial to understand how people these days are eager to use social media as their personal library in order to explore a plethora of knowledge and make it an essential tool for self-education. Social media is an extensive educational platform for history buffs, science fanatics, language learners, and tech enthusiasts. Now-a-days even financial literacy finds space on social media via budgeting tips on TikTok, investment strategies on YouTube, and online communities like Investopedia for expert advice.

According to the OECD (2022), financial literacy is the combination of an individual's knowledge, skills, awareness, behavior and attitude required for making wise financial decisions that will ultimately lead to financial prosperity. On the other hand, Lusardi (2012) believes, financial literacy represents a life skill that all individuals must possess in order to raise their living standard and sustain in the challenging economic climate of today. It is crucial to raise awareness regarding financial literacy because it may minimize the possibilities of being deceived in investment decisions (Braunstein & Welch, 2002).

Hence in order to achieve society's long-term financial goals and to promote financial equality, financial literacy is essential. This is consistent with social media's inclusive nature, which removes hurdles of inclusivity faced by traditional media because of its cost and physical constraints, and allows users from a variety of backgrounds to access a plethora of information (Ridho, 2022). Brick by brick, financial literacy had been built prior to the digital era. Books and brochures about investment, financial management, and budgeting were kept in libraries. Financial professionals were approached for tailored assistance, while courses and seminars held in person provided instruction. Financial sections were featured in newspapers, and personal economic issues were discussed on radio shows. These tried and tested techniques, although still relevant, provided the groundwork for financial literacy and paved the way for tech-driven solutions we have today. Gone are the days of confined learning spaces—with technology, education has transformed into a dynamic, mobile experience. Social media among other solutions provide a vast learning landscape with just a click and swipe.

## 2. THE ROLE OF SOCIAL MEDIA COMPONENTS IN SHAPING FINANCIAL LITERACY

The subsequent elements delineate various social media components that exert an impact on financial literacy. The categories have largely been adapted from Csordas's model of social media categorization (Csordás *et al.*, 2014).

***Microblogs:*** Microblogs like Twitter, Tumblr, and Mastodon are the platforms for sharing short, real-time updates and news, including financial information, like budgeting hacks, investment news, or upcoming seminars. They spark discussions, encourage questions, and provide immediate feedback, promoting active learning and peer support. A study by Ante (2022), found that tweets from influential figures such as Elon Musk can have a significant impact on financial markets, such as increasing crypto currency prices and trading volume. Conversely, Reed (2016) found that increased social media discussions about economic issues can negatively affect stock prices.

***Blogs:*** Unlike microblogs, platforms like WordPress, Blogger, and Medium offer in-depth explorations of financial topics, including detailed guides, analyses, and personal stories to help readers understand complex concepts and make sound decisions. For example, Mr. Money Moustache, a popular blog advocating for a minimalist lifestyle and early financial independence, has gained popularity due to its detailed guides and personal stories. Studies show frequent readers have higher financial literacy scores (*Mr. Money Mustache*, n.d.), demonstrating the potential of blogs to contribute to financial education significantly.

***Social News Website:*** Reddit, Digg, and Hacker News are examples of social news websites that combine user-submitted content and community voting to provide a unique perspective on financial information, encouraging research, trend identification and peer learning. The impact of social media on the stock market was demonstrated in January 2021, when the Reddit forum Wallstreetbets had a significant influence on the price of GameStop stock. According to Buz & de Melo (2021), following highly promoted stocks on such platforms can result in higher returns, but it also comes with inherent risks. Therefore, users should conduct their own research before making investment decisions based solely on online content.

***Social Networking Sites:*** Social networking sites such as Facebook, Instagram, and TikTok, which are primarily used to connect with friends and family, can also be effective platforms for promoting financial literacy, given their viral nature. Financial institutions and educators can use the "word-of-mouth" effect to reach a larger audience and encourage discussions within familiar circles (Ridho, 2022). Furthermore, platforms like TikTok helps users to explore a wide range of financial information and perspectives using hashtags such as #StimulusCheck, which has received over 904 million views. This system serves as an alternative to traditional search engines, allowing users to find relevant and engaging financial content (Gleason, 2013). As a result, social networking sites can play an important role in raising financial awareness and engagement.

***Commerce Communities:*** Commerce communities such as Etsy, Amazon Handmade, and Shopify provide a unique opportunity to combine financial education and online commerce. These platforms offer convenient financial products, educate users on making informed financial decisions, promote responsible spending, and encourage community discussions. Managers can set up financial literacy programmes, collaborate with experts, and host financial socialization events (Ridho, 2022). For instance, Etsy, a marketplace for handcrafted and vintage items, indirectly promotes financial literacy by allowing users to run their own businesses, developing valuable skills in pricing, marketing, inventory management, and customer service, demonstrating commerce communities' role in responsible financial decision-making.

***Content Communities:*** YouTube, Twitch, and Pinterest are popular platforms for sharing financial education in multimedia formats such as explainer videos and infographics. These platforms improve information retention and reach a larger audience, promoting deeper learning and comprehension of financial concepts (Mayer, 2003). Research shows that platforms such as YouTube have a significant impact on their followers' financial decisions and are frequently regarded as credible sources of information. Sokolova & Kefi (2020) found a positive correlation between influencers' perceived credibility and users' purchase intentions, highlighting the power of content communities to educate and guide people in making sound financial decisions.

***Collaborative Projects:*** Collaborative platforms such as Wikipedia, Github, and Google Docs make it easier to create and share open-source financial education resources, encouraging innovation and knowledge exchange among diverse communities. For instance, Khan Academy is an innovative platform that uses a collaborative approach to provide interactive micro-courses on complex financial topics, overcoming geographical and economic barriers. This gamified approach makes financial literacy accessible to a global audience, demonstrating the potential of collaborative platforms for a financially empowered future.

Social media platforms have a noticeable impact on financial literacy, influencing users' financial knowledge and behaviour. The advent of finfluencers brings a dynamic aspect to this environment, as they have a major influence on and direction of financial literacy in the internet realm.

## 3. THE RISE OF FINFLUENCER: IS IT HARMONY OR CHAOS FOR FINANCIAL LITERACY?

The digital age has seen the fascinating emergence of financial influencers, or finfluencers, who use their social media clout to guide, inspire, and sometimes mislead the public on their financial journeys. Guan (2022) defines a "finfluencer" as an individual or entity who has a significant influence on investment choices through social media. According to Charles Schwab (2021), 15% of stock market investors began investing in 2020. According to Bloomberg Intelligence (2020), retail investors traded 19.5% of all stocks in the first six months of 2020, nearly doubling the rate a decade ago. With COVID-19 keeping people indoors, demand for investment information increased, particularly on social media platforms such as YouTube and TikTok. This resulted in the rise of "finfluencers" who provide financial advice and content. Examining the effectiveness of finfluencers in promoting financial literacy reveals a mix of positive insights and potential pitfalls which are as follows:

### 3.1 Positive Aspects

- ***Accessibility:*** Finfluencers simplify complex financial concepts into bite-sized, digestible content, making financial literacy more accessible to the digitally savvy generation (Business Today, n.d.).
- ***Diversity of Voices:*** Unlike traditional financial institutions, finfluencers provide a variety of perspectives, catering to a wide range of demographics and financial objectives (Lake, 2023).
- ***Engagement and Community:*** Social media's interactive nature encourages discussions, questions, and a sense of community around financial well-being.

### 3.2 Negative Aspects

- ***Misinformation and Scams:*** A lack of transparency and verification can expose users to false information, misleading advice, and even financial scams (Oosting, 2022).
- ***Unrealistic Portrayals:*** Finfluencers may promote unsustainable spending habits or unrealistic quick-fix solutions, distorting financial reality and potentially encouraging risky behaviour (Shanteau, 1992).
- ***Conflicts of Interest:*** Sponsored content and affiliate marketing arrangements can introduce biases and conflicts of interest, compromising the objectivity of the financial advice provided (Parthasarathy, 2023).

## 4. NAVIGATING THE FINANCIAL SYMPHONY: HOW TO EVALUATE FINFLUENCER ADVICE?

In a rapidly evolving financial landscape driven by influencers, determining the credibility of financial advice is critical. Figure 1 digs into key ways for effectively evaluating finfluencer advice. Navigating this digital arena necessitates a critical eye to distinguish insightful guidance from possible risks, ensuring that individuals can make informed financial decisions in an age where internet influence plays a big part in shaping financial literacy.

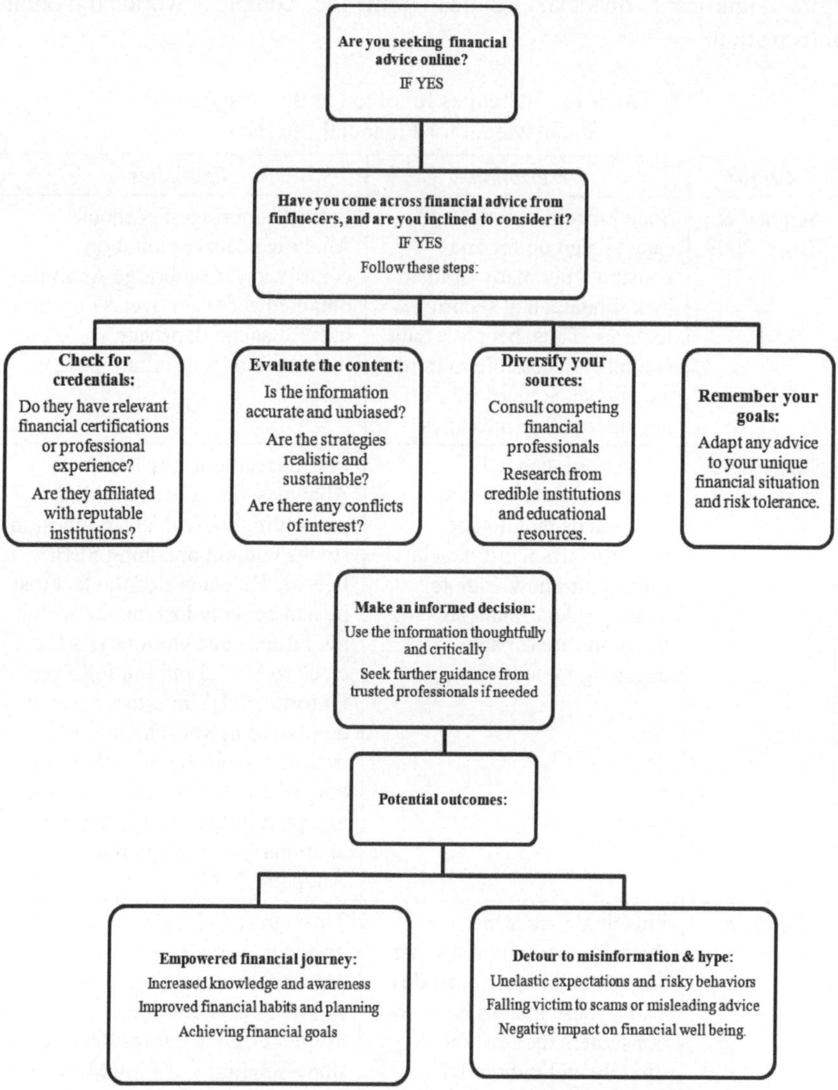


**Figure 1:** Decision Tree for Evaluating Finfluencer Advice

(*Source:* Developed by the authors.)

**Remember:** You are the conductor of ***your*** Financial Journey. Use finfluencers as guides, not gurus, and always prioritize reliable information and responsible decision-making.

# 5. CHALLENGES PERTAINING TO UTILIZATION OF SOCIAL MEDIA FOR FINANCIAL LITERACY

Addressing the following challenges as described in Table 1, is critical in the digital era for encouraging ethical engagement and allowing consumers to draw significant financial insights from the complex world of online information.

**Table 1:** Challenges Involved in the Usage of Social Media for Financial Literacy

| *Author* | *Description* | *Examples* |
|---|---|---|
| Acquisti & Gross, 2009 | Social media websites are easy to sign up for and consume, but many of them lack fundamental security features. Thus, people's data is readily accessible to third parties, since there aren't adequate safety measures. | In the Cambridge-Facebook Analytica data exploitation controversy, Cambridge Analytica obtained access to over 87 million users' Facebook private information (McCallum, 2022). |
| Skagerlund *et al.*, 2018 | As a consequence of increasing accessibility, individuals that do not possess sufficient financial literacy or knowledge to make prudent financial decisions are capable of engaging in poor choices. | Finfluencer and YouTuber Abhishek Kar was accused of persuading individuals to invest in stocks without obtaining SEBI license. He concealed the fact that he had actually lost money within the Futures and Options (F&O) stock to his 1.5 million followers. Unfortunately, investors became engrossed in Kar's high-risk trading lessons because they were enticed by the fast money notions and paid little attention to safety examinations (Anupam & Anupam, 2023). |
| Chen *et al.*, 2011 | Phishing attacks are one of the major security risks that social media users must deal with. These attacks have cost consumers money both directly and indirectly. People are refraining from adopting social media for personal finance to a greater extent because of these perceived hazards and challenges. | Through social media, fake celebrities employ urgent and persuasive messaging to make promises of increasing cryptocurrency returns. Online impersonations of Elon Musk, a well-known figure in the digital currency movement, occur regularly. These impersonators took almost $2 million as cryptocurrency frauds in 2021 itself (Camu, 2022). |

| ***Author*** | ***Description*** | ***Examples*** |
|---|---|---|
| Situngkir, 2011; Vosoughi *et al.* 2018 | The quick exchange of information on social media could disseminate misinformation and hoaxes. False news spreads six times quicker than accurate content online, and 70% of consumers are unable to discern the difference between real and fake news. | Social media posts aided in hastening Silicon Valley Bank withdrawals in March 2023, leading to depositors withdrawing $42 billion in just a span of 10 hours. Moreover, during the run phase, unfavourable tweets caused immediate losses in the stock market as well (Cookson et al., 2023). |
| Douglas *et al.*, 2019; Bancroft & Scott Reid, 2016; Serracino-Inglott, 2013; Colton *et al.,* 2016 | Doxxing is defined as the deliberate disclosure of a person's personal information online by some third party, typically with the goal of defaming, threatening, intimidating, or punishing that individual. Doxxing focuses on using it either against certain groups or within particular fora, such as hacker networks and cryptomarkets. | At the beginning of 2023, X was the target of doxxing when hackers insisted on a $200,000 ransom, revealing the email addresses of a staggering 200 million users onto a hacker forum (What Is Doxxing? \| Examples & Prevention Tips, n.d.). |

## 6. CONCLUSION

Social media has emerged as a powerful double-edged sword in the realm of financial literacy. While it provides unparalleled accessibility, diverse perspectives, and engaging educational formats, it also introduces significant risks such as misinformation, scams, and security vulnerabilities. Recognizing potential pitfalls is critical to safely navigating this complex landscape. Finfluencers, the new financial gurus, provide a us with plentiful amounts of benefits and drawbacks. They can simplify complex concepts and promote community engagement, but their credibility and potential conflicts of interest must be carefully considered. It is crucial for users to understand that they hold the reins in steering their financial paths, with finfluencers acting as guides rather than oracles.

Several challenges impede the responsible use of social media for financial education. The influx of unqualified individuals, the prevalence of misleading content, and the ease of data breaches and scams necessitate strict user awareness and platform regulations. Combating misinformation and protecting user privacy are critical components of creating a secure and trustworthy learning environment.

Moving forward, cultivating a culture of critical thinking and responsible content creation is critical. Platforms can enforce stricter verification procedures, promote financial literacy initiatives, and provide users with digital literacy training. Users, on the other hand, are advised to be cautious, diversify their information sources, and prioritize fact-checking before making financial decisions based on social media content. Finally, harnessing the power of social media to promote financial literacy requires a collaborative effort. We can develop social media into a valuable tool for building a financially empowered future for all by acknowledging the challenges, encouraging responsible content creation, and equipping users with critical thinking skills.

## REFERENCES

[1] Adomako, S., Danso, A. and Ofori Damoah, J. (2015, October 29). The moderating influence of financial literacy on the relationship between access to finance and firm growth in Ghana. Venture Capital, 18(1), 43–61. https://doi.org/10.1080/13691066.2015.1079952

[2] Alalwan, A.A., Rana, N.P., Dwivedi, Y.K. and Algharabat, R. (2017, November). Social media in marketing: A review and analysis of the existing literature. *Telematics and Informatics*, *34*(7), 1177–1190. https://doi.org/10.1016/j.tele.2017.05.008

[3] Ante, L. (2022). How Elon Musk's Twitter Activity Moves Cryptocurrency Markets. *SSRN Electronic Journal*. https://doi.org/10.2139/ssrn.4065313

[4] Anupam, S. and Anupam, S. (2023, October 14). Can SEBI Clear The Murky Waters of Finfluencers In India? Inc42 Media. https://inc42.com/features/can-sebi-clear-the-murky-waters-of-finfluencers-in-india/#:~:text=Ghanshyam%20Tech%20(Yadav)%2C%20another,into%20investing%20in%20specific%20stocks.

[5] Bancroft, A. and Scott Reid, P. (2016, May 20). Challenging the techno-politics of anonymity: the case of cryptomarket users. Information, Communication & Society, 20(4), 497–512. https://doi.org/10.1080/1369118x.2016.1187643

[6] Bloomberg Intelligence. (2020). Individual-Investor Boom Reshapes the U.S. Stock Market. https://ofdollarsanddata.com/wp-content/uploads/2020/08/wsj_feature_nmaggiulli.pdf

[7] Braunstein, S. and Welch, C. (2002). Financial Literacy: An Overview of Practice, Research, and Policy. Federal Reserve Bulletin, 88(11), 0–0. https://doi.org/10.17016/bulletin.2002.88-11

[8] Brownhilder Ngek, N. (2016, July 14). Performance implications of financial capital availability on the financial literacy—performance nexus in South Africa. Investment Management and Financial Innovations, 13(2), 354–362. https://doi.org/10.21511/imfi.13(2-2).2016.10

[9] Business Today. (n.d.). *Rise of the Finfluencers*. Businesstoday. Retrieved February 15, 2024, from https://www.businesstoday.in/interactive/immersive/rise-of-the-finfluencers

[10] Buz, T. and de Melo, G. (2021). Should You Take Investment Advice from WallStreetBets? A Data-Driven Approach. *Cornell University- ArXiv*. https://doi.org/10.48550/arxiv.2105.02728.

[11] Camu, M. (2022, September 23). 9 examples of social media phishing schemes and how to avoid it. Red Points. https://www.redpoints.com/blog/social-media-phishing/

[12] Charles Schwab. (2021). *The Rise of the Investor Generation*. https://www.aboutschwab.com/generation-investor-study-2021

[13] Chen, X., Bose, I., Leung, A. C. M. and Guo, C. (2011, March). Assessing the severity of phishing attacks: A hybrid data mining approach. Decision Support Systems, 50(4), 662–672. https://doi.org/10.1016/j.dss.2010.08.020

[14] Colton, J. S., Holmes, S. and Walwema, J. (2016, December 7). From NoobGuides to #OpKKK: Ethics of Anonymous' Tactical Technical Communication. Technical Communication Quarterly, 26(1), 59–75. https://doi.org/10.1080/10572252.2016.1257743

[15] Cookson, J. A., Fox, C., Gil-Bazo, J., Imbet, J. F. and Schiller, C. (2023, January 1). Social Media as a Bank Run Catalyst. Social Science Research Network. https://doi.org/10.2139/ssrn.4422754

[16] Csordás, T., Markos-Kujbus, É. and Gáti, M. (2014). The attributes of social media as a strategic marketing communication tool. *Journalism and Mass Communication*, *4*(1), 48–71.

[17] Douglas, H., Harris, B.A. and Dragiewicz, M. (2019, January 9). Technology-facilitated Domestic and Family Violence: Women's Experiences. The British Journal of Criminology, 59(3), 551–570. https://doi.org/10.1093/bjc/azy068

[18] Gleason, B. (2013, March 15). #Occupy Wall Street. *American Behavioral Scientist*, *57*(7), 966–982. https://doi.org/10.1177/0002764213479372

[19] Guan, S. (2023). The Rise of the Finfluencer. *SSRN Electronic Journal*. https://doi.org/10.2139/ssrn.4400042

[20] Hastings, J.S., Madrian, B. C. and Skimmyhorn, W. L. (2013, August 2). Financial Literacy, Financial Education, and Economic Outcomes. Annual Review of Economics, 5(1), 347–373. https://doi.org/10.1146/annurev-economics-082312-125807

[21] Kemp, S. (2024, January 31). *The time we spend on social media — DataReportal – Global Digital Insights*. DataReportal—Global Digital Insights. https://datareportal.com/reports/digital-2024-deep-dive-the-time-we-spend-on-social-media#:~:text=Research%20from%20GWI%20reveals%20that,per%20day%20using%20social%20platforms.&text=On%20average%2C%20that%20means%20that,attributed%20to%20social%20media%20platforms.

[22] Lake, R. (2023, April 29). *Personal Finance Influencers You Should Know*. Investopedia. https://www.investopedia.com/financial-influencers-to-know-5217608

[23] Lusardi, A. (2012, January). Numeracy, Financial Literacy, and Financial Decision-Making. Numeracy, 5(1). https://doi.org/10.5038/1936-4660.5.1.2

[24 McCallum, B. S. (2022, December 23). Meta settles Cambridge Analytica scandal case for $725m. BBC News. https://www.bbc.com/news/technology-64075067

[25] *Mr. Money Mustache.* (n.d.). Mr. Money Mustache. https://www.mrmoneymustache.com/

[26] OECD. (2022). OECD/INFE Toolkit for Measuring Financial Literacy and Financial Inclusion 2022. Retrieved from http://www.oecd.org/financial/education/2022-INFE-ToolkitMeasuring-Finlit-Financial-Inclusion.pdf

[27] Oosting, J. (2022). Finfluencers and their impact on the Stock Market.

[28] Ortiz-Ospina, E. (2023, December 28). *The rise of social media.* Our World in Data. https://ourworldindata.org/rise-of-social-media#:~:text=There%20were%2C%20of%20course%2C%20earlier,make%20friends%20with%20other%20users.

[29] Parthasarathy, S. (2023, September 5). *Rise of 'finfluencers' sparks debate over influence and accountability.* Frontline. https://frontline.thehindu.com/society/rise-of-finfluencers-sparks-debate-over-influence-and-accountability-personal-finance-sebi-asci/article67273277.ece#:~:text=%E2%80%9CSocial%20media%20continues%20to%20grow,of%20potential%20scams%20and%20losses.%E2%80%9D

[30] Reed, M. (2016, October). A Study of Social Network Effects on the Stock Market. *Journal of Behavioral Finance, 17*(4), 342–351. https://doi.org/10.1080/15427560.2016.1238371

[31] Reich, C.M. and Berman, J. S. (2014, December 9). Do Financial Literacy Classes Help? An Experimental Assessment in a Low-Income Population. Journal of Social Service Research, 41(2), 193–203. https://doi.org/10.1080/01488376.2014.977986

[32] Ridho, W. F. (2022). Comparison of Social Media as a means of financial literacy source. *Jurnal Aplikasi Manajemen dan Bisnis*, 3(1), 1–14. https://doi.org/10.5281/zenodo.7260311%20

[33] Serracino-Inglott, P. (2013, January). Is it OK to be an Anonymous? Ethics & Global Politics, 6(4), 22527. https://doi.org/10.3402/egp.v6i4.22527

[34] Shanteau, J. (1992, November). Competence in experts: The role of task characteristics. *Organizational Behavior and Human Decision Processes, 53*(2), 252–266. https://doi.org/10.1016/0749-5978(92)90064-e

[35] Situngkir, H. (2011, January 1). Spread of Hoax in Social Media. Social Science Research Network. https://doi.org/10.2139/ssrn.1831202

[36] Skagerlund, K., Lind, T., Strömbäck, C., Tinghög, G. and Västfjäll, D. (2018, June). Financial literacy and the role of numeracy–How individuals' attitude and affinity with numbers influence financial literacy. Journal of Behavioral and Experimental Economics, 74, 18–25. https://doi.org/10.1016/j.socec.2018.03.004

[37] Sokolova, K. and Kefi, H. (2020, March). Instagram and YouTube bloggers promote it, why should I buy? How credibility and parasocial

interaction influence purchase intentions. *Journal of Retailing and Consumer Services*, *53*, 101742. https://doi.org/10.1016/j.jretconser.2019.01.011

[38] What Is Doxxing? | Examples & Prevention Tips. (n.d.). SoSafe. https://sosafe-awareness.com/glossary/doxxing/

# Navigating Financial Markets: A Study of Investors Rationality and Behavioral Finance

G. Kavitha[1] and P. Suryadevi[2]
[1]Assistant Professor & Head, Department of Commerce,
PSGR Krishnammal College for Women, Coimbatore, India
[2]Research Scholar, Department of Commerce,
PSGR Krishnammal College for Women, Coimbatore, India

***ABSTRACT:*** *The study investigates the investors' rational decision-making and the pervasive influence of behavioral factors in the financial market. The data have been collected from a sample of 150 investors through a structured questionnaire. The influence of various behavioral biases has been studied and found that various cognitive and emotional biases have supremacy in investment decisions of investors. From this study, it can be concluded that a substantial number of respondents agree that their investment decisions are influenced by mental accounting and recency biases. While acknowledging the study's limitations, we propose future research directions to further unravel the complexities inherent in financial decision-making. This study underscores the imperative synthesis of rationality and behavioral finance for cultivating a resilient and informed financial ecosystem in an ever-evolving market landscape.*

**Keywords:** Behavioral Finance, Biases, Decision Making, Financial Market, Investor Rationality.

## 1. INTRODUCTION

Financial markets represent a complex and dynamic environment where investors constantly encounter challenges and opportunities. Navigating these markets effectively requires a nuanced understanding of decision-making processes, combining rational analysis with an awareness of behavioral biases. Investors frequently exhibit deviations from rational behavior, leading to decisions that are often illogical (Birau, 2012). Investor rationality and behavioral finance are two concepts that explore the decision-making processes of individuals in financial markets (Ahmad & Ibrahim, 2017). They represent contrasting perspectives on how investors make choices and respond to market conditions. Investor rationality, rooted in traditional economic theories, posits that individuals make choices by carefully weighing the costs and benefits of available options. However, the assumption of complete rationality has been increasingly challenged by the field of behavioral finance, which recognizes that cognitive and emotional factors can introduce biases into decision-making (Boda & Sunitha, 2018). The cognitive and emotional biases taken for the study are mental accounting, recency, illusion of control, optimism, anxiety and panic, and trust biases.

The title of our study, "Navigating Financial Markets", encapsulates the notion that investors face a journey full of twists and turns, requiring a strategic approach to make informed decisions. The study aims to contribute to the ongoing discourse on investor behavior by examining the extent to which rationality guides decision-making and the impact of behavioral biases on market dynamics. The main assumption being considered was that investors' decisions are always rational and that the markets are lined up with expected utility maximization (Boda, 2018). We will explore how investors navigate through the sea of information, considering factors such as market efficiency, information asymmetry, and the role of emotions in shaping financial choices. By combining insights from both rational and behavioral perspectives, our study seeks to provide a comprehensive understanding of the multifaceted nature of decision-making in financial markets. As we embark on this exploration, it is crucial to recognize the evolving nature of financial markets and the need for adaptive strategies. Through a careful analysis of investor behavior, we aim to shed light on the complexities inherent in financial decision-making, offering valuable insights for investors, policymakers, and researchers alike.

## 2. STATEMENT OF THE PROBLEM

It has been seen over time that a variety of biases impair investors' ability to make rational investment decisions. As a result, it is imperative that stakeholders are aware of these biases (Joo & Durri, 2018). The study aims to investigate the intricate interplay between traditional economic rationality and the emerging field of behavioral finance within the context of financial markets. As investors continually face complex decision-making scenarios, understanding the factors influencing their choices becomes paramount. This research seeks to identify and analyze the extent to which investors adhere to rational decision-making and how behavioral biases may deviate them from optimal choices.

## 3. OBJECTIVES OF THE STUDY

- To analyze investor rationality while taking investment decisions.
- To know the effect of behavioral finance on investment decisions.

## 4. METHODOLOGY

The area of the study is Coimbatore district, Tamil Nadu, India. The respondents for the study are investors. Primary data have been collected from 150 respondents using structured questionnaires employing snowball sampling technique.

## 5. REVIEW OF LITERATURE

**Mukherjee & De (2018)** proposed a theory between rationality and inherent behavior biases, where they claim that no investor is fully rational or fully behavioral, it is a choice that the investors make after momentous mental calculations. The study concludes by claiming that information do not make investors completely rational, rather they claim that the biases will get stifle to an great extend when investors have access to ample set of information.

**Mitroi & Oproiu (2014)** review relevant psychological theories to understand the correlation and causation between psychology and finance. The study focuses on demonstrating whether investor psychological biases affect investment performance in the long run. Analyzing the data of the study shows that the market doesn't "random walk" the investor's psychological biases and differences have an important relation with the investment decision-making process.

**Birau (2012)** described the presence of biases in investment decision-making. It is a descriptive study where the researcher explains the classical finance paradigm and its imperfection and behavioral finance approach to the capital market. In this study, the researcher opines that investors may deviate from rational behavior, which often results in illogical reasoning. The paper also studies classical finance and behavioral finance theories in which the researcher found that both theories have indisputable arguments and both are not a perfect replacement for each other.

**Byrne & Brooks (2008)** review the various concepts that are relevant to practitioners of investment management, personal finance planning, or corporate finance. The study reviews the traditional finance concepts and concludes that certain facts such as aggregate stock market, cross-section of average return, etc are not clear in that framework. The paper also explains that behavioral finance is an alternative where it points out that at least a significant minority of investors are subject to biases that and the investments are less than fully rational.

**Gajjala (2005)** provides a review of development in behavioral finance also it explains about Efficient Market Hypothesis (EMH) where each individual makes rational choices that maximise their satisfaction. However, due to the volatility of the market that could not be explained by rational choice theory, behavioral finance put forward the psychological explanation for the irrational behavior of investors.

## 6. PERSONAL PROFILE OF RESPONDENTS

- Out of 150 respondents, 38 per cent of respondents is in the age group of 21–30 years, followed by 31–40 years (26 per cent).
- Most of the respondents are male (66 per cent) and 31 per cent of the respondents are female.

- Majority of the respondents have bachelor's degrees (52 percent), and 40 per cent of the respondents have master's degrees.
- 42 per cent of the respondents are working in the public sector where as 28 per cent of the respondents are private sector employees.
- The majority of the respondents are married and, 28 per cent of the respondents are unmarried.
- 38 per cent of the respondents have a monthly income of Rs. 50000 – Rs. 100000, and 36 per cent is having Less than Rs. 50000 as a monthly family income.
- Most of the respondents invest 10–20% of their salary, and 36 per cent invest Less than 10% of their salary.
- 94 per cent of the respondents invest from, their earnings. Whereas 4 per cent invest from other sources and 2 per cent of respondents from the borrowed source.

## 7. MULTIPLE DICHOTOMY

A total of nine investment avenues have been given to know in which investment avenue the investors have mostly invested. Multiple choice questions have been used to find the number of responses in each avenue.

| *Investment Avenues* | *Responses* | |
|---|---|---|
| | *N* | *Percent* |
| Share | 129 | 28.9% |
| Derivative | 18 | 4.0% |
| Bond | 15 | 3.4% |
| Gold | 48 | 10.7% |
| Mutual Fund | 102 | 22.8% |
| Fixed Deposit | 63 | 14.1% |
| Public Provident fund | 27 | 6.0% |
| Pension Find | 18 | 4.0% |
| Cryptocurrencies | 27 | 6.0% |
| **Total** | 447 | **100%** |

A total of 447 responses have been received from respondents using multiple dichotomy analysis. From this table, it can be interpreted that 28.9 per cent have chosen "Shares" as the investment avenue that is having highest number of investors. The second highest (22.8 per cent) investment avenue that most of investors invest in is "Mutual Funds". The next best investment avenue as per the responses is "Fixed Deposits" (14.1 per cent) followed by "Gold" with 10.7 per cent of response. 6 per cent of respondents invest in "provident find and crypto currencies" followed by 4 per cent in derivatives and pension fund. The least number of investors is invested in Bonds (3.4 per cent).

## 8. DESCRIPTIVE STATISTICS

A total of twelve statements have been considered to test the investors rationality and decision making. The descriptive table shows that high mean scores have been found for "short-term vs. Long term perspective matters" (Mean 4.52) followed by "understanding and managing risk perception is crucial" (Mean 4.34) and the least mean score has been found for "overconfidence in prediction can affect decisions". Further ANOVA have been employed to analyse the investor rationality and decision making.

### 8.1 ANOVA

H0: The average score of respondents on investor rationality and decision making do not vary significantly for the personal factors.

Personal Factors vs. Investors Rationality and Decision Making

| *Personal Factors* | *Investors Rationality and Decision Making* | | | | | | |
|---|---|---|---|---|---|---|---|
| | | *N* | *Mean* | *Std. Deviation* | *F* | *Sig.* | |
| Age | 21–30 years | 57 | 48.58 | 6.196 | 2.623 | .053 | NS |
| | 31–40 years | 39 | 49.54 | 4.006 | | | |
| | 41–50 years | 33 | 46.45 | 5.075 | | | |
| | 51 years and above | 21 | 46.71 | 5.302 | | | |
| Educational qualification | Matriculation | 3 | 50.00 | .000 | 3.041 | .031 | S |
| | Bachelor's degree | 78 | 46.85 | 6.030 | | | |
| | Master's degree | 60 | 49.40 | 4.626 | | | |
| | Ph.D. | 9 | 49.67 | 2.500 | | | |
| Occupation | Business | 21 | 47.00 | 4.517 | 3.237 | .008 | S |
| | Private sector | 42 | 48.29 | 5.628 | | | |
| | Public sector | 63 | 48.90 | 5.034 | | | |
| | Pensioner | 9 | 50.67 | 2.784 | | | |
| | Professionals | 12 | 43.00 | 7.311 | | | |
| | Homemaker | 3 | 49.00 | .000 | | | |

| *Personal Factors* | *Investors Rationality and Decision Making* | | | | | | |
|---|---|---|---|---|---|---|---|
| | | *N* | *Mean* | *Std. Deviation* | *F* | *Sig.* | |
| Marital Status | Married | 105 | 47.51 | 5.691 | 2.200 | .114 | NS |
| | Unmarried | 42 | 49.57 | 4.618 | | | |
| | Divorced | 3 | 48.00 | .000 | | | |
| Average monthly Income | Less than Rs. 50000 | 54 | 47.72 | 5.189 | 1.571 | .199 | NS |
| | Rs .50000 – Rs.100000 | 57 | 48.32 | 4.218 | | | |
| | Rs. 100000 – Rs. 150000 | 33 | 47.55 | 7.517 | | | |
| | Above Rs.150000 | 6 | 52.50 | .548 | | | |
| Level of Investment | Less than 10% of the salary | 54 | 45.56 | 5.269 | 11.820 | .000 | S |
| | 10–20% | 63 | 48.24 | 5.139 | | | |
| | 20–30% | 18 | 51.83 | 4.382 | | | |
| | 30% and above | 15 | 52.20 | 2.396 | | | |
| Procurement of Fund for Investment | From personal earnings | 141 | 48.17 | 5.498 | .272 | .763 | NS |
| | From borrowed source | 3 | 46.00 | .000 | | | |
| | Others | 6 | 47.50 | 4.930 | | | |

The ANOVA table indicates that for personal factors like age, marital status, average monthly income and procurement of funds for investment the null hypothesis is accepted at 5% and for factors like educational qualification, occupation, and level of investment the null hypothesis is rejected.

## 9. DESCRIPTIVE STATISTICS

A total of six statements have been considered to test the behavioral finance in investment decision. From the descriptive table, it can be inferred that the highest mean score (Mean 4.50) is for the statement "money can be used from any available source to cover any unforeseen expenses" followed by "impulsive buying or selling decisions that are not aligned with long term, fundamentals of investment" (Mean 4.20). The lowest mean score has been found for "rushed and fear-driven decisions that are not aligned with long-term fundamentals of investment" (Mean 3.76). Further ANOVA have been employed to analyse the behavioral finance on investment decision.

## 9.1 ANOVA

H0: The average score of respondents on Behavioral Finance on Investment Decision do not vary significantly for the personal factors.

Personal Factors vs. Behavioral Finance on Investment Decision

| Personal Factors | Behavioral Finance on Investment Decision | | | | | | |
|---|---|---|---|---|---|---|---|
| | | N | Mean | Std. Deviation | F | Sig. | |
| Age | 21–30 years | 57 | 23.79 | 3.755 | 2.723 | .047 | S |
| | 31–40 years | 39 | 25.31 | 3.286 | | | |
| | 41–50 years | 33 | 24.00 | 2.250 | | | |
| | 51 years and above | 21 | 23.14 | 2.220 | | | |
| Educational qualification | Matriculation | 3 | 26.00 | .000 | .459 | .711 | NS |
| | Bachelor's degree | 78 | 24.00 | 3.121 | | | |
| | Master's degree | 60 | 24.15 | 3.318 | | | |
| | Ph.D. | 9 | 24.67 | 4.000 | | | |
| Occupation | Business | 21 | 24.14 | 2.816 | .620 | .685 | NS |
| | Private sector | 42 | 24.29 | 3.300 | | | |
| | Public sector | 63 | 24.10 | 3.449 | | | |
| | Pensioner | 9 | 22.67 | 1.000 | | | |
| | Professionals | 12 | 24.50 | 3.802 | | | |
| | Homemaker | 105 | 24.09 | 2.896 | | | |
| Marital Status | Married | 42 | 23.86 | 3.706 | 5.463 | .005 | S |
| | Unmarried | 3 | 30.00 | .000 | | | |
| | Divorced | 105 | 24.09 | 2.896 | | | |
| Average monthly Income | Less than Rs. 50000 | 54 | 24.89 | 2.873 | 2.801 | .042 | S |
| | Rs. 50000 – Rs. 100000 | 57 | 23.42 | 3.229 | | | |
| | Rs. 100000 – Rs. 150000 | 33 | 23.82 | 3.264 | | | |
| | Above Rs. 150000 | 6 | 26.00 | 4.382 | | | |
| Level of Investment | Less than 10% of the salary | 54 | 24.89 | 3.100 | 3.816 | .011 | S |
| | 10–20% | 63 | 23.14 | 3.146 | | | |
| | 20–30% | 18 | 24.50 | 2.956 | | | |
| | 30% and above | 15 | 25.20 | 3.364 | | | |
| Procurement of Fund for Investment | From personal earnings | 141 | 23.96 | 3.214 | 4.171 | .017 | S |
| | From borrowed source | 3 | 28.00 | .000 | | | |
| | Others | 6 | 26.50 | 1.643 | | | |

The ANOVA table depicts that except for the factors of educational qualification and occupation for all other factors, the null hypothesis has been rejected at a 5 % level of significance.

## t-Test

t-Test have been utilized to test the significant difference between investor rationality and behavioral finance with the gender of respondents.

$H_0$: "There is no significant difference between investor rationality and behavioral finance concerning the gender of respondents".

Gender vs. Investor Rationality and Behavioral Finance

| *Personal Factors* | *Groups* | | *Investor Rationality* | | | | | *Behavioral Finance* | | | | |
|---|---|---|---|---|---|---|---|---|---|---|---|---|
| | | *N* | *Mean* | *SD* | *t-Value* | *Sig.* | | *Mean* | *SD* | *t-Value* | *Sig.* | |
| Gender | Male | 99 | 48.27 | 5.210 | .524 | .697 | NS | 24.00 | 3.061 | -.709 | .245 | NS |
| | Female | 51 | 47.76 | 5.833 | | | | 24.41 | 3.517 | | | |

It is inferred from the table that, the high mean score with respect to investor rationality is for male respondents (Mean 48.27) and the high mean score with respect to behavioral finance is for female respondents (Mean 24.41).

However, with the t-value it has been found that the respondents have not varied significantly in investor rationality and behavioral finance, Hence, the null hypothesis has been accepted at 5 percent level.

## 10. FINDINGS OF THE STUDY

- It is evident from the percentage analysis that most of the respondents are in the age group of 21–30 years and male respondents are more compared to females, possessing bachelor's degrees, and most of them are married.
- Majority of the respondents are working in the public sector having an average monthly income of Rs. 50000 – Rs. 100000. Most of the respondents are investing 10-20 % of their earnings and they are using personal earnings for their investment.
- The ANOVA results for the first objective show that educational qualification, occupation, and level of investment have significant differences with investor rationality while taking investment decisions.
- The ANOVA results for the second objective show that age, marital status, average monthly income, level of investment, and procurement of funds for investment vary significantly with behavioral finance.
- The t-test result shows that there is no significant difference between dependent factors with gender of the respondents.

## 11. SUGGESTIONS

- Enhance advisory services by training financial professionals to recognize and address clients' behavioral biases, fostering more informed and rational decision-making.
- Explore the development of technology solutions that leverage behavioral insights to guide investors through decision-making processes.
- Integrate behavioral finance concepts into finance and business education programs to equip future professionals with a more holistic understanding of market dynamics.

## 12. CONCLUSION

In conclusion, this study delves into the intricate dynamics of financial markets by examining the interplay between investors' rational decision-making and the pervasive influence of behavioral factors. Notably, this study contributes to the evolving field of behavioral finance by shedding light on specific behavioral patterns exhibited by investors. From this study, it can be concluded that a substantial number of respondents agree that their investment decisions are influenced by mental accounting and recency biases. For investors, this study offers practical insights into refining their decision-making processes, emphasizing the importance of self-awareness and strategic risk management. Financial institutions and advisors can leverage these insights to tailor their services, fostering a more empathetic and effective approach. Regulators and policymakers, armed with a deeper comprehension of behavioral dynamics, can implement measures to enhance investor protection and market resilience. While this study provides valuable insights, we acknowledge its limitations and propose avenues for future research to continue unraveling the complexities inherent in financial decision-making. Ultimately, the synthesis of rationality and behavioral finance is imperative for cultivating a resilient and informed financial ecosystem.

## REFERENCES

[1] Ahmad, Z. and Ibrahim, H. (2017). Institutional investor behavioral biases: syntheses of theory and evidence, *Management Research Review*, Volume 40, Issue 5, pp. 578–603

[2] Birău, F.R. (2012). The Impact of Behavioral Finance on Stock Markets, Annals of the "Constantin Brâncuşi" University of Târgu Jiu, *Economy Series*, Issue 3, pp. 45–50.

[3] Boda, J.R. and Sunitha, G. (2018). Investor's Psychology in Investment Decision Making: A Behavioral Finance Approach, *International Journal of Pure and Applied Mathematics*, Volume 119, Issue 7, pp. 1253–1261.

[4] Byrne, A. and Brooks, M. (2008). Behavioral Finance: Theories and Evidence, *The Research Foundation of CFA Institute Literature Review*, pp. 1–26.

[5] Gajjala, S. (2005). Behavioral Finance: Is Investor Irrationality the Norm? OSMANIA *Journal of Management,* Volume 2, Issue 2, pp. 13–20.

[6] Joo, B.A. and Durri, K. (2018). Impact of Psychological Traits on Rationality of Individual Investors, *Theoretical Economics Letters,* Volume 8, pp. 1973–1986.

[7] Mitroi, A. and Oproiu, A. (2014). Behavioral Finance: New Research Trends, Socionomics and Investor Emotions, *Theoretical and Applied Economics*, Volume 21, Issue 4(593), pp. 153–166.

[8] Mukherjee, S. and De, S. (2018). When Are Investors Rational? *Journal of Behavioral Finance*, pp. 1–18, DOI: 10.1080/15427560.2018.1443936

# The Association between Financial Literacy and Income Inequality—A Study on the Salaried Individual of Lucknow

**Avnare Singh**[1] **and Alka Singh**[2]
[1]Research Fellow, Institute of Management Commerce and Economics, Shri Ramswaroop Memorial University, Lucknow, Uttar Pradesh, India
[2]Professor, Institute of Management Commerce and Economics, Shri Ramswaroop Memorial University, Lucknow, Uttar Pradesh, India
E-mail: [1]avnare22@gmail.com; [2]alkavinay@gmail.com

***ABSTRACT:*** *The present paper delves into the intricate relationship between financial literacy and income inequality, exploring the dynamics, mechanisms, and implications of their association. Income inequality persists as a pressing socio-economic challenge worldwide, posing significant implications for individual well-being, social cohesion, and economic stability. In recent years, increasing attention has been directed towards financial literacy as a potential tool for addressing this disparity. To this end, this research undertakes a meticulous synthesis of the existing literature and empirical studies to investigate the extent to which financial literacy influences income distribution and inequality levels. The study scrutinizes the pathways through which financial literacy can impact income inequality, including its effects on employment prospects, income generation, wealth accumulation, and financial decision-making.*

*The objective of this study is to examine the correlation between financial literacy and income inequality among salaried individuals of Lucknow. The research delves into the influence of varying levels of financial literacy, on the levels of income and income inequality, and whether this interaction intensifies or mitigates disparities within communities.*

*The findings of this paper demonstrate a strong correlation between financial literacy and income inequality. This presents a valuable opportunity for policymakers, educators, and advocates of economic inclusion to advance greater equity, opportunity, and prosperity for every member of society. By comprehending the intricate interplay between these two factors, we can strive towards a future that is fair and prosperous for all.*

**Keywords:** Financial Literacy, Income Inequality, Lucknow, Poverty, SDG's.

## 1. INTRODUCTION

Unprecedented economic growth brings into existence unprecedented complexities in the economy, these complexities emerge in the form of inequalities. The world has witnessed an extensive surge in the inequalities in income on a global landscape. In the present scenario, the resourceful conduct of money and wealth is of paramount significance. It is no longer about counting coins, but rather having a discerning intellect towards making sound financial decisions. This ability varies from person to person, one might possess a higher ability to administer money, while the other might possess unsubstantial intellect to administer money.

In order to tackle these complexities to ensure societal and individual prosperity and overcome this surge in income inequality, financial literacy may prove to be a key variable in the alleviation of this irregularity. "Financial literacy alludes to an individual's competence toward understanding fundamental financial concepts, such as budgeting, saving, investment, and retirement planning". Those with the knowledge and skills in this aspect tend to prosper through exceptional economic outcomes. Thus, Financial literacy is vital as it empowers individuals to skillfully tread through the financial system enabling them to make well-judged financial decisions and consequently attain economic equity.

This research explores the association between financial literacy to the inequalities in income, and to illuminate whether financial literacy will prove to be a remedial factor in the reduction of these inequalities. When we talk about income inequality, we are essentially explaining the "unequal distribution of income across individuals of a specific region, country, or at a global scale including the inequality between the rich and poor". These inequalities in income have severe consequences for the individual and society. Economic instability emerges as a consequence of income inequality, increasing inequality negatively influences consumer spending and reduces economic growth. With the presence of income inequality access to adequate education, quality healthcare, and standard of living is negatively affected. Which in turn impacts society in the form of poverty, crime, and reduced innovation.

Poverty is associated with inequalities in income, individuals with lower incomes struggle to fulfill their needs, such as housing, healthcare, food, and education this is a leading cause of poverty expansion. On the contrary individuals with higher earning capacity have access to better education, housing, and healthcare to name a few, and even after fulfilling their basic needs they have a certain amount of income left at their disposal. Access to credit and financial services is convenient for higher-income individuals which further enhances their capacity to make investments, this capacity is lost to individuals with lower incomes as their access to credit is hindered further trapping them into poverty. Income inequality becomes an obstacle in achieving economic well-being or financial well-being as it places barriers that cause predicaments for individuals and households trying to avoid poverty.

The objective of this paper is to understand the association of Income inequality with financial literacy in Lucknow and how financial literacy aids in inequality reduction. The findings of this research will contribute to the existing literature and the methodology would be suitable for conducting similar research in other parts of the country and world which demonstrate similar characteristics as that of Lucknow. Lucknow is a Tier 2 (Y) city (Government of Uttar Pradesh, n.d.) with a population of approximately 3,945,409 (World Population Review, n.d.).This research seeks to disclose the evidence that contributes to explaining that disparities in income emerge as a result of a deficiency in financial intellect. Financial literacy can impact the economic outcomes of the individual and society and due to a lack of financial education people are often met with conundrums while making a financial decision, as a result of which inequality is reflected in their state of financial well-being.

Financial literacy enables an individual to make well-thought-out choices in the context of money-related matters. They have an improved propensity to save, invest, and budget their financial resources efficiently, resulting in an improved overall economic position. Adequate financial knowledge facilitated access to economic opportunities and credit facilities, while also ensuring long-term financial prosperity through adequate planning in terms of retirement and investments resulting in a secure financial position in the future. Financial literacy assists in the differentiation process of separating good and bad financial choices which might prove to be catastrophic if made without due diligence, it also encourages skill development leading to an increased earning potential and improved knowledge further increasing the potential to reduce unemployment and ultimately disparity in income.

Addressing income inequality remains a significant challenge in reducing poverty. Income inequality is responsible for enforcing a restraint on financial well-being and escaping poverty. Inequality reduction is beneficial since a higher income enables individuals to access essential resources. Access to quality education at an affordable cost leads to potential prosperity for future generations. Improved health resulting from increased income that was previously beyond an individual's means leads to a healthier population, resulting in the emergence of robust human capital. Higher income provides opportunities for better skill development, improving employment and earning potential. By addressing income inequalities, a more equitable society can be created, one where each person has an equal opportunity to relish and prosper.

Therefore, this paper will give us a better understanding of financial literacy and its role in reducing income inequality, which will help in building a society where individuals benefit through exposure to a balanced economic landscape.

## 2. LITERATURE REVIEW

### 2.1 Evidence of Income Inequality

Inadequate financial literacy hinders the decision-making capability of individuals concerning financial matters, as the complexity of financial decisions is increasing lack of financial literacy disrupts their economic well-being and at large contributes to inequality in wealth and income (Annamaria Lusardi, 2023). The problem of unequal wealth distribution has become apparent in recent times, it is often observed that wealth is disproportionately distributed and widely dispersed as a result several workers upon their retirement, unfortunately, are unable to acquire personal assets for financial stability, causing financial stress on their lives. Thus, it becomes crucial to understand and address this issue (Maarten van Rooij, 2011).

One of the major challenges in the world right now is the widening gap between the rich and the poor and has thus, recently garnered significant attention such that it has found its place in the tenth sustainable development goal (UNDP, 2020), "targeting a reduction in inequality in order to promote social inclusion and sustainable universal economic growth". There is a persisting issue of poverty and income inequality in Asia and the Pacific despite the fact that over the last few decades, there has been rapid economic growth in the region (Cyn-Young Park, 2015). "At global levels, 76% of the total household wealth and 52% of total income is accumulated by the top 10% population, the middle 40% owns 22% of total household wealth and 39% of total income and the bottom 50% owns just 2% of the total household wealth and 8% of total income." (Lucas Chancel, 2022). "Being one of the most rapidly growing economies in the world India is also one of the most unequal countries, increasing inequality in the past thirty years has resulted in the accumulation of 77% wealth of the nation with the top 10%, the number of billionaires in India has increased from 9 in 2000 to 119 in 2020, for a minimum wage worker to earn equal to the annual earning of top paid executives, it would take him/her 941 years" (OXFAM, 2020).

### 2.2 Significance of Financial Literacy

In the present times, with the financial markets offering new and complex financial products, individuals must assume increased responsibility for their finances. Just as seeking success in the modern world, it is vital to be literate (ability to read and write), without the fundamental knowledge of finance and economics (financial literacy) it would be impossible to succeed in the current financial system (Lusardi, 2009). Studies show that a higher financial literacy leads to increased participation in the stock market resulting in better economic outcomes, those with greater financial literacy are equipped with better skills to analyze and understand the market trends enabling them to make better decisions in comparison to those individuals with low levels of financial literacy (LUIGI GUISO, 2015)

The income at the disposal of an individual is reflected in their spending capacities, individuals with higher spending capacity tend to have more unspent income, thus spending more and contributing towards economic growth, relying upon their ability to understand financial concepts and principles they were able to make informed decisions in financial matters (Leora Klapper, 2012). Investigating the results of financial literacy levels of young adults and correlating it to the Inequalities in GDP, the findings suggest that in the course of examining the levels of financial literacy and its association with inequalities, financial literacy has emerged as a crucial key variable to understand these inequalities (Gian Paolo Stella, 2020).

## 2.3 Financial Literacy as a Means to Reduce Income Inequality

The remedy to every issue lies in the identification of its root cause, similarly in order to reduce inequalities we must understand the reason behind its existence, only then we will be able to implement corrective measures through the development of strategies to overcome inequalities (Prete, 2012). The studies report that an increment in financial literacy levels has diversified implications for distinct groups, these outcomes have the potential of greatly reducing inequality among the weakest groups, highlighting the significance of financial literacy, such an effort can lead to improved financial well-being for individuals and groups, financial literacy empowers individuals to improve their financial condition through making informed decisions, contributing to an equitable society where everyone prospers (Gallo & Sconti, 2023).

Engagement of individuals in financial planning renders higher net worth, planning enables an individual to establish financial goals and means to achieve them, ascertaining greater wealth accumulation and financial security (Ameriks, 2003). Planning for retirement is likely to accumulate three times more wealth for individuals in comparison to those who do not (Annamaria Lusardi, 2011). The inability to plan is associated with a lack of financial knowledge and financial literacy, as financial planning often involves complex financial calculations and financially unsophisticated individuals lack a clear understanding of financial concepts such as compounding of interest and often find themselves selecting the wrong financial tools with high service charges (Annamaria Lusardi, 2011). Improving financial literacy through the means of financial inclusion programs is an effective measure in combating poverty and income inequality, the findings suggest that through implementation of policies aimed towards financial inclusion has a significant contribution in reducing income inequality and poverty rates in developing countries, through financial inclusion an improved financial literacy leads to promotion of economic growth via increased accessibility to financial services (Md Abdullah Omar, 2020). Millions remain ousted from the financial system in developing regions as a consequence of low levels of income, financial inclusion narrows the gap leading to increased demand for resources, increased investment and consumption, resulting in economic growth, enabling efficient resource allocation, reduced cost, improved financial management, reduction in debt (Demirgüç-Kunt A, 2013).

### 2.4 Emerging Gaps

While existing literature proves that inequalities in income exist and that there is a correlation between income inequality and poverty, through several pieces of evidence it can be known that financial literacy is, in fact, a contributing factor resulting in an improvement in the financial state of an individual, there remains a notable gap as the majority of these studies are centred in the regions where the population composition and economic factors differ from those of the population selected for the purpose of this study. Moreover, there is extensive evidence establishing the relationship between financial literacy and its effect on the economic outcomes of individuals, yet so far, very few studies have made an investigation into the association of financial literacy with the inequalities in income, thus, there lies a need to further extend the research to various other regions of the globe to establish robust evidence that financial literacy is in fact a solution towards reducing income inequality. This study is the first of its kind in the region of Lucknow, Uttar Pradesh.

## 3. RESEARCH METHODOLOGY

### 3.1 Objective

The primary objective of this research is to ascertain the relationship between income inequality and levels of financial literacy, in order to know the effect that financial literacy might have on reducing income inequality.

### 3.2 Hypothesis

$H_0$: "There is no association between financial literacy and income inequality."

$H_1$: "There is an association between financial literacy and income inequality."

### 3.3 Sample Design and Size

The sample for this research has been drawn from the population of salaried individuals of Lucknow, the capital city of the state of Uttar Pradesh, India. The sample has been drawn using the Stratified Random Sampling technique of the Probability Sampling method. The sample size for this study taking into consideration the confidence level to be 95% and margin of error to be 5% the sample (n) is 250.

### 3.4 Data Collection

This study is based on primary data, collection of which was done via questionnaire to obtain information about the financial literacy of respondents based on the "**Big Three**" questions which have been used as a measure of financial literacy in several studies across 20 countries designed by (Annamaria Lusardi, 2011), the questionnaire also obtained information about the income of individuals for comparison of the gaps in income and also ascertain the correlation between income inequality and financial literacy.

### 3.4 Analysis

For the analysis of data collected via questionnaire, the financial literacy of the respondents is determined through univariate analysis using descriptive statistics. The financial literacy of the respondents will be ascertained based on the correct response to the aforementioned "Big Three" questions. To understand the relationship between financial literacy and income inequality a bivariate analysis is performed using descriptive statistics. The income of the respondents has been categorized into three levels namely, "Low, Middle, and High" Pearson's coefficient of correlation will determine the relationship between financial literacy and income.

## 4. DATA ANALYSIS

To ascertain whether or not financial literacy can be a useful tool in reducing the inequalities in income, the levels of income of the respondents were compared alongside their levels of financial literacy. The overall financial literacy percentage of respondents in correspondence to their response to the big three questions is illustrated in Figure 1.

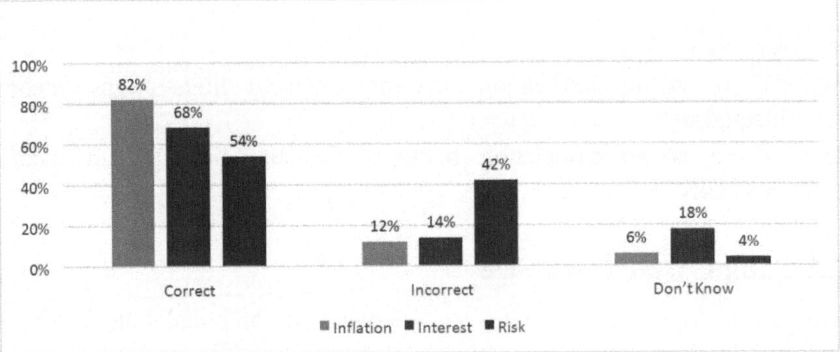


**Figure 1:** Response to the "Big Three"

(*Source:* Computed.)

In Figure 1 it can be observed that the response to the inflation question "Suppose you had Rs. 1,000 in a savings account and the interest rate was

2% per year. After 5 years, how much do you think you would have in the account if you left the money to grow?" consists of 82% of the individuals giving the right answer "More than Rs. 1,000", while 12% answer incorrectly "Exactly Rs. 1,000 and Less Than Rs. 1,000" and 6 % of the respondents don't know the correct answer. In addition to that the response to the second question on Interest "Imagine that the interest rate on your savings account was 1% per year and inflation was 2% per year. After 1 year, how much would you be able to buy with the money in this account?" the correct response to this question "Less than today" was opted by 68% of the respondents, 14% of the respondents choose incorrectly "More than today and Exactly the same" while the percentage of respondents not knowing the correct answer to this question were 18%. The response to the third and the last question "Please tell me whether this statement is true or false. Buying a single company's stock usually provides a safer return than a stock mutual fund." 54% of the respondents answered correctly "False", while 14% answered incorrectly "True" and 4% of the respondents didn't know the correct answer.

A significant percentage of the total respondents gave correct answers to the financial literacy question, however, in order to understand the financial literacy levels of the respondents the individuals with correct responses to all three questions will be considered to be financially literate.

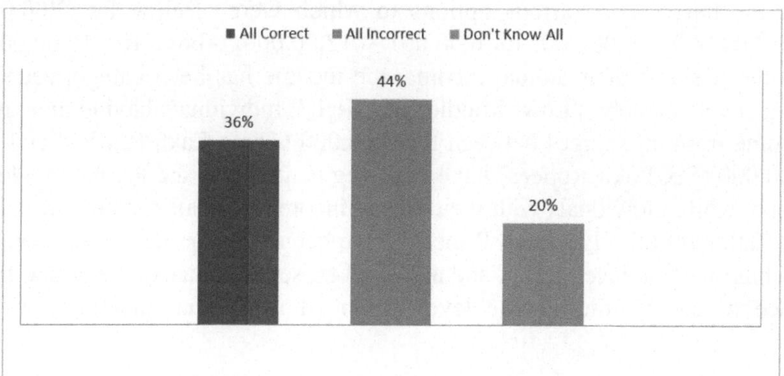


**Figure 2:** Combined Correct, Incorrect and Don't Know Response to All Three Question

(*Source:* Computed.)

Figure 2 gives information about the total percentage of respondents who answered all the "Big Three" questions correctly is 36%, while 44% of the respondents answered all three questions incorrectly and 20% of the total respondents do not know the correct answer to all three questions. This gives us information about their level of financial literacy, which is illustrated in Figure 3.

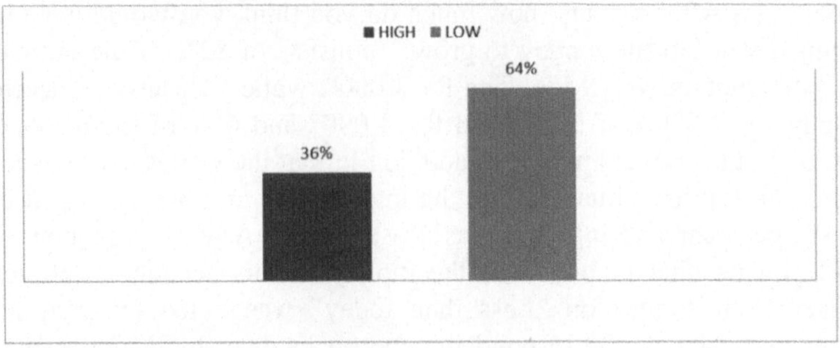


**Figure 3:** FInancial Literacy Levels

(*Source:* Computed.)

The financial literacy of the individuals is determined based on the correct response to all three questions, as observed in Figure 2, the financial literacy of 36% of the respondents is high as they answered all three questions correctly and 64% of the total participants show low levels of financial literacy as they either answered all the questions incorrectly or did not know the correct answer to the question.

In addition to questions aimed at measuring financial literacy levels, the respondents were also asked to give information about their income levels "Please select the range within which your annual income from all sources fits the best." The various options to which were "Below Rs. 3,00,000; Rs. 3,00,000 – 6,00,000; Rs 6,00,001 – 12,00,000; Above Rs. 12,00,001." On the basis of their annual income, the income has been categorized into three levels namely, "Low, Middle, and High," Individuals having an annual income from all sources between Rs. 3,00,000 (Three Lakh Rupees) and Rs. 6,00,000 (Six Lakh Rupees) have been segmented into the lowincome level group, while individuals with their annual income from all sources exceeding Rs.12,00,000 (Twelve Lakh Rupees) have been categorized as belonging to the high-income level group, and at last all those individuals have found their place in the Middle-income level group whose annual income from all

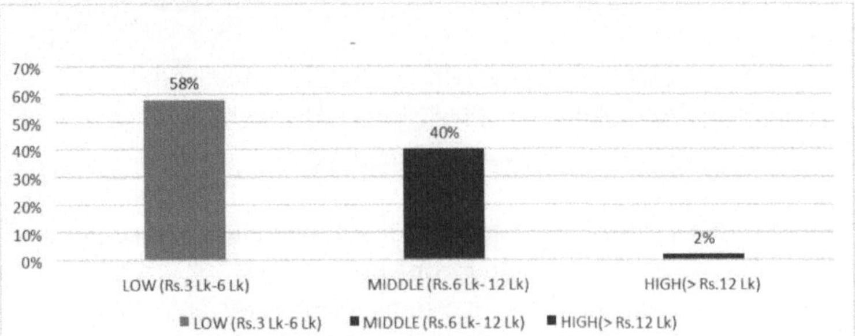


**Figure 4:** Income Levels

(*Source:* Computed.)

sources fall between Rs. 6,00,000 (Six Lakh Rupees) and Rs. 12.00,000 (Twelve Lakh Rupees). The data on the income of the respondents is summarised in Figure 4.

Among the total number of responses that formed the data for income levels it was found that there was a massive inequality in the incomes of the individuals, the analysis further revealed that out of the total respondents only 2% were in the High-Income level group, while 58% of them belonged to the Low- income level group, while the remaining 40% belong to the middle level income group. This data highlights the prevailing inequalities in income. For facilitating the identification of inequality in income the data base was only the salaried individuals, which allows for much accurate comparison. It can be clearly observed that there is a wide gap in the income levels of the salaried individuals.

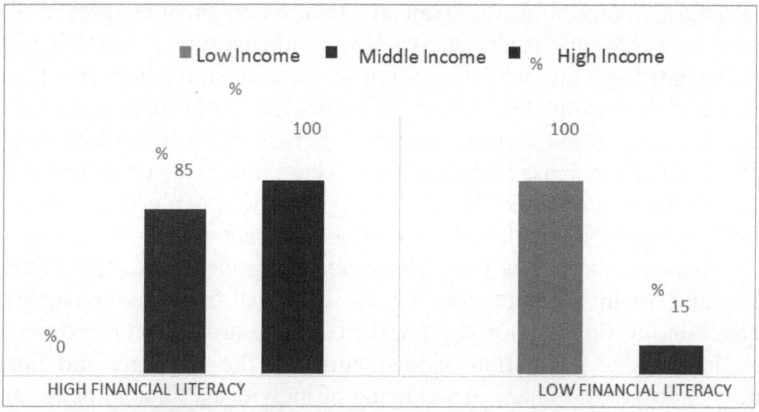


**Figure 5:** Financial Literacy and Income Levels
(*Source:* Computed)

The data in Figure 5 renders information about the distribution of income based on the financial literacy of the respondents, it can be observed that among the group of respondents who possess high levels of financial literacy consists of 100% of the high-income earners, 85% of the middle-income earners and none from the low-income bracket. While the group with low levels of financial literacy having answered one, two or all three questions incorrectly, consists of 100% of low-income earners, 15% of the middle-income earners and none of the high-income earners.

There is a difference in the levels of financial literacy and there is an observable inequality in income, but are they related to each other and does one variable have an influence over the other, this can be ascertained by testing the relationship between the two variables that are financial literacy and income inequality. To determine the relationship between financial literacy and income levels we make use of "Pearson's Correlation."

**Table 1:** Correlation Analysis

| | | *Financial Literacy* | *Income Level* |
|---|---|---|---|
| Financial Literacy | Pearson Correlation | 1 | .726** |
| | Sig. (2- tailed)<br>N | 250 | <.001<br>250 |
| Income Level | Pearson Correlation | .726** | 1 |
| | Sig. (2-tailed)<br>N | <.001<br>250 | 250 |

**. Correlation is significant at the 0.01 level (2-tailed).
(*Source:* Computed.)

Pearson's correlation of financial literacy and income level is Highly Positive ($r = .726$) and is also statistically significant with ($p < 0.05$) Table 1. Thus, suggesting that there is a significant association between financial literacy and the income level of an individual. This information also clarifies that an increase in the level of financial literacy of an individual would be followed with an increase in their income. These results are consistent with the study of (Gian Paolo Stella, 2020); (Leora Klapper, 2012) where the researcher suggests that low levels of income are prevalent among those whose financial literacy is low. Moreover, alongside its positive effects on income and wealth accumulation, it is also seen that financial literacy leads to a reduction in financial stress (Annamaria Lusardi, 2011). Low-income levels lead to the generation of inequalities in the economy and financial literacy improves the financial wellbeing of individuals through better returns on investments and the overall ability to manage their economic affairs and financial position (Annamaria Lusardi, 2023). Greater financial literacy assists an individual in absorbing economic shocks in events of unexpected macroeconomic distress (Leora Klapper, 2012). It is also seen that with an increase in the financial literacy of an individual, their disposable income also increases further expanding their ability to spend, thus leading to a reduction in the inequalities in income among groups (Gallo & Sconti, 2023).

As inequalities are a result of a disproportionate increase in income with respect to economic growth, an increment in income will result in reduced income inequalities, as observed earlier financial literacy is a helpful measure in this direction, as financial literacy promotes human development (Annamaria Lusardi, 2023), and improvement in the level of human development leads to lower inequalities in income (Francisco J. Oliver-Márquez, 2021). The outlook that financial literacy leads to an improvement in financial well-being will reduce the inequalities in income and further reduce the poverty level, and that financial literacy along with a positive impact on reducing income inequalities has a significant role in poverty reduction is supported by (Md Abdullah Omar, 2020); (Media Wahyudi Askar, 2020).

Thus, following the results of this research and the available literature, it can be ascertained that financial literacy is a positive and impactful approach to reducing the inequalities in income.

## 5. CONCLUSION

The present study offers a comprehensive analysis of the intricate relationship between financial literacy and income inequality, shedding light on its multifaceted dynamics and implications. The findings underscore the critical role of financial literacy in shaping income distribution and societal inequality, emphasizing its potential as a proactive tool for addressing disparities and fostering economic empowerment.

Drawing on the insights gleaned from this research, several recommendations emerge for policymakers seeking to mitigate income inequality through financial literacy initiatives. Firstly, there is a pressing need to prioritize financial education within formal schooling systems, integrating comprehensive curriculum components that equip students with essential financial management skills from an early age. Additionally, targeted interventions should be developed to reach vulnerable and marginalized populations, including low-income individuals, minorities, and those with limited access to traditional financial services.

Furthermore, policymakers should invest in the design and implementation of innovative financial literacy programs that are tailored to the specific needs and circumstances of diverse communities. These initiatives should leverage technology and digital platforms to enhance accessibility and engagement, ensuring that individuals from all backgrounds have the opportunity to build their financial knowledge and capabilities. Moreover, efforts to promote financial inclusion and economic empowerment should be coupled with broader policy measures aimed at reducing structural barriers and enhancing socio-economic mobility. This includes initiatives to increase access to affordable housing, healthcare, and education, as well as measures to address systemic inequalities in employment, wages, and wealth distribution.

In conclusion, by integrating financial literacy into policy frameworks and adopting a holistic approach to addressing income inequality, policymakers can pave the way for a more equitable and inclusive society. Through strategic investments, targeted interventions, and concerted efforts to tackle underlying structural challenges, societies can move towards a future where financial empowerment is truly accessible to all, regardless of income or background.

## REFERENCES

[1] Ameriks, J. A. (2003). Wealth Accumulation and the propensity to plan. *Quarterly Journal of Economics*.

[2] Annamaria Lusardi, O.S. (2011). Financial Literacy Around the World: An Overview. *National Bureau of Economic Research*.

[3] Annamaria Lusardi, O.S. (2023). The Importance of Financial Literacy: Opening a New Field. *National Bureau of Economic Research*.

[4] Cyn-Young Park, R.V. (2015). Financial Inclusion, Poverty, and Income Inequality in Developing Asia. *ADB Economics Working Paper Series*.

[5] Demirgüç-Kunt A, K.L. (2013). Measuring financial inclusion: explaining variation in use of financial services. *Brook Pap Econ Activ*, 279–340.

[6] Francisco J. Oliver-Márquez, A. G.-R.-F.-N. (2021). Is Income Inequality Influenced by Financial Knowledge? A Macroeconomic and Longitudinal Analysis. *Journal of the Knowledge Economy*.

[7] Gallo, G. and Sconti, A. (2023). How much financial literacy matters? A simulation of potential influences on inequality levels.

[8] Gian Paolo Stella, U.F. (2020). Could Financial Literacy Become a Key Variable to Examine Social and Economic Inequalities? A Study on Italian Regions. *International Journal of trade, Economics and Finance*.

[9] Government of Uttar Pradesh. (n.d.). Retrieved from https://sects.up.gov.in.

[10] Leora Klapper, A.L. (2012). Financial Literacy and the Financial Crisis. *Network of studies on pension, aging and retirement.*

[11] Lucas Chancel, T.P. (2022). *World Inequality Report.* Harvard Univ Press.

[12] Luigi Guiso, E.V. (2015). How Much Can Financial Literacy Help? *Review of Finance*.

[13] Lusardi, A. (2009). The importance of financial literacy. *National Bureau of Economic Research*.

[14] Maarten van Rooij, A.L. (2011). Financial Literacy, Retirement Planning, and Household Wealth. *National Bureau of Economic Research*.

[15] Md Abdullah Omar, K.I. (2020). Does financial inclusion reduce poverty and income inequality in developing countries? A panel data analysis. *Journal of Economic Structures*. doi: https://doi.org/10.1186/s40008-020-00214-4

[16] Media Wahyudi Askar, B. O.-F. (2020). Financial Literacy and Poverty Reduction: The Case of Indonesia. *ADBI Working Paper Series*.

[17] OECD INFE (2011). Measuring Financial Literacy: Core Questionnaire in Measuring Financial Literacy: Questionnaire and Guidance Notes for conducting an Internationally Comparable Survey of Financial literacy. Paris: OECD.

[18] Oxfam, I. (2020). India: Extreme inequality in numbers. *Oxfam International.*

[19] Prete, A.L. (2012). Economic literacy, inequality, and financial development. *Economics Letters*.

[20] UNDP, U.N. (2020). Goal 10: Reduce inequality within and among countries. Retrieved from Sustainable Development Goals: https://www.un.org/sustainabledevelopment/inequality/

[21] World Population Review (n.d.). Retrieved from worldpopulationreview.com

# Job Burnout and Psychological Well-being: A Study on Academicians of Higher Educational Institutions

**Manjeet Kaur[1], Rekha Khosla[2] and Masood Siddiqui[3]**
[1]Research Scholar, Department of Management, Amity Business School, Amity University, Lucknow, India
[2]Assistant Professor, Department of Management, Amity Business School, Amity University, Lucknow, India
[3]Professor, Department of Statistics, University of Lucknow, Lucknow, India
E-mail: [1]manjeet.kaur066@gmail.com; [2]rkhosla@lko.amity.edu; [3]mhsiddiqui@gmail.com

***ABSTRACT:*** *Job burnout is a situation in which an individual undergoes fatigue or frustration created by high job demands and expectations at the workplace where a person feels, that one is mentally, emotionally, and physically exhausted, feels his energy has depleted, reduced sense of motivation, and distant in his work or work relations. Psychological well-being consists of acceptance of one's self, positive Interpersonal relationships, autonomy, environmental mastery, a feeling of purpose and meaning in life, and personal growth and development. The purpose of this paper is to study the factors of job burnout and Psychological well-being. A questionnaire-based study was conducted on academicians working in higher educational Institutions. Data was collected using the Maslach Burnout Inventory and RYFF Psychological well-being scale. Descriptive research design was used. This study tries to find the linkage between Job burnout and Psychological well-being. The findings stated that Job burnout has a significant impact on the Psychological well-being of higher educational institutions.*

**Keywords:** Academicians, Education, Job Burnout, Psychological Well-being, Stress, Teachers.

## 1. INTRODUCTION

Job burnout is one of the most crucial problems emerging among the employees within the organization. The employees are continuously subjected to different demands at the workplace, and the work culture where they are exposed may result to an increased amount of stress and burnout and the teachers of higher educational institutions are no exception. Earlier burnout studies were restricted to the Health Industry i.e. nurses and hospital staff were supposed to be more affected by it but nowadays it also spreads in the teaching profession due to advancements in teaching technology used in the classroom and the work culture existing among the higher educational institutions.

## 2. JOB BURNOUT

Job burnout is a result of conflict with one's work, and interpersonal stressors at the workplace. Maslach Inventory Burnout comprises of professional inefficacy, emotional exhaustion, and cynicism. The American psychologist Herbert Freudenberger introduced the term "Burnout" in academics in 1974. Freudenberger described Job Burnout as an eventual physiological and psychological depletion and low productivity and commitment. According to him, the first symptom of burnout is when an individual works hard in an organization but his achievements appear too less comparatively to himself.

Workplace inefficacy or reduced personal accomplishment means an individual employee judges themselves negatively and is ineffective at work and with interpersonal interaction too. Emotional or Occupational exhaustion deteriorates the employee's capability to function and operate efficiently and effectively.

Cynicism or depersonalization means skeptical and cold behavior towards other employees and individuals and, a lack of personal attachment while dealing with them.

Physiological well-being is the subjective experience that an individual goes through it is related to life satisfaction, happiness, and a positive attitude having a sense of self-worth and capability. Psychological well-being is related to the emotional and mental health of an individual.

### 2.1 Physiological Well-being

An individual is Psychologically well if he feels confident about oneself, accepts one's ideas and beliefs, has fulfilling relationships, and has a goal or motive in life.

To further study Physiological Well-Being, a Ryff Physiological Well-being scale was used. Ryff (1989) gave six dimensions of Psychological well-being which is self-acceptance, autonomy, environmental mastery, personal growth, purpose of life, and Positive relation with others.

### 2.2 Dimensions of Ryff Psychological Well-being

***Autonomy:*** When an Individual has confidence in their beliefs and opinions even if they are different from the general beliefs of individuals. They have the capability of making their own decisions.

***Self-acceptance:*** An individual is aware and accepts his traits, strengths, and weaknesses and is in peace with most dimensions of their personality. A person's overall satisfaction with his life, control, and emotional stability is referred to as self-acceptance.

***Environmental Mastery:*** When an individual is responsible for the environment where he resides, he has a sense of managing his surroundings, he can manage his life and everyday circumstances and he is capable of efficiently utilizing and creating opportunities to benefit his needs and well-being.

***Personal Growth:*** When an individual believes that it is important to have new experiences in life and is more open to such experiences, he understands that change is the only thing that is dynamic and he takes steps towards continuous self-improvement in his attitude and behavior.

***Purpose in Life:*** An individual has goal clarity. He knows what he wants from his life he does not wander without a purpose in his life.

***Positive Relations with Others:*** An individual has healthy and meaningful relations with others he understands the essence of intimacy, affection, and empathy. He is a person who believes in giving and sharing whatever he has.

## 3. LITERATURE REVIEW

According to Seligman and Sikszentmihalyi (2000) Psychological well-being is the result of two dimensions one is positive emotion and engagement in purposeful activities. As per this study higher level of Psychological well-being is seen in individuals who are actively engaged in meaningful activities and those who feel positive emotions frequently.

Malek and colleagues conducted a cross-cultural study on the Psychological well-being of Malaysian and British (Malik and Collagress 2001) firefighters .1053 was the sample size. It was found that Occupational stress is negatively correlated with Psychological well-being. The coping strategies are different in Malaysian and British firefighters.

Oyku and colleagues (2017) conducted a study on teachers' Psychological well-being which was Psychological well-being: comparison among teachers in the USA, Turkey, and Pakistan. There were 990 teachers from Turkey, 403 teachers from the USA, and 715 teachers from Pakistan. The findings stated that the teachers of the U.S have high Psychological well-being followed by teachers of Turkey and Pakistan.

Suleman and colleagues (2018) performed a research on the linkage between Occupational stress and Psychological well-being among the teachers of secondary schools in Pakistan. 260 male and 142 female teachers participated, in total the sample was 402. Occupational Stress Index questionnaire was utilized. The findings stated that female and male teachers were stressed with respect to work overload, unfavorable working conditions, unreasonable political pressure, unprofitability, and lack of participation in management. Occupational stress is negatively correlated with Psychological well-being and there is a medium correlation between all the sub-scales of Occupational stress and Psychological well-being.

Toro and Peieto (2014) conducted a study, to analyze differences concerning gender level of burnout, absenteeism, work stress, and depression in academicians. The total sample size was 71 secondary teachers, including 40 women and 51 men. Data was collected using the Teachers Burnout (CBP-R) scale, the Beck Depression Inventory (BDI), the symptomatology checklist-90R (SCL-90-R) and a Socio-demographic and work situation scale. The finding stated that there is no different patterns of Burnout and Depression between the different genders of teachers.

According to Cordes and Dougherty (1993), Harrington *et al.,* 2001, and Mac Dougall, 2000 Job burnout occurs when there is a lot of workload, reduced personal control inadequate and improper reward and recognition system biased and partial behavior of the management breakdown of working community and difference or conflict in the belief system of values.

## 4. RESEARCH METHODOLOGY

A descriptive research design is utilized for the present research study. Random and convenient sampling has been used for the study. A total sample of 330 was utilized, who were the faculty members of higher educational Institutions of districts of Uttar Pradesh. The present study was been done using primary data, Maslach Burnout Inventory, and the RYFF Psychological well-being scale has been used for the data collection ..More than 420 questionnaires were sent to respondents out of which 330 questionnaires were found useful.

## 5. OBJECTIVE

The main purpose of this study is to:

1. To find any linkage between Job Burnout & Psychological well-being of the faculty.
2. To analyze the impact of Job Burnout on the Psychological well-being of the faculty.

## 6. HYPOTHESIS

$H_1$: There is a significant relationship between Job Burnout & Psychological well-being of the faculty.

$H_2$: There is a significant impact of Job Burnout & Psychological well-being of the faculty.

## 7. DATA ANALYSIS

The 22 items of Job Burnout has a Cronbach alpha coefficient of .850, Occupational exhaustion (OE), 9 items have a Cronbach alpha coefficient of .866, Depersonalisation (DP), 5 items have a have a Cronbach alpha coefficient of .645, Personal accomplishment assessment (PAA), 9 items have a Cronbach alpha coefficient of .742.

**Table 1:** Reliability of Data (Job Burnout)

| *Variable* | *Cronbach Alph* | *No. of Items* |
|---|---|---|
| Job Burnout | .850 | 22 |
| Occupational exhaustion (OE) | .866 | 09 |
| Depersonalisation (DP) | .645 | 05 |
| Personal accomplishment assessment (PAA) | .742 | 08 |

*Source:* Primary data.

**Table 2:** Reliability of Data (Psychological well-being)

| *Variable* | *Cronbach's Alpha* | *No. of Items* |
|---|---|---|
| Psychological well-being | .883 | 42 |
| Autonomy (A) | .717 | 07 |
| Environmental Mastery (EM) | .725 | 07 |
| Personal Growth (PG) | .699 | 07 |
| Positive relations (PR) | .751 | 07 |
| Purpose of Life (PL) | .738 | 07 |
| Self-acceptance (SA) | .682 | 07 |

The 42 items of Psychological well-being have a Cronbach alpha coefficient of .883, Autonomy (A), and 9 items have a Cronbach alpha coefficient of .717. Environmental Mastery (EM), 7 items have Cronbach alpha coefficient of .725, Personal Growth (PG), 7 items have a Cronbach alpha coefficient of .699, Positive relations (PR), 7 items have a have a Cronbach alpha coefficient of .751, Self-acceptance (SA), 7 items have a have a Cronbach alpha coefficient of .682.

**Objective 1:** To find any linkage between Job Burnout & Psychological well-being of the faculty.

$H_1$: There is a significant relationship between Job Burnout & Psychological well-being of the faculty.

**Table 3:** Correlation Coefficient

| *Independent Variable* | *Dependent Variable* | *Pearson Correlation* | *Significance* |
|---|---|---|---|
| Job Burnout | Psychological well-being | .797 | .000** |

*N*=330 **correlation is significant at 0.01 level.

Table 3, shows a positive correlation between Job Burnout and the Psychological well-being of faculties of higher educational Institutions. The significant p-value is 0.000. Correlation is significant at 0.01 level (2-tailed).

Hence the hypothesis (H1) gets accepted and it can be inferred that there is a significant relationship between Job Burnout and Psychological well-being.

**Objective 1:** To analyze the impact of Job Burnout on the Psychological well-being of the faculty.

There is a significant impact of Job Burnout & Psychological well-being of the faculty.

**Table 4:** Regression Analysis

| *Independent Variable* | *Dependent Variable* | *R square* | *Adjusted R square* | *Significance* |
|---|---|---|---|---|
| Job Burnout | Psychological well-being | .635 | .634 | .000** |

*N*=330 ** correlation is significant at 0.01 level.

Table 4, shows the impact of Job burnout on Psychological well-being. The R square value in the table is 0.635 and the adjusted R square value is .0.634. Job burnout significantly impacts the Psychological well-being of faculties of higher educational Institutions.

## 8. FINDINGS OF THE STUDY

According to this study, there is a significant positive correlation between Job burnout and Psychological well-being. Also, Job burnout has a significant impact on the Psychological well-being of faculties of higher educational Institutions. Hence the organizations and the faculty themselves need to make necessary efforts to address these problems at the workplace. The institutions should alleviate the stressors and encourage the Psychological well-being of teachers by minimizing the stress at work.

## 9. DISCUSSION

Job Burnout has a Cronbach alpha coefficient of .850, which indicates they have a high level of consistency, Occupational exhaustion (OE), 9 items have a Cronbach alpha coefficient of .866, Depersonalisation(DP), 5 items have a Cronbach alpha coefficient of .645, Personal accomplishment assessment(PAA), 9 items have a Cronbach alpha coefficient of .742.

The 42 items of Psychological well-being have a Cronbach alpha coefficient of .883, which indicates they have a high level of consistency. Autonomy (A), 9 items has a Cronbach alpha coefficient of .717. Environmental Mastery, 7 items has a Cronbach alpha coefficient of .725. For personal Growth, 7 items have a Cronbach alpha coefficient of .699, Positive relations (PR), 7 items have a have a Cronbach alpha coefficient of .751, Self-acceptance, 7 items have a have a Cronbach alpha coefficient of .682.

The scale and the data collected are considered as reliable and the reliability coefficient of .60 is considered acceptable.

## 10. CONCLUSION

This study attempts to find the relationship and Impact of Job burnout on the Psychological well-being of faculty members of higher educational Institutions. This research shows that Job burnout has a significant positive relationship with Psychological well-being. Job burnout has a significant impact on the Psychological well-being of faculty members of higher educational Institutions. Therefore appropriate action should be taken to lessen the stress at work which prevents Job burnout, it can be done by a stress management program which in turn will not only reduce the stress but it can also help teachers to mitigate work stress effectively and will reduce the effects of Job burnout. The individual teacher should also understand the level of their stress and what is causing it and should effectively try to cope with it before it starts to affect their work and well-being.

## REFERENCES

[1] Arnold, B. Bakker and Patrícia, L. Costa, Chronic job burnout and daily functioning: A theoretical analysis Burnout, Research, Volume 1, Issue 3, 2014, Pages 112119, ISSN22130586, https://doi.org/10.1016/j.burn. 2014.04.0. 03. (https://www.sciencedirect.com/science/article/pii/S2213058614000096)

[1] Bermejo-Toro, L. and Prieto-Ursúa, M. (2014). Absenteeism, burnout and symptomatology of teacher stress: sex differences. *International Journal of Educational Psychology.*

[2] Chowdhury, Rahat (2018). Burnout and its Organizational Effects: A Study on Literature Review. *Journal of Business & Financial Affairs*. 07. 10.4172/2167-0234.1000353.

[3] Christina, Maslach and Michael, P. Leiter, It's time to take action on burnout, Burnout Research, Volume 2, Issue 1, 2015, Pagesivv, ISSN22130586, https://doi.org/10.1016/j.burn.2015.05.002. https://www.sciencedirect.com/science/article/pii/S2213058615000157)

[4] Cordes, C.L. and Dougherty, T.W. (1993). A review and an integration of research on job burnout. Academy of Management Review, Vol. 18, No. 4, pp. 621–656.

[5] De-Juanas, Á., Bernal Romero, T. and Goig, R. (2020). The Relationship between Psychological well-being and Autonomy in Young People According to Age. Front. Psychol. 11:559976. doi: 10.3389/fpsyg.2020. 559976

[6] Dhanabhakyam, M. and Sarath, M. (2022). Impact of Occupational Stress on Job Satisfaction and Psychological Wellbeing. *International Journal of Advanced Research in Science, Communication and Technology (IJARSCT)*, 270–275.

[7] Lubbadeh, Tareq (2020). Job Burnout: A General Literature Review. *International Review of Management and Marketing,* 10. 7–15. 10.32479/irmm.9398.

[8] Dhanabhakyam, M. and Sarath, M. (2023). Psychological Wellbeing: A systematic Literature Review, 603–607. 10.48175/IJARSCT-8345.

[9] Malek, M.D., Kamil, I.M. and Fahrudin, A. (2009). A cross-cultural study of psychological wellbeing among British and Malaysian Firefighters. Asian school work and policy review, 143–154. Retrieved from doi:10.1111/j.1753- 1411.2009.00030.x

[10] Oyku. O., Zepeda, S., Iigan, A., Jimenez, A.M., Ata, A. and Akram, M. (2017). Teachers psychological wellbeing: A comparison among teachers in U.S.A, Turkey and Pakistan. *International journal of mental health promotion*, 19(3), 144–158.

[11] Seligman, M.E.P. (2002). Positive psychology, positive prevention, and positive therapy. In

[12] Dhanabhakyam, C.R., M., and Sarath, M. (2022). Impact of Occupational Stress on Job Satisfaction.

[13] Suleman, Q., Hussain, I. and Jumani, N.B. (2018). Occupational stress among the secondary school heads A gender-based comparative study. *Journal of education and educational development,* 5(2), 240–258.

[14] World Health Organization (2021). Mental Health. Retrieved from https://www.who.int/health- topics/mental-health/#tab=tab https://en.wikipedia.org/wiki/Sixfactor_model_of_psychological_wellbeing#:~:text=Psychological%20well%2Dbeing%20consists%20of, and%20personal%20growth%20and%20development

# Relationship between Product Differentiation and Brand Equity

T.D. Hemamalini[1] and M. Kamaraj[2]

[1]Ph.D. Research Scholar, Department of Business Administration, Annamalai University, Annamalai Nagar, Chidambaram, Tamil Nadu, India

[2]Associate Professor, Department of Business Administration, Annamalai University, Annamalai Nagar, Chidambaram, Tamil Nadu, India

***ABSTRACT:*** *In today's fiercely competitive market, creating a distinctive product that stands out from the crowd is essential for building a strong brand. Product differentiation lies at the heart of attracting customers, gaining their loyalty, and ultimately, maximizing brand equity. Product differentiation refers to the process of highlighting the unique features and benefits of a product or service that distinguishes it from competitors. It involves creating a perception of value, superiority, and innovation in the minds of target consumers. Brand equity represents the intangible value and strength that a brand possesses. It encompasses the positive associations, perceived quality, and emotional connection established with consumers over time. Product differentiation is instrumental in driving brand equity by creating a unique position in the marketplace. The purpose of this study is to understand the relationship between product differentiation and brand equity. Sample size was 272 laptop users of Tiruchirappalli City. Data were gathered and analyzed through correlation to test relationship between the study variable. It was concluded that increased deployment of product differentiation dimensions will lead to brand equity of laptop market.*

**Keywords:** Brand Equity, Product Differentiation, Product Price, Product Quality.

## 1. INTRODUCTION

Product differentiation is the key to unlocking brand equity. By analyzing the market, identifying consumer needs, and highlighting unique selling proposition, organizations position their brand as a frontrunner in the marketplace. Pairing superior quality with a compelling brand story and fostering an engaged community further strengthens brand equity. Companies and manufacturers must concentrate on products that are launched well in the market. The company must deal well with existing competitors, and handle and manage customers, both existing customers and potential customers. The more variety of product choices, it makes customers more selective in choosing products. In other way it will say that, customers will look for products with better value than competing products. By noting that the current competition is getting tougher, it is a must that the company must adopt a strategy to make customers more engaged, and more loyal to the company. So based on the explanation above, the purpose of this research is to increase and brand equity through the implementation of strategies to improve product differentiation, and sharpen loyalty from customers and expected to increase revenue of the company.

Farquhar (1989) defined brand equity is the added value endowed by the brand to the product. To maintain a competitive edge, it's crucial to continuously innovate and adapt to changing market dynamics. Monitor trends, anticipate customer needs, and proactively introduce new features or product variations to stay ahead of the curve. By demonstrating a commitment to innovation and staying relevant, organizations strengthen product differentiation and sustain brand equity over the long term. With continuous innovation and adaptation, brand can carve out a lasting presence, capturing the hearts and minds of consumers. Embrace differentiation; unleash brand's potential, and turbocharger success. A differentiated product is unique by itself. Philip Kotler defined product differentiation is the act of designing a set of meaningful differences to distinguish the company's products from competitors' products as well as the company's own services .In today's world there has been an extraordinary competition between countries, products, and even among the brands themselves.

## 2. REVIEW OF LITERATURE

Yue and Chanchai (2023) investigated the influence of marketing mix strategy on brand equity enhancement of Chinese dried forest fruit brands based on customer mind model. The objective of the research aimed to study the influence of a marketing mix strategy on brand equity enhancement (brand loyalty) among Chinese dried forest fruit brands, brand utility as a mediator of the relationship between the marketing mix and brand equity enhancement (brand awareness, brand association, perceived quality and perceived value), and the effect of brand equity dimensions on the willingness of customers to pay a price premium. This study gathers responses from a sample of 480 consumers, with Structural Equation Modeling (SEM) being employed to analyze the data. The results showed that product, promotion and place had positive impacts on both brand utility and brand equity dimensions. The research also revealed that brand utility positively impacts both brand value dimensions and brand loyalty, serving as an intermediary for the association between the marketing mix (product, place) and brand loyalty. Finally, the study concluded that both brand equity dimensions and brand equity enhancement positively influence customers' willingness to pay a price premium.

Nwe Ni Aye (2022) examined the effect of marketing practices on brand equity and consumer buying behavior of bossini fashion products. The specific objectives of this study are to examine the effect of marketing practices on brand equity and to analyze the effect of brand equity on customer buying behavior of Bossini fashion products in Yangon. The structured questionnaire is used to collect primary data. Data were analyzed through Descriptive statistics and regression analysis. According to the analysis, product quality, perceived value and customer communication have positive and significant effect on brand equity. It is also found that among the four elements of brand equity has positive and significant effect on buying behavior. This study suggests that Bossini brand must be keep product quality, perceived value and customer communication to build brand equity and thereby, it can lead to encourage buying behavior of customer on Bossini fashion products.

Wahyuni *et al.* (2019) studied the role of brand equity in influencing rural bank depositors. This study evaluates the elements of brand equity used by rural banks. The study used sample size of 61. The study adopted structural equation modelling for analysis. The study found that affected rural bank depositors on brand loyalty were perceived quality. This research cannot explain the influence of trust, brand awareness and brand association on brand loyalty. The study concluded that the role of perceived quality in influencing brand loyalty is high, and rural banks have not maximized the use of other elements in brand equity in their business activities.

Nedka and Mariana (2015) examined the opportunities for increasing brand equity by applying the concept of product differentiation. The main objective of the paper was a theoretical systematization of the possibilities for increasing brand equity by applying the concept of product differentiation. The study concluded that to create a sustainable competitive advantage, a brand and its products must be well differentiated, and marketing must reflect and enhance that differentiation. Brands with well differentiated products set the trends for their category or transcend it; they act differently and stand out from their competition.

Murtiasih (2013) examined how word of mouth influence brand equity for automotive products in Indonesia. The study sample size was 214. Structural equation modelling was used for analytical purpose. The study results indicated that positive information through WOM increases brand awareness, brand associations, perceived quality and brand loyalty. The study findings concluded that positive WOM helps companies to build strong brand equity. But management should be aware of WOM diffusion as it could be in negative or positive, especially on internet. Satisfied customers theoretically distribute positive WOM, but dissatisfy customer on the reverse will diffuse negative WOM.

Mosarrat (2012) investigated brand elements lead to brand equity: differentiate or die. The methodology adopted was relevant research reviews (Secondary Data) for analysis. The study concluded that brand is a mental game where each element tells a story about the brand itself and these stories are destined together to a single goal to draw a distinct image in the consumer's mind. Differentiation is an inevitable part of the brand management, which can be done by positioning and integrated marketing communication

Shahram (2011) studied impact of selected marketing elements on strategic brand management for improving brand equity. The sample size of study was 424. The analytical methodology used was structural equations modelling. The study concluded that different marketing mix elements impact the creation of brand equity with different levels of intensity, as well as that some elements of marketing mix can negatively affect the creation of brand equity. Furthermore, the research results indicate that managers, in their efforts to build the equity of the brands they are managing, should primarily focus on the creation of brand awareness and a positive brand image.

Goi and Fayrene (2011) studied dimensions of customer-based brand equity: a study on Malaysian brands. The study sample size was 489. The analytical methodology adopted was Cronbach's alpha, factor analysis and correlation. The study concluded that conceptualizing brand equity from the consumer's perspective is useful because it suggests both specific guidelines for marketing strategies and tactics and areas where research can be useful in assisting managerial decision making. Two important points emerge from this conceptualization. Primarily marketers should consider a broad view of marketing activity for a brand and recognize the various effects on its brand knowledge and the same time how changes in brand knowledge affect more traditional outcome measures such as sales. Second, markets must realize that the long-term success of all future marketing programs for a brand is affected by the knowledge about the brand in memory that has been established by the firm's short-term marketing efforts.

Tanmay (2010) examined marketing mix elements influencing brand equity and brand choice. The sample size of study was 302.Structural Equation Model was adopted by the study for analysis. The study found that for any economy, brand consumers price, distribution intensity, celebrity endorsement, event sponsorship, non-price promotion, WOM and country-of-origin of the brand are important parameters. The study concluded that perceived pricing efforts may create illusive reflections on brand equity, distinct from the actual pricing efforts.

Xiao and Jana (2009) studied measuring customer-based brand equity: empirical evidence from the sportswear market in china. This study seeks to examine the practicality and applications of a customer-based brand equity model in the Chinese sportswear market. The study sample size was 304. Structural equation modelling was used by study for analytical purpose. The study found that brand association and brand loyalty are influential dimensions of brand equity. The study concluded that when concentrating on creating brand association and brand loyalty, managers should not undervalue the effects of perceived quality and brand awareness.

## 3. STATEMENT OF THE PROBLEM

Several studies have been conducted world-wide on investigating the product differentiation traits and their effect on brand equity. Product differentiation is the specific way that one organization's products can be identified from another organization's products or services in a business. This helps in adding dedicated customers and generates brand equity. Brand equity shows "Customers willingness to pay a premium price for the brand and/or willingness to continue to purchase" (Ambler, 2008).Though the concept of Product differentiation traits have been considered as essential antecedents of Brand Equity. Studies on relationship between Product differentiation and Brand equity were found very few in literature. Brand equity can be improved and promoted through product differentiation. So, the researchers investigate relationship between product differentiation and brand equity.

## 4. CONCEPTUAL FRAMEWORK OF THE STUDY

The present study is aimed to investigate the relationship between Product Differentiation and Brand Equity. Hence, the researcher has designed this following frame work to study the relationship between Product Differentiation and Brand Equity.

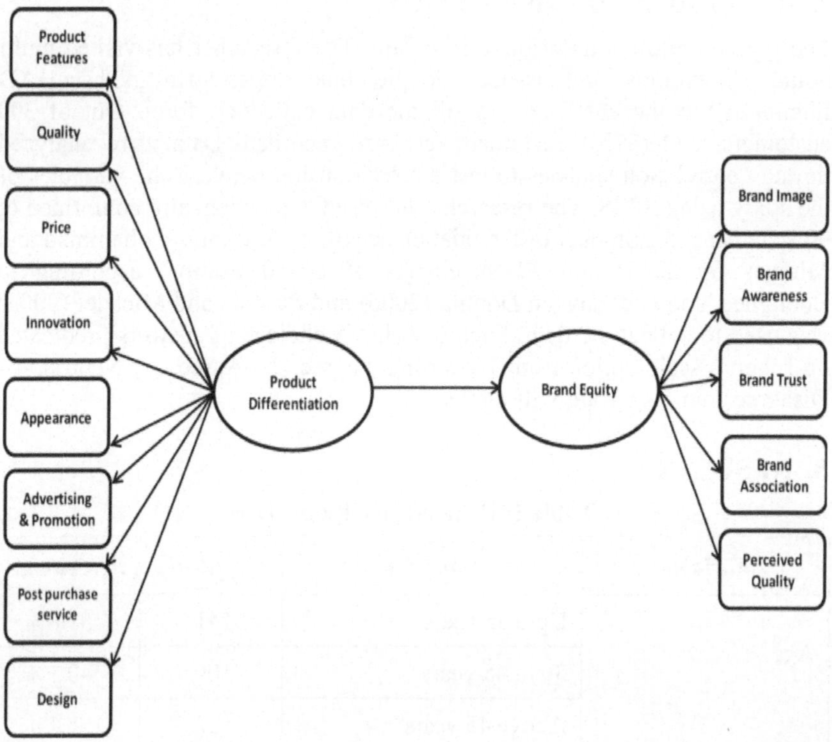

## 5. SCOPE OF THE STUDY

The present study is aimed to investigate the relationship between Product differentiation and Brand equity. Product differentiation is independent variable and Brand equity is dependent variable. The present study is undertaken in various brand Laptop users of Tiruchirappalli City. The commoditization of laptop industry has created a big challenge for marketers to survive in market. They need to find out the purchasing criteria set by the customers on which they are making decisions. Any laptop company can increase the sales by increasing brand valuation that is brand equity. Hence, the researcher intended to know the relationship between Product differentiation and Brand equity.

## 6. OBJECTIVE OF THE STUDY

The objective of the study is to find out the relationship between the Product Differentiation dimensions and Brand Equity.

### 6.1 Hypothesis of the Study

Product differentiation dimensions have significant positive relationship with Brand Equity.

## 7. RESEARCH METHODOLOGY

The type of study is descriptive in nature. The researcher has visited multi brand showrooms and issued Google link https://forms.gle/hseqHAD fihcninAy9 to the customers to fill the data collection form. Out of 300 customers, 272 (91%) customers response recorded. Data were analyzed through correlation analysis to test the relationship between the variables of the study using SPSS. The researcher has used a questionnaire conformed of 90 statements for product differentiation according to (Amin mohammad and Mingya Gu 2013) and 37 statements of Brand Equity according to Boonghee Yoo and Naveen Donthu (2000) and Particia and Michael (2003) was used to collect the data. Each item has 5 choices of answers predicated on Likert's scale option from 1 - Strongly agree, 2 - Agree, 3 - Neutral, 4 - Disagree, and 5 - Strongly disagree.

## 8. RESULTS

**Table 1:** Demographic Profile Data

| *Variable* | *Category* | *Frequency* | *Percentage* |
|---|---|---|---|
| Age | Upto 35 years | 141 | 51.8% |
| | 36 to 45 years | 109 | 40.1% |
| | Above 45 years | 22 | 8.1% |

| *Variable* | *Category* | *Frequency* | *Percentage* |
|---|---|---|---|
| Gender | Female | 101 | 37.1% |
| | Male | 171 | 62.9% |
| Marital Status | Married | 191 | 70.2% |
| | Unmarried | 81 | 29.8% |
| Educational Qualification | Graduate | 129 | 47.4% |
| | Post Graduate | 54 | 19.9% |
| | Professional Course | 41 | 15.1% |
| | School level / Diploma | 48 | 17.6% |
| Occupation | Government Employee | 32 | 11.8% |
| | Home maker | 12 | 4.4% |
| | Own business | 27 | 9.9% |
| | Private Employee | 149 | 54.8% |
| | Student | 52 | 19.1% |
| Monthly Income | Upto 20000 | 77 | 28.3% |
| | 20001 to 35000 | 63 | 23.2% |
| | 35001 to 75000 | 73 | 26.8% |
| | Above 75000 | 59 | 21.7% |
| Family Type | Joint | 120 | 44.1% |
| | Nuclear | 152 | 55.9% |
| **Total** | | **272** | **100.0%** |

Table I explains the distribution of respondents. Majority of the respondents in age variable 51.8% is from "Up to 35 years", in Gender variable 62.9% is from "Male", 37.1% is from "Female", in Marital Status variable 70.2% is from "Married", in Educational Qualification variable 47.4% is from "Graduate", in Occupation variable 54.8% is from "Private employees", in Monthly income variable 28.3% is from "Up to Rs.20,000", in Family type variable 55.9% is from "Nuclear family".

**Table 2**

| WEIGHTED SUM & ITS PERCENTAGE CONTRIBUTION | | | | | | | | |
|---|---|---|---|---|---|---|---|---|
| **Brand** | **Innovation** | **Quality** | **Design** | **Post Purchase Service** | **Price** | **Advert & Promotion** | **Appearance** | **Features** |
| Acer | 1944 / 15.0% | 1100 / 17.0% | 646 / 12.0% | 866 / 10.4% | 501 / 12.0% | 640 / 14.8% | 800 / 18.9% | 461 / 10.7% |
| Apple | 4278 / 33.0% | 1876 / 29.0% | 1669 / 31.0% | 1499 / 18.0% | 460 / 11.0% | 779 / 18.0% | 728 / 17.2% | 992 / 23.0% |
| Asus | 736 / 5.7% | 776 / 12.0% | 592 / 11.0% | 850 / 10.2% | 235 / 5.6% | 446 / 10.3% | 690 / 16.3% | 741 / 17.2% |
| Dell | 2243 / 17.3% | 970 / 15.0% | 770 / 14.3% | 2082 / 25.0% | 710 / 17.0% | 498 / 11.5% | 542 / 12.8% | 754 / 17.5% |
| HP | 1633 / 12.6% | 841 / 13.0% | 539 / 10.0% | 1249 / 15.0% | 815 / 19.5% | 1112 / 25.7% | 571 / 13.5% | 582 / 13.5% |
| Lenovo | 1867 / 14.4% | 647 / 10.0% | 845 / 15.7% | 1541 / 18.5% | 1333 / 31.8% | 762 / 17.6% | 665 / 15.7% | 681 / 15.8% |
| Others | 262 / 2.0% | 259 / 4.0% | 323 / 6.0% | 242 / 2.9% | 134 / 3.2% | 90 / 2.1% | 237 / 5.6% | 99 / 2.3% |
| Grand Total | **12963 / 100%** | **6468 / 100.0%** | **5385 / 100.0%** | **8329 / 100.0%** | **4188 / 100.0%** | **4326 / 100.0%** | **4233 / 100.0%** | **4311 / 100.0%** |

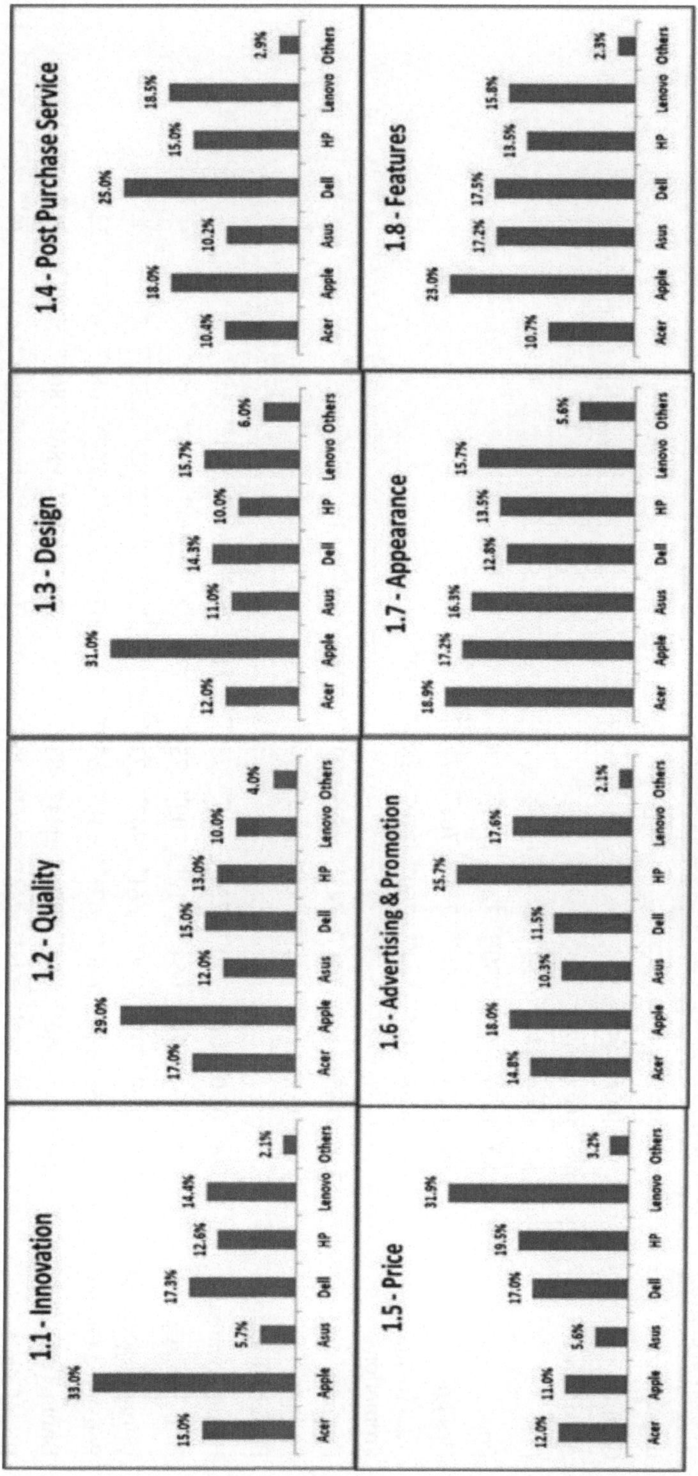
1.1 - Innovation
15.0% 33.0% 5.7% 17.3% 12.6% 14.4% 2.1%
Acer Apple Asus Dell HP Lenovo Others
1.2 - Quality
17.0% 29.0% 12.0% 15.0% 13.0% 10.0% 4.0%
Acer Apple Asus Dell HP Lenovo Others
1.3 - Design
12.0% 31.0% 11.0% 14.3% 10.0% 15.7% 6.0%
Acer Apple Asus Dell HP Lenovo Others
1.4 - Post Purchase Service
10.4% 18.0% 10.2% 25.0% 15.0% 18.5% 2.9%
Acer Apple Asus Dell HP Lenovo Others
1.5 - Price
12.0% 11.0% 5.6% 17.0% 19.5% 31.9% 3.2%
Acer Apple Asus Dell HP Lenovo Others
1.6 - Advertising & Promotion
14.8% 18.0% 10.3% 11.5% 25.7% 17.6% 2.1%
Acer Apple Asus Dell HP Lenovo Others
1.7 - Appearance
18.9% 17.2% 16.3% 12.8% 13.5% 15.7% 5.6%
Acer Apple Asus Dell HP Lenovo Others
1.8 - Features
10.7% 23.0% 17.2% 17.5% 13.5% 15.8% 2.3%
Acer Apple Asus Dell HP Lenovo Others

**Figure 1.1–1.8**

**Table 3:** Descriptive Statistics and Correlations between the Study Variables

| *Variables* | *Mean* | *S.D* | *1* | *2* | *3* | *4* | *5* | *6* | *7* | *8* | *9* | *10* | *11* | *12* | *13* | *14* | *15* |
|---|---|---|---|---|---|---|---|---|---|---|---|---|---|---|---|---|---|
| Innovation | 4.00 | 0.59 | 1 | | | | | | | | | | | | | | |
| Quality | 3.98 | 0.65 | .696** | 1 | | | | | | | | | | | | | |
| Appearance | 3.98 | 0.67 | .698** | .783** | 1 | | | | | | | | | | | | |
| PPS | 3.87 | 0.64 | .679** | .754** | .784** | 1 | | | | | | | | | | | |
| Price | 3.89 | 0.70 | .679** | .730** | .721** | .787** | 1 | | | | | | | | | | |
| Design | 3.99 | 0.64 | .677** | .716** | .748** | .761** | .791** | 1 | | | | | | | | | |
| Advertising & Promotion | 3.92 | 0.68 | .711** | .744** | .760** | .770** | .787** | .780** | 1 | | | | | | | | |
| Features | 3.98 | 0.65 | .645** | .741** | .743** | .758** | .771** | .778** | .778** | 1 | | | | | | | |
| Product Differentiation | 3.95 | 0.58 | .817** | .876** | .887** | .894** | .893** | .888** | .900** | .884** | 1 | | | | | | |
| Brand Awareness | 3.96 | 0.70 | .661** | .750** | .726** | .691** | .733** | .694** | .753** | .769** | .821** | 1 | | | | | |
| Brand Image | 3.88 | 0.74 | .661** | .664** | .712** | .709** | .731** | .737** | .727** | .790** | .814** | .727** | 1 | | | | |
| Brand Association | 3.93 | 0.69 | .701** | .709** | .661** | .743** | .726** | .717** | .736** | .813** | .824** | .766** | .767** | 1 | | | |
| Perceived Quality | 3.98 | 0.66 | .684** | .640** | .631** | .638** | .659** | .719** | .676** | .728** | .762** | .681** | .680** | .752** | 1 | | |
| Brand Trust | 3.94 | 0.58 | .840** | .895** | .901** | .904** | .889** | .835** | .852** | .828** | .986** | .805** | .786** | .798** | .733** | 1 | |
| Brand equity | 3.94 | 0.62 | .757** | .774** | .766** | .780** | .799** | .803** | .810** | .869** | .903** | .890** | .894** | .920** | .867** | .875** | 1 |

**- Correlation is significant at the 0.01 level.

Figures 1.1, 1.2, 1.3, 1.8 explains that Apple brand dominates out of other brands in Innovation, Quality, Design and Features dimensions and contributes 33%, 29%, 31% and 23% respectively. Figure 1.4 depicts that in "Post Purchase Service" dimension, Dell brand is topping with 25% weighted sum contribution. Figure 1.5 details that Lenovo brand demonstrates high weighted sum contribution with 31.9%in "Price" dimension. Figure 1.6 exhibits that HP brand contributes higher weighted sum with 25.7% in "Advertising & Promotion" dimension. Figure 1.7 shows that Acer brand contributes with 18.9% higher weighted sum in "Appearance" dimension.

## 9. FINDINGS

It is understood from the results of descriptive analysis that product differentiation dimensions namely, Innovation (mean=4.00; S.D. =0.59) and Design (mean=3.99; S.D. =0.64) are found to be higher than other traits. Quality (mean =3.98;S.D.=065),Appearance (mean=3.98;S.D.=0.67) and Features (mean=3.98;S.D.=0.65) are found to be higher for Advertising and Promotion (mean=3.92,S.D.=068),Price (mean=3.89;S.D.=0.70) and Post Purchase Service (mean=3.87;S.D.=0.64).

Innovation has significant correlation at the 0.01 level with the factors namely, Brand Awareness (r=0.661), Brand Image (r=0.661), Brand Association (r=0.701), Perceived quality (r=0.684), Brand Image (r=0.840) and Brand Equity (r=0.757). Quality has significant correlation at the 0.01 level with the other factors namely, Brand Awareness (r=0.750), Brand Image (r=0.664), Brand Association (r=0.709), Perceived quality (r=0.640), Brand Image (r=0.895) and Brand Equity (r=0.774). Appearance has significant correlation at the 0.01 level with the other factors namely, Brand Awareness (r=0.726), Brand Image (r=0.712), Brand Association (r=0.661), Perceived quality (r=0.631), Brand Image (r=0.901) and Brand Equity (r=0.766). Post purchase service has significant correlation at the 0.01 level with the other factors namely, Brand Awareness (r=0.691), Brand Image (r=0.709), Brand Association (r=0.743), Perceived quality (r=0.638), Brand Image (r=0.904) and Brand Equity (r=0.780). Price has significant correlation at the 0.01 level with the other factors namely, Brand Awareness (r=0.733), Brand Image (r=0.731), Brand Association (r=0.726), Perceived quality (r=0.659), Brand Image (r=0.889) and Brand Equity (r=0.799). Design has significant correlation at the 0.01 level with the other factors namely, Brand Awareness (r=0.694), Brand Image (r=0.737), Brand Association (r=0.717), Perceived quality (r=0.719), Brand Image (r=0.835) and Brand Equity (r=0.803). Advertising and Promotion has significant correlation at the 0.01 level with the other factors namely, Brand Awareness (r=0.753), Brand Image (r=0.727), Brand Association (r=0.736), Perceived quality (r=0.676), Brand Image (r=0.852) and Brand Equity (r=0.810). Features has significant correlation at the 0.01 level with the other factors namely, Brand Awareness (r=0.769), Brand Image (r=0.790), Brand Association (r=0.813), Perceived quality (r=0.728), Brand Image (r=0.828) and Brand Equity (r=0.869).

## 10. DISCUSSIONS

In the previous studies undertaken by the researchers Nedka and Mariana (2015), Nwe Ni Aye (2022), Abu-Aliqah (2012), Felly (2015), Murtisih (2013), Goi and Fayrane (2011), Murain (2020) are similar with the findings of the present study. In this study it is observed that hypothesis of all direct connections are supported by findings.

Product differentiation has positive and significant relationship with brand equity, which indicated that when customers are communicated well about the product differentiation dimensions, it produce brand equity. It is observed that true customers will continue to buy and support the brand. Likewise, they will produce a good carriage and feeling because it is delegate to imagine disappointed customers having a positive carriage toward the companies.

## 11. MANAGERIAL IMPLICATIONS

This study provides valuable implications for marketing people. In a practical context, Marketing people can use the findings of this study to see their strengths and weaknesses of their product differentiation dimensions and can improve their performance accordingly at the local market level. Marketing people must concentrate on developing product differentiation strategies that must successfully make loyal customers and it will lead to brand equity. From this study it can be understood that, how important is product differentiation in getting desired marketing output that is brand equity.

## 12. LIMITATIONS AND RECOMMENTATIONS FOR FUTURE RESEARCH

First this study does not cover in-depth the relationship between demographic variables and study variables. Secondly, this study was focused on Tiruchirappalli district and additional research is necessary to generalize the relationship between variables to other areas. Thirdly, population of this study represented a fairly homogeneous group of individuals in terms of both cultural and ethnic diversity in this case additional research is needed to determine if the findings can be generalized to across cultural and racial boundaries. Finally, the sample size for this study was relatively small (n = 272); future, large-scale research will be instrumental in determining whether these findings can be replicated. To conclude, this research has solely examined the relationship of product differentiation to brand equity.

## 13. CONCLUSIONS

Product differentiation is one of the important factors that affect brand equity in numerous aspects. Present study showed that product differentiation has positive relationship with brand equity. Brand Equity is ultimate result that an organization wants its customers to attain, which will be influenced by product differentiation. Thus institutions must try to achieve brand equity by preciously designing their product differentiation features like, styles, quality, shape, appearance and other factors get affected directly and in directly. Eventually, it is proposed that there is a considerable relationship between brand equity and product differentiation.

## REFERENCES

[1] NedkaNikolova and MarianaMurzova (2015). "Opportunities for increasing brand Equity by applying the concept of product differentiation", Volume 2, Issue 6, June 2015, pp. 64–70 ISSN 2349-4751 (Print) & ISSN 2349-476X (Online).

[2] Nebojsa, S. Davcik and Piyush, Sharma (2015). "Impact of product differentiation, Marketing and brand investments equity on pricing strategies—A brand level investigation", *European Journal of Marketing* 49(5/6):760 -78.DOI:10.1108 / EJM-03-2014-0150 7(1): 1 - 24 DOI: 10.4018 / ijmhci.2015010101.

[3] Chin-Lung, Hsu and Judy, Chuan-Chuan Lin (2015). "An Empirical Study of Smartphone User Behavior: The effect of Innovation Characteristics, Brand Equity and Social Influence", *International Journal of Mobile Human Computer Interaction (IJMHCI),* IGI Global, Vol. 7(1), pp. 1–24, January.

[4] Mosarrat, Farhana (2012). "Brand elements lead to brand equity: differentiate or Die", *Information Management and Business Review,* 4(4):223-233 DOI: 10.22610/imbr.v4i4.983

[5] Wei-Tsong, Wang and Hui-Min, Li (2012). "Factors influencing mobile services Adoption: A brand-equity perspective", *Internet Research,* 22(2) DOI: 10.1108/10662241211214548.

[6] Shahram, Gilani nia; Kambiz, Shahroudi; Naser, Pahlevanzadeh and Seyed, JavadMousavian, (2011). "Impact of selected marketing elements on strategic brand management for improving brand equity", *Journal of Basic and Applied Scientific Research,* ISSN 2090-424X .

[7] Goi, Chai Lee and Fayrene, Chieng Yew Leh (2011). "Dimensions of customer-Based brand equity: A study on Malaysian brands", *Journal of Marketing Research and Case Studies,* http://www.ibimapublishing.com/journals/JMRCS/jmrcs.html Vol.2011 (2011), Article ID 821981, 10 pages DOI: 10.5171 / 2011.821981

[8] Tanmay, Chattopadhyay; Shraddha, Shivani and Mahesh, Krishnan (2011). "Marketing mix elements influencing brand equity and brand choice", *Vikalpa 35(3), DOI: 10.1177 / 0256090920100305.*

[9] Xiao Tong Jana M. Hawley (2009), "Measuring customer-based brand equity: Empirical evidence from the sportswear market in China", *Journal of Product and Brand Management,* ISSN: 1061-0421.

[10] Boonghee, Yoo Naveen Donthu Sungho Lee (2008). "An examination of selected Marketing mix elements and brand equity". *Journal of the Academy of Marketing Science,* Volume 28, Article number: 195 (2000).

[11] Ravi, Pappu; Pascale, G. Quester and Ray, W. Cooksey (2005). "Consumer-based Brand equity: improving the measurement—empirical evidence". *Journal of Product and Brand Management,* ISSN: 1061-0421.

[12] Chris, A. Myers (2003). "Managing brand equity: a look at the impact of Attributes". Journal of Product & Brand Management 12(1):39–51 DOI: 10.1108/10610420310463126

[13] Eda, Atilgan; Safak, Aksoy and Serkan, Akinci (2005). "Determinants of the brand Equity: a verification approach in the beverage industry turkey". *Marketing Intelligence and planning*, ISSN-0263-4503.

[14] Yue, Huang and Chanchai, Bunchapattanasakda (2023). "Influence of marketing mix strategy on brand equity Enhancement of Chinese dried forest fruit brands based on customer mind model". *ABAC Journal,* Vol. 43, No. 4 (October-December 2023, pp. 318–339).

[15] New, Ni Aye (2022). "The Effect of Marketing Practices on Brand Equity and Consumer Buying Behavior of Bossini Fashion Products", MBA Thesis, Yangon University of Economics.

# Management

# Consumers' Perceived Risk to Visit Restaurants: A Perspective from Theory of Planned Behaviour

**Prachi Patil**
Assistant Professor Dr. Ambedkar Institute of Management Studies and Research, Nagpur

***ABSTRACT:*** *The COVID-19 pandemic has considerably impacted various sectors across India, including restaurant and tourism. To curb the spread of coronavirus, travel restrictions, lockdowns, and social distancing have become the norm of the society. This study investigates consumer's intention to visit restaurants during the pandemic period. This study tries to explore the impact of factors like affordability, revenge dining, consumers risk & perception, and the attitude that has guided the Indian consumer's intention to visit restaurants during the pandemic. A detailed questionnaire is developed using Likert scale. 440 responses have been collected from different locations of Maharashtra, India. The data is collated through random sampling to understand the consumer's intention of visiting restaurants. The study was undertaken to analyse the factors which guides the consumer behaviour towards visiting restaurant during pandemic. The finding of the study reveals that brand trust, revenge dining and covid risk perception influence the consumer's intention to visit the restaurant. The study concludes that brand trust influences consumers to visit the restaurants rather than covid risk and perception.*

**Keywords:** Brand India, Consumers, Covid Pandemic, Food, Hospitality, Restaurants, Revenge Dining.

## 1. INTRODUCTION

Covid 19 pandemic has wrecked the progression made by humankind and has caused severe impairment to the communal and economic life of people across the globe. (Mandala, G.N. (2022)). The year 2020 will be etched in the minds of many generations to come as the year that was worst hit by the Covid-19 Pandemic, which eventually changed the whole diaspora of global economy. The service sector was the most affected sector. In the wake of the pandemic, many countries implemented various remedial measures like lockdowns, social distancing, home quarantine, and precautionary measures like use of masks and sanitizers in each city, to reduce the transmission of deadly coronavirus. The series of lockdowns and restrictions imposed in the cities, human deployment remained primarily affected and rendered the hotels and restaurants with zero footfall (Song *et al.*, 2021). The pandemic transformed people's lives and created mayhem in national and international trade that witnessed a decline in tourism and restaurant businesses, bringing them to a trembling end. Countless restaurants were compelled to briefly shut down or restrict themselves to takeaway options and order food online due to the lockdown announced by the government or constraints on mobility to curtail the spate of infection (Gursoy & Chi, 2020). On 11$^{th}$ March 2020, WHO pronounced Covid-19 as a Pandemic. Many restaurants were already running at 10–20% less capacity in terms of customer footfall in comparison to previous years. This mighty announcement by WHO further hindered customers' mind-sets about dining out (Dube *et al.*, 2020). The ordeal did not end there. To control operating expenses, almost about 10,000 restaurants in U.S were forced to shut down, rendering 3 million employees jobless (National Restaurant Association, 2020).

Many countries started imposing curbs on travel and indoor dining, and thus started facing a shortage of labour, and as a result, there was a downfall in customer footfalls. This also instilled fear in the customers' minds about the virus's transmission from the restaurant staff. Hence, many restaurants switched to takeaways and online deliveries. In the wake of these concerns, many restaurants reformed their safety and health measures to control the virus's rapid spread and hence, encouraged customers to visit restaurants (Seyitoğlu & Ivanov, 2020). The hospitality sector was the worst hit due to the pandemic. A number of government imposed restrictions were in place to prevent the disease from spreading further. The hospitality industry was the primary target of the pandemic. Travel restrictions resulted in reduction of the number of persons venturing out of their homes, leading to a sudden drop in occupancy rates of the hotels. Many restaurant staffs were laid off on account of less or no business. Eight million people were rendered jobless in the restaurant industry alone. (National Restaurant Association, 2020.) After the slowdown of the risk posed by the coronavirus in June 2020, maximum states started permitting restaurants to reopen with restrictions such as limited sitting capacity, no mask no entry policy, limitation on the number of people attending a party or get-together, and norms for maintaining stringent social distancing in restaurants. These constraints have changed the mindsets of customers and they are less like to visit restaurants even now. Researches show that over 50% of the population is not in favor of dinning out anymore (Gursoy *et al.*, 2020).

## 2. LITERATURE REVIEW

Very often, people find it challenging to get involved with others in any sort of social or physical communication; covid has worsened this situation and has forced people to stay indoors and adapt to a new normal. Restaurants and the hospitality industry are considered among the vital socio-economic support systems of any economy, as they play a crucial role in revenue generation, and the pandemic caused devastating effect on them (Dube *et al.*,

2020). Hence, it is imperative to understand and study the menace that COVID-19 has created in terms of the behaviours and intentions of people in dining out. In certain cities, where the impact of the pandemic was very catastrophic, many people lost their near and dear ones and in some cases, whole families too. It created fear in people's minds, and hence they preferred to venture out of the house, only in case of dire necessity. People's hesitancy to meet each other has affected the communal upbringing and social value system of the societies at large (Bilge and Bilge, 2020). By implementing various safety and health protocols, restaurant owners have encouraged customers to visit the restaurants. It may also lead to a positive attitude in the customers' minds about that particular restaurant. Ponnam and Balaji (2014) indicated that the packaging of food, adherence to the safety protocols, educating the restaurant staff on the safety measures, and undertaking the necessary precautions can impact customers' perception regarding casual dining. Dedeoglu (2022) & Bogan (2021) in their study conducted in Turkey found that trust plays a moderating role in government and risk perception of dining out. Goyal & Verma (2021) revealed that perceived economic wellbeing, knowledge about covid19 and self-efficacy influenced the consumer perception for consumption. Lakshmi *et al.* (2020) in their study found that concern about hygiene, food safety and convenience offered by food service providers affect the consumer attitude towards outside dining. Pradana *et al.* (2021) revealed that brand name of restaurants, perceived risk and safety and comfort offered by food service providers influence the consumer perception for outside dining. Patra (2020) highlighted about change in consumer attitude towards consumption post covid era and its effect on tourism and hospitality sector.

**Table 1:** Meta Data

| ***Author/'s*** | ***Methodology*** | ***Study Area*** | ***Factors Identified*** |
|---|---|---|---|
| Dedeoglu BB2022, Bogan 2021 | Multifactorial consideration | Turkey | Moderating role of trust in government and risk perception |
| Goyal A., Verma P.*, 2021 | Online Survey, structural equation modelling (SEM) | India | Perceived economic well-being; knowledge about Covid-19, self-efficacy |
| Ms. Sainaz Sardar | Case Study methodology | India | Marketing strategies; Covid-19; pandemic; lockdown |
| Lakshmi B. *M et al.*, 2020 | Structured questionnaire and secondary data | India | Hygiene and safety; food services aggregators; operations |
| Pradana *et al.*, 2021 | Partial Least Squares SEM (PLS-SEM) with the help of Smart PLS3 software | Indonesia | Health Scrutiny Trust; perceived risk and safety and brand name of the restaurant; cohesion with The Food Services |

| *Author/'s* | *Methodology* | *Study Area* | *Factors Identified* |
|---|---|---|---|
| Dube, Nhamo & Chikodzi, 2021 | Qualitative Analysis | South Africa | Hospitality industry; COVID19; restaurants; tourism industry; coronavirus |
| Hoang T. & Suleri J., 2021 | Statistical Package for the Social Sciences (SPSS), Correlation and Regression | Netherlands | customer satisfaction, customer loyalty, customer behavior during COVID-19 |
| Memon, *et al.*, 2021 | Quantitative & qualitative methodologies | China and India | Sustainable supply chain; |
| Patra N., 2020 | Demographic survey | India | Tourism and hospitality; post-epidemic, behavior change in consumers |
| Vig s *et al.*, 2021 | Qualitative analysis | India | Innovation; challenges for the small restaurant entrepreneurs; new trends in restaurant entrepreneurship |

## 3. METHODS

In this paper, authors have focussed on the factors that affect the customers' intentions (1) to visit the restaurants (2) order food online'. A theoretical model has been developed by drawing inferences from the Theory of Planned Behavior (TPB) Model, to study the factors responsible for determining consumer intention. Through this study, an attempt has been made to answer the below mentioned research questions under the various factors considered for the Indian market, with 'Attitude' as a mediating variable.

1. Does the restaurants' brand affect the customers' attitude to visit restaurants during the pandemic?
2. Does revenge dining impact the attitude of customers visiting restaurants during the pandemic?
3. How the pandemic has affected the restaurant sector in terms of customers' intentions and attitudes toward visiting restaurants?
4. Does affordability have any impact on the intention of the consumers in visiting restaurants?

In light of the aforesaid questions no study was conducted on the effect of revenge dining on customers and their willingness to visit the restaurant during the pandemic. It is in this regard, the current study approaches the consumers' intention in visiting restaurants after COVID-19 with reference to affordability and revenge dining. Thus, significant contribution offered by this study includes revenge dining and brand trust, which motivate the consumer to visit restaurants. Thus, the study emphasizes on managing COVID-19 risk perceptions and taking effective steps for building consumer trust.

The novelty of the paper is linked to three factors. First, it explores the influence of brand trust among consumers during the pandemic, where hygiene and safety have occupied prime importance in their decision making. Second, the study considered revenge dining, which has still not been explored among Indian consumers. Third, the research focuses on affordability, which is a very important factor in Indian context, given the price-sensitive nature of the market. (Gupta, 2011).

## 3.1 Development of Questionnaire & Data Collection

To predict the factors, which guided the consumers in visiting restaurants during the pandemic, a wide-ranging questionnaire was designed using google form. The questionnaire was framed using recent literature reviews on the content available. Initially, the questionnaire was shared with an expert panel comprising of people from the industry, academicians, and research scholars to discard any vagueness and uncertainty. Their suggestions were duly incorporated in the questionnaire, which improved its accuracy and authenticity. Then it was shared with 650 participants, consisting a wide range of people exploring all categories. The questionnaire consisted of two parts. The first part includes questions relating to the personal details like

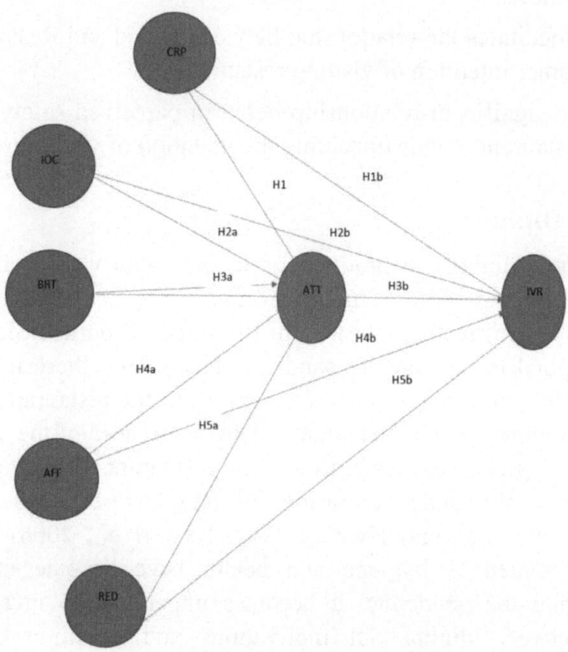


**Figure 1:** Theoretical Model

name, age, education, and income, while the second part comprises of constructs with detailed questionnaires. A five-point Likert scale was used to avoid binary responses, offering participants a wide range of options. In order to ensure huge responses from the participants, diverse methods were carried out, such as clearing doubts about questionnaires and personalized interaction. We collected a total of 523 responses, out of which 440 were taken into consideration.

## 4. CONSTRUCTS & HYPOTHESIS DEVELOPMENT

### 4.1 Brand and Restaurant Trust

Aaker (1991) described a brand as an identity imparted through sign, symbol, name, logo with an intention to ascertain the tangible product or services of a specific seller, or a group of sellers, and to enable to distinguish those tangible product or services from those of the competitors. A brand plays a crucial role in distinguishing one product from the other. Customers rely on products with strong brand names and positive brand images. The prime objective of any product/service design is to create a strong brand association in the customers' minds, resulting in quick brand recall and brand loyalty (Wheeler, 2017). In a study conducted by Han, Nguyen, and Lee (2015), it was found that brand associations can positively impact the brand image, which is a significant factor in defining a reliable brand. Thus, we propose the following hypothesis:

H1a: Attitude meditates the relationship between Brand and Restaurant trust and consumer intention of visiting restaurants.

H1b: There is a significant relationship between perceived safety and well-known restaurant brands impacting the intention of visiting restaurants.

### 4.2 Revenge Dining

The pre-pandemic dining out motivations incorporated various factors like hedonic values, pricing, word of mouth, events, safety, social gathering, ease of availability. However, the new way of life imposed on us because of the restrictions applied to contain the pandemic has altered these motivational elements. People's preferences have changed from the restaurants that they used to visit, to more upscale restaurants. Perhaps because of the concern for health, quality, hygiene, and taste, in upscale restaurants. This concern was present during the pre-pandemic era too, but they have elevated during and after the pandemic (Lee and Hwang, 2011; Kim *et al.*, 2006). Since the apprehensions related to hygiene and health have become much more significant during the pandemic, it becomes imperative to investigate the relationship between dining out motivations and intention of visiting restaurants (Lee and Hwang, 2011).

Motivation plays a mammoth role in dining out expectations regarding the choice of restaurant, service evaluation, and food quality. (Ponnam & Balaji, 2014) state that consumption of food is considered a complicated behaviour in terms of socio-cultural and economic factors. Many other factors are also considered to encourage the population in dining out, such as stepping out from boredom routine, meeting with friends and dining out with family. From the above study, we propose the following hypothesis:

H2a: Attitude mediates the relationship between revenge dining and consumers' intention in visiting restaurants.

H2b: Revenge dining has a significant relationship with consumers' intention in visiting restaurants.

## 4.3 Impact of COVID-19 on the Restaurant Sector

In last two years, there has been a significant dip in number of customers visiting restaurants. However, it was not the case before the pandemic hit the mankind. People enjoyed eating out occasionally, with family and friends. Eating out was considered a significant socializing event. Nevertheless, the pandemic has changed the face of the restaurant industry, drawing it to shambles (Nielsen *et al.*, 2016). The pandemic has been very harsh on the restaurant industry, where in the wake of restrictions, all the restaurants were partly/permanently closed. Customers were forced to resort to online delivery food services through apps or otherwise. Some restaurants that had the access and agility to resort to the new way of delivery somehow managed to survive, but many had to die a painful death in the form of loss of business, which later resulted in the complete closure. From the above literature, we propose the following hypothesis:

H3a: Attitude mediates the relationship between impact of Covid-19 and consumers' intention of visiting restaurants.

H3b: COVID-19 has significantly impacted the consumers' intention of visiting restaurants.

## 4.4 COVID-19 Risk & Perception

In the initial phase, very less information was available on the Covid-19 pandemic across the globe. Hence, the statistics on the impact of the pandemic, longevity of the pandemic and corresponding cure were not available. With the rapid spread of the virus, information and misinformation about the virus spread alike. With everyone trying to preach a cure, much anxiety and apprehension were created in every person's minds about the risks involved (Torales *et al.*, 2020). This ambiguity perhaps led to an endangered feeling (Taha *et al.*, 2014). Strict guidelines and protocols were in place to combat this risk posed by the pandemic. Government protocols on Covid Appropriate Behavior (CAB) in the form of restriction in movement, avoiding social gathering, using sanitizers and wearing a mask further instilled a sense of fear in the people's minds. Hence, we propose the following hypothesis:

H4a: Attitude mediates the relationship between Covid-19 risk and perception and intention of consumers' in visiting restaurants.

H4b: Covid-19 risk and perception have a positive effect on consumers' intention of visiting restaurants.

## 4.5 Affordability

The affordability of visiting any restaurant depends on the disposable income of individuals. Almedia *et al.* (2021) in their study revealed that Covid-19 had significantly impacted the disposable income of households. It could significantly affect the footfall in restaurants. Sushanto and Jaya (2014) in their study, found that affordability is not significantly related to loyalty for any restaurant. Spending on eating outs drastically reduced during the pandemic Gangu Naidu Mandala et.al (2022). Frisbee and Madeira (1986) revealed that convenience rather than affordability was the prime factor guiding people in visiting restaurants. In their research, Shinde *et al.* (2018) found that affordability is strongly related to customer satisfaction and retention.

Based on above review we propose the following hypothesis:

H5a: Attitude mediates the relationship between affordability and consumers' intention of visiting restaurants.

H5b: Affordability has a significant relationship with consumers' intention of visiting restaurants during COVID-19.

## 4.6 Attitude

Attitude is a state of mind which is developed through experiences one learns through his/her life. This experience helps an individual establish a state of readiness or organized behavior towards an object, situation, or individual. In other words, attitude has a direct role in forming an individual's response toward something (Allport, G.W., 1935). Study suggests that attitudes can be divided into two categories—essential and unimportant. Important attitudes seem to change less over a period of time in comparison to unimportant attitudes. Some studies shows that individuals whose attitude is shaped based on the foundations of direct behavioural interaction with the prime object of the attitude, will exhibit considerable attitude-behaviour constancy compared to those, whose attitudes were shaped based on other factors (Regan, D.T., & Fazio, R., 1977). Hence we propose the following hypothesis:

H6: Attitude has a significant relationship with consumers' intention of visiting restaurants during COVID-19.

## 4.7 Theory of Planned Behavior

The Theory of Planned Behaviour (TPB) is an advanced version of the Theory of Reasoned Action (TRA) (Fishbein & Ajzen, 1975). TPB and TRA are based on the judgment that individuals arrive at any rationale or well-thought decision to exhibit a specific behaviour by assessing the data available to them at any given point and time. In this paper, we have extensively made use of TPB. TPB is a philosophy used to foresee and comprehend behaviours. It postulates that behaviours are closely determined by behavioural intents, which are further determined by a blend of three factors – attitude toward the behaviour, subjective norms, and perceived behavioural control. TPB is a powerful persuasive theory in the likelihood of social and well-being behaviours (Rivis *et al.*, 2009). The foundation of TPB is that individuals articulate diverse information to arrive at a decision. Individuals greatly rely on word-of-mouth communication (positive or negative) while taking any decision.

From the extensive literature review done by the authors, the TPB model can be concomitant with this research in the following ways:

1. ***Attitude:*** It is the level of understanding of a particular object or situation. In our paper, the fear created in the customers' minds due to the pandemic is a major driving force in forming an intention whether to visit a restaurant or not.
2. Behavioural intention concerns the motivational factors that may encourage a customer to visit restaurants. Factors such as CAB imposed by the government may be considered in this respect.
3. ***Subjective Norms:*** This is concerned with the beliefs of the customers. If they visit the restaurant physically, how the peers would view their decision? Will it be approved or disapproved? This becomes an essential factor in arriving at any decision.
4. ***Social Norms:*** This deals with the standard behaviour in which one is expected to behave in a society. When all others are sitting at home and ordering food, how will society treat a particular individual, if she/he/they dines out? Hence, people may resort to the standard practices that everybody in society (friends/relatives) follow.
5. ***Perceived Power:*** This refers to the customers' perceptions or beliefs about the presence of any factors encouraging or discouraging a customer from dining out. Perhaps the fear of being infected while in the restaurant was discouraging. In contrast, strict impositions of CAB could have encouraged the customers to dine out.
6. ***Perceived Behavioural Control:*** This is associated with perceived risk or safety. It refers to a perceived notion of the ease or difficulty of carrying out a particular task. If the customers find it easy and safe to sit at home and order food online, they will exhibit this behaviour. On the other hand, if the customers want to socialize and have a delightful dining experience, they may exhibit this behaviour.

## 5. DATA ANALYSIS & DATA INTERPRETATION

The data was analysed in various steps. Exploratory factor analysis was done to measure the construct's reliability. Convergent and discriminant validity tests were performed through Confirmatory factor analysis and hypothesis testing, through Structural Equational Modelling.

### 5.1 EFA (Exploratory Factor Analysis)

EFA is performed to improve the accuracy and understating of constructs. The adequacy of sample and to test the appropriateness of data Kaiser – Meyer – Olkin (KMO) and Bartlett's test of Sphericity was performed. The KMO value was 0.569 and Bartlett's test of Sphericity value was 0.00, which suggest that the data is meaningful and suitable for further analysis. Previous studies have proved that minimum acceptable value for KMO was 0.5 (Field, 2000; Kaiser, 1974). Cronbach Alpha test was conducted to test the reliability of each constructs. The value of Cronbach Alpha lies within the range of 0.638–0.786 which is well within the acceptable limit of 0.6 (Kerlinger & Lee, 2000) (Table 4). The EFA was done by conducting Factor loading, Varimax Rotation, Eigen Value>1(Kaiser 1958). Indicators with value less than 0.6 were removed to increase the accuracy of the data (Awang, 2015). Indicator BRT1 was removed as its value was less than the desired level (Table 3).

### 5.2 CFA (Confirmatory Factor Analysis)

CFA was performed using AMOS 26. Mean and standard deviation of the data were calculated. Low value of SD in comparison to the mean indicates a high-reliability index of data (Table 3). AVE (Average Variance Extracted) and CR (Composite reliability) was calculated to test the reliability and validity of data. The AVE value for the constructs was >0.5 and the CR value was >0.7, which were well within the acceptable limit (Fornell & Larcker, 1981) (Table 4). A discriminant validity test was performed in which the diagonal values were found to lower than the square root of AVE, which signifies that values are acceptable (Fornell & Larcker, 1981) (Table 5).

### 5.3 SEM (Structural Equational Modelling)

To test the hypothesis, SEM was performed using AMOS 26. In the test, Brand and Restaurant trust, revenge dining, affordability, impact of Covid, and risk perception were considered exogenous variables, while the intention to visit the restaurant was considered as an endogenous variable. Those hypotheses whose P value was less than 0.5 were accepted, and whose value was greater than 0.5 were rejected. T-test and Path coefficient (β) were analysed to test the validity of the model (Table 6).

**Table 2:** Demographic Profile of Respondents

| *Sl. No.* | *No. of Items* | *Total (in counts)* | *Percentage* |
|---|---|---|---|
| Gender | Male | 27 | 54% |
| | Female | 23 | 46% |
| Age (in years) | 18–25 years | 13 | 26% |
| | 25–35 years | 22 | 44% |
| | 35–50years | 15 | 29% |
| | 50 years and above | 0 | 0 |
| Education | Under graduate | 6 | 12% |
| | Post Graduate | 31 | 62% |
| | Doctorate | 9 | 18% |
| | Doctorate and above | 3 | 6% |
| Annual Income | 1–2 lakhs per year | 8 | 16% |
| | 3–5 lakhs per year | 15 | 30% |
| | 5–10 lakhs per year | 10 | 20% |
| | 10–15 lakhs per year | 6 | 12% |
| | 10–15 lakhs and above | 2 | 4% |

## 5.4 Demographic Profile

From table 2, we can observe that while 54% of the participants are men, 46% are women. While the percentage of participants between the age 18–25 years is 26%, between the age 25–35 years is 44%, and between the age 35–50 years is 29%, While the percentage of under graduates is 12%, the percentage of postgraduates is 62%. The percentage of doctorate is 18%. While the percentage above doctorates is 6%. While 16% of the respondents earn an annual income of 1–2 lakhs per year, 30% of the participants earn an annual income of 3–5 lakhs per year, 20% of the participants earn an annual income of 5–10 lakhs per year, 12% of the respondents earn an annual income of 10–15 lakhs per year, while 4% of the participants earn an annual income of 10–15 lakhs and above.

**Table 3:** Mean and Standard Deviation

| | *Mean* | *Std. Deviation* | *Factor Loading* |
|---|---|---|---|
| CRP1 | 3.70 | 0.814 | 0.665 |
| CRP2 | 3.90 | 0.707 | 0.727 |
| IOC1 | 3.08 | 1.104 | 0.623 |
| ICO2 | 3.54 | 1.073 | 0.666 |

| | Mean | Std. Deviation | Factor Loading |
|---|---|---|---|
| IOC3 | 2.90 | 0.863 | 0.728 |
| RED1 | 3.84 | 0.997 | 0.745 |
| RED2 | 2.78 | 1.112 | 0.645 |
| RED3 | 4.38 | 0.635 | 0.84 |
| RED4 | 3.70 | 1.165 | 0.677 |
| BRT1 | 3.78 | 0.790 | 0.47 |
| BRT2 | 3.38 | 0.805 | 0.69 |
| BRT3 | 3.92 | 0.528 | 0.715 |
| AFF1 | 2.84 | 0.213 | 0.685 |
| AFF2 | 3.62 | 0.751 | 0.712 |
| IVR1 | 4.04 | 0.669 | 0.706 |
| IVR2 | 3.62 | 0.697 | 0.764 |

**Table 4:** Composite Reliability, Average Variance Extracted, and Cronbach Alpha

| | CR | AVE | Cron bach Alpha |
|---|---|---|---|
| Covid and Risk Perception (CRP) | 0.721 | 0.552 | 0.638 |
| (Revenge Dining) RED | 0.784 | 0.672 | 0.659 |
| Impact of Covid-19 (IOC) | 0.845 | 0.534 | 0.648 |
| Brand & Restaurant Trust (BRT) | 0.754 | 0.645 | 0.786 |
| Affordability (AFF) | 0.769 | 0.589 | 0.762 |

**Table 5:** Discriminant Validity Test of Constructs

| | CRP | RED | IOC | BRT | AFF |
|---|---|---|---|---|---|
| CRP | 0.735 | | | | |
| RED | –0.748 | 0.801 | | | |
| IOC | 0.646 | –0.731 | 0.714 | | |
| BRT | 0.737 | 0.764 | 0.658 | 0.796 | |
| AFF | 0.621 | 0.739 | 0.687 | 0.723 | 0.758 |

**Table 6:** Hypotheses Testing Using SEM

| *Hypothesis* | *Path* | *P value* | *T test* | *β* | *Comment* |
|---|---|---|---|---|---|
| H1a | CRP → ATT | 0.049 | .078 | 0.08 | Supported |
| H2a | RED → ATT | 0.036 | –1.315 | –0.62 | Supported |
| H3a | IOC → ATT | 0.043 | –0.46 | –.035 | Supported |
| H4a | BRT → ATT | 0 | 1.205 | 2.53 | Supported |
| H5a | AFF → ATT | 0.974 | 0.53 | 0.74 | Not Supported |
| H6a | ATT → IVR | 0.039 | 0.67 | .087 | Supported |

**Table 7:** Mediating Effect

| | | *Direct Effect* | | *Indirect Effect* | | | *Total Effect* | |
|---|---|---|---|---|---|---|---|---|
| *Hypo-thesis* | *Structural Path* | *B* | *p-value* | *Mediating Construct* | *β* | *p-value* | *β* | *p-value* |
| H1b | CRP → IVR | 0.53 | 0 | Attitude | 0.16 | NS | 0.69 | NS |
| H2b | RED → IVR | 0.68 | 0.043(***) | Attitude | 0.0158 | 0.032 | 0.6958 | 0.087(**) |
| H3b | IOC → IVR | 0.73 | 0.0037(***) | Attitude | 0.0038 | 0.01 | 0.7338 | 0.0047(***) |
| H4b | BRT → IVR | 0.545 | 0.0019(***) | Attitude | 0.13 | NS | 0.675 | 0.0028(***) |
| H5b | AFF → IVR | 0.027 | NS | Attitude | 0.0158 | NS | 0.0428 | 0.002(***) |

## 6. RESULTS

The results obtained after performing SEM have been shown in the form of regression weight (β), t values and p values which have been shown in table 6. Hypothesis H1a revealed that Covid risk perception has a positive relationship with the attitude of consumers intending to visit restaurants ($P<0.05$, β= 0.08). Similarly, we investigated the relationship between revenge dining and the attitude of consumers intending to visit restaurants. The results of Hypothesis H2a reveal that there is a strong relationship between revenge dining and the attitude of consumers intending to visit restaurants ($P<0.05$, β= –.062). Hypothesis H3a, which defined the relationship between the impact of Covid-19 and the attitude of consumers towards visiting restaurants, was found to be significant ($P<0.05$, β= –.035). Hypothesis H4a revealed that brand and restaurant trust had a significant relationship with the attitude of consumers willing to visit restaurants ($P<0.05$, β= 2.53). However, Hypothesis H5a, which highlights the relationship between affordability and attitude to visit restaurants, was not found to be significant. Hypothesis H6 showed that the relationship between consumer attitude and intention of visiting the restaurant is significant ($P<0.05$, β= 0.87). Results exhibited in table 7 shows that Hypothesis H1b, which discusses the relationship between Covid-19 risk and perception, has a significant relationship with the intention to visit a restaurant. In their study, Dube *et al.* (2020) revealed that due to Covid protocols like lockdowns, social distancing, and restrictions in the movement of people negatively impacted the footfalls in restaurants. Interestingly, hypothesis H2b showed that revenge dining has significant relationships with the intention to visit the restaurant ($P<0.05$, $\beta= 0.68$). Nguyen and Chao (2021) revealed a V-shaped bounce back in a visit to the restaurant and fast food joints. Hypothesis H3b revealed that the Impact of Covid 19 has a significant relationship with the intention to visit the restaurant ($P<0.05$, $\beta= 0$). Dedeoglu *et al.* (2022) found that Covid-19 negatively impact the motivation of consumers in visit restaurants. Hypothesis H4b showed that Brand and Restaurant Trust had a significant relationship with the intention of visiting restaurants ($P<0.05$, $\beta= 0.54$). Espinosa *et al.* (2018) in their study found that restaurant brand image and trust significantly influence the customers' intention in revisiting restaurants. Interestingly, hypothesis H5b did not find any support, which means that affordability did not have any significant relationship with the intention of visiting restaurants.

## 6.1 Theoretical Implications

Our study focuses on restaurant brands, revenge dining, and perceived safety and risk associated with dining in restaurants and hence the resultant consumer intention.

On the basis of the above findings, we can draw the conclusion that the intention to visit restaurants during and perhaps immediately after the pandemic that hit India and the world was primarily based on the trust, brand, and cohesion of the consumers in the specific restaurants. This is a new area of concern, as the pandemic may continue to hamper the restaurant business for the long term. Consumers have been concerned about safety right from the onset of the pandemic, but safety cannot be accounted as a major factor in framing consumer intent. According to a typical consumer mindset, the safety standards are accessed more on account of foul smell from food, crockery not being cleaned well, and hygiene factors in the restaurant. More-so-ever, to arrive at the exact standard of cleanliness, the consumers have to visit the kitchen, where the actual cooking happens, however, this area is not accessible in many restaurants. Hence the consumers can judge the safety standards of any restaurant from the physical protocols that are followed (CAB – Covid Appropriate Behavior), such as social distancing in seating, placement of sanitizers, ventilation, use of safety gear like gloves, masks, and shower caps by waiters. In such cases, the restaurants are bound to adhere to all the rules, regulations, and policies set by the government. These undertakings by the restaurant owners will help the consumers to frequently visit the restaurants and eventually reduce the negative economic consequences due to the pandemic.

## 6.2 Practical Implications

Concerning health, opening restaurants during the pandemic itself was a matter of apprehension for all. Despite Covid Appropriate Behavior being followed by restaurants and consumers, the chances of the spread of the virus in crowded places is higher. Hence, to draw the consumers to the restaurants, the restaurant owners should focus on safety conventions and adhere to the safety and security decorum put forward by the government as a primary concern. If any customer notices that the restaurant staff is not following the safety protocols, it may draw him away from visiting the restaurant the next time. Brands instil a sense of security and trust in the minds of the consumers; a small mistake on the part of any restaurant staff can cost the entire restaurant. The image of the restaurant may dwindle in the mind of the consumer, and therefore he/she may no longer patronize that restaurant. Also, if word of mouth can be a method of spreading a quick positive word, it can also work the other way and spoil the image of the restaurant more quickly than it builds. The second most important concern for visiting a restaurant during a pandemic is 'Affordability'. Our test results have rejected the hypothesis. Hence, we can safely conclude that affordability does not have a significant relationship with consumers' intention of visiting restaurants. However, there could be other factors, such as 'Safety and Health' which are of primary concern in the minds of the restaurant goers. Another reason that we account for as to why people are staying away from restaurants is economic uncertainty. With increasing economic ambiguity like salary cuts, and job losses, consumers have become more price-conscious and perhaps want to stay away from making unnecessary expenditures. Some of this behaviour may persist even after the pandemic is over.

## 7. CONCLUSION

Through this research the authors have studied the possible causes that could affect the intention of consumers to visit restaurants during or immediately after the pandemic. The factors under consideration are: brand of the restaurant, safety, revenge dining, risk involved, and affordability that influence the decision of consumers. However, during the course of this research, it has come to the knowledge of the researchers that affordability has no significant relationship with intention to visit restaurants during the pandemic. Other factors such as health and safety, the brand of the restaurant, and associated risk have significant relationships with consumers' intention of visiting restaurants. It is a well-understood fact that the intention of consumers varies according to the prevailing situations. Covid-19 pandemic itself is dynamic, and its intensity varies from location to location and time to time. The restaurant owners must follow the CAP and must also adhere to all the rules, regulations, and protocols laid down by the government in terms of the restaurant business. It is challenging to predict the future, but one must note that the behaviour of the consumers is not momentary and that it may be carried well beyond the pandemic. The restaurant owners have to prepare themselves accordingly.

## Limitations & Scope for Future Research

Through this study we have tried to bridge the gap pertaining to the intention of consumers wanting/not-wanting to visit restaurants during/immediately after the pandemic. However, every study has a scope of improvement. The survey was conducted online through Google forms, which perhaps may have led to biased responses in comparison to face-to-face collection of data. Our study is restricted to Maharashtra. The pandemic situation is dynamic and changing day-by-day, month-by-month and also varies from place-to-place. The first wave in India had thrown different challenges in terms of newness of the disease and lockdown scenarios. The second wave was more fatal and people and the government were not prepared to handle the disease of this magnitude. In the third wave most of the people were vaccinated and the government apparently was more prepared to handle this disease. As a result, consumer trust and perception may vary rapidly. Consequently, this will again affect the intention of the consumer to dine out.

## Disclosure Statement

No potential conflict of interest was reported by the authors.

## Funding

This is not a funded research.

## REFERENCES

[1] Aaker, A., "Brand equity. La gestione del valore della marca," 1991, pp. 347–356.

[2] Ajzen, I., "The Theory of Planned Behavior," *Organizational Behavior and Human Decision Processes*, Vol. 50, No. 2, pp. 179–211, Dec. 1991.

[3] Ajzen, I. and Fishbein, M., "A Bayesian Analysis of Attribution Processes," *Psychological Bulletin*, Vol. 82, No. 2, pp. 261–277, Mar. 1975.

[4] Almeida, V., Barrios, S., Christl, M., De Poli, S., Tumino, A. and Wielen, W. Van Der, "The Impact of COVID-19 on Households' Income in the EU," *The Journal of Economic Inequality*, Vol. 19, No. 3, pp. 413–431, Sep. 2021.

[5] Andersson, T.D. and Mossberg, L., "The Dining Experience: Do Restaurants Satisfy Customer Needs?" *Food Service Technology*, Vol. 4, No. 4, pp. 171–177, Dec. 2004.

[6] Awang, P., "SEM made simple: A gentle approach to learning Structural Equation Modeling," *MPWS Rich Publication,* Bangi, 2015.

[7] Verma, A., Verma, M., Boaler, M.S. and Mandala, G.N. "Determinants of consumer intention towards Covid vaccination: The mediating role of attitude," *Academy of Marketing Studies Journal*, Vol. 26, No. 3, 2022.

[8] Bartik, A. *et al.*, "How Are Small Businesses Adjusting to COVID-19? Early Evidence from a Survey," Cambridge, MA: National Bureau of Economic Research, Apr. 2020.

[9] Van Bavel, J.J. *et al.*, "Using Social and Behavioural Science to Support COVID-19 Pandemic Response," *Nature Human Behaviour*, vol. 4, no. 5, pp. 460–471, Apr. 2020.

[10] Berg-Weger, M. and Morley, J.E., "Loneliness and Social Isolation in Older Adults during the COVID-19 Pandemic: Implications for Gerontological Social Work," *The Journal of Nutrition, Health & Aging*, Vol. 24, No. 5, pp. 456–458, May 2020.

[11] Cahyanto, I., Wiblishauser, M., Pennington-Gray, L. and Schroeder, A., "The Dynamics of Travel Avoidance: The Case of Ebola in the U.S.," *Tourism Management Perspectives*, Vol. 20, pp. 195–203, Oct. 2016.

[12] Cheng, S., Lam, T. and Hsu, C.H.C., "Negative Word-of-Mouth Communication Intention: An Application of the Theory of Planned Behavior," *Journal of Hospitality & Tourism Research*, Vol. 30, No. 1, pp. 95–116, Feb. 2006.

[13] Dedeoğlu, B.B. and Boğan, E., "The Motivations of Visiting Upscale Restaurants during the COVID-19 Pandemic: The Role of Risk Perception and Trust in Government," *International Journal of Hospitality Management*, Vol. 95, May 2021.

[14] Dedeoğlu, B.B. *et al.*, "The Impact of COVID-19 on Destination Visit Intention and Local Food Consumption," *British Food Journal*, Vol. 124, No. 2, pp. 634–653, Jan. 2022.

[15] Dowd, K.D. and Burke, K.J., "The Influence of Ethical Values and Food Choice Motivations on Intentions to Purchase Sustainably Sourced Foods," *Appetite*, Vol. 69, pp. 137–144, Oct. 2013.

[16] Dube, K., Nhamo, G. and Chikodzi, D., "COVID-19 Cripples Global Restaurant and Hospitality Industry," *Current Issues in Tourism*, Vol. 24, No. 11, pp. 1487–1490, Jun. 2021.

[17] Espinosa, J.A. *et al.*, "I'll Have the Usual: How Restaurant Brand Image, Loyalty, and Satisfaction Keep Customers Coming Back," *Journal of Product & Brand Management*, Vol. 27, No. 6, pp. 599–614, Sep. 2018.

[18] Fornell, C. and Larcker, D.F., "Evaluating Structural Equation Models with Unobservable Variables and Measurement Error," *Journal of Marketing Research*, Vol. 18, No. 1, Feb. 1981.

[19] Frisbee, W.R. and Madeira, K., "Restaurant Meals – Convenience Goods or Luxuries?" *The Service Industries Journal*, Vol. 6, No. 2, pp. 172–192, Jul. 1986.

[20] Goyal, A. and Verma, P., "Do It Yourself Effect on Restaurants – The Pandemic Effect: Driven by the Fear Appeal Theory," *Journal of Hospitality and Tourism Management*, Vol. 48, pp. 76–87, Sep. 2021.

[21] Gupta, N., "Extent of Susceptibility to Interpersonal Influence and Price Sensitivity among Indian Youth: Is There a Relationship between These Two Constructs?" *Young Consumers*, Vol. 12, No. 4, pp. 361–369, Nov. 2011.

[22] Gursoy, D. and Chi, C.G., "Effects of COVID-19 Pandemic on Hospitality Industry: Review of the Current Situations and a Research Agenda," *Journal of Hospitality Marketing & Management*, Vol. 29, No. 5, pp. 527–529, Jul. 2020.

[23] Hakim, M.P., D'Avoglio Zanetta, L. and Da Cunha, D.T., "Should I Stay, or Should I Go? Consumers' Perceived Risk and Intention to Visit Restaurants during the COVID-19 Pandemic in Brazil," *Food Research International*, Vol. 141, Mar. 2021.

[24] Han, S.H., Nguyen, B. and Lee, T.J., "Consumer-Based Chain Restaurant Brand Equity, Brand Reputation, and Brand Trust," *International Journal of Hospitality Management*, Vol. 50, Sep. 2015.

[25] Hoang, T. and Suleri, J., "Customer Behaviour in Restaurants before and during COVID-19: A Study in Vietnam," *Research in Hospitality Management*, Vol. 11, No. 3, pp. 205–214, Sep. 2021.

[26] "Investigation of the Effects of Corona Virus Pandemic and Social Isolation on Psychological Symptoms in Terms of Psychological Resilience and Coping Styles (Tur)," *Journal of Clinical Psychiatry*, 2020.

[27] Jeong, E. and (S.) Jang, S. "Price Premiums for Organic Menus at Restaurants: What Is an Acceptable Level?" *International Journal of Hospitality Management*, Vol. 77, pp. 117–127, Jan. 2019.

[28] Kaiser, H.F., "The Varimax Criterion for Analytic Rotation in Factor Analysis," *Psychometrika*, Vol. 23, No. 3, pp. 187–200, Sep. 1958.

[29] Kang, Y. and Park, S., "The Perfection of the Narcissistic Self: A Qualitative Study on Luxury Consumption and Customer Equity," *Journal of Business Research*, Vol. 69, No. 9, pp. 3813–3819, Sep. 2016.

[30] Kim, W.G., Lee, Y.-K. and Yoo, Y.-J., "Predictors of Relationship Quality and Relationship Outcomes in Luxury Restaurants," *Journal of Hospitality & Tourism Research*, Vol. 30, No. 2, pp. 143–169, May 2006.

[31] Knight, D.W. *et al.*, "Impact of COVID-19: Research Note on Tourism and Hospitality Sectors in the Epicenter of Wuhan and Hubei Province, China," *International Journal of Contemporary Hospitality Management*, Vol. 32, No. 12, pp. 3705–3719, Nov. 2020.

[32] Krosnick, J.A., "Attitude Importance and Attitude Change," *Journal of Experimental Social Psychology*, Vol. 24, No. 3, pp. 240–255, May 1988.

[33] Kwun, D.J., Hwang, J.H. and Kim, T. "Eating-Out Motivations and Variety-Seeking Behavior: An Exploratory Approach on Loyalty Behavior," *Journal of Hospitality Marketing & Management*, Vol. 22, No. 3, pp. 289–312, Apr. 2013.

[34] Lakshmi, R. and Shareena, P. "Impact of COVID 19 on the Restaurants," *Journal of Interdisciplinary Cycle Research*, Vol. 12, No. 8, pp. 1327–1334, 2020.

[35] Lee, J.H. and Hwang, J., "Luxury Marketing: The Influences of Psychological and Demographic Characteristics on Attitudes toward Luxury Restaurants," *International Journal of Hospitality Management*, Vol. 30, No. 3, pp. 658–669, Sep. 2011.

[36] Espinosa, A. *et al.*, "I'll Have the Usual: How Restaurant Brand Image, Loyalty, and Satisfaction Keep Customers Coming Back," *Journal of Product & Brand Management*, Vol. 27, No. 6, pp. 599–614, Sep. 2018.

[37] Fornell, C. and Larcker, D.F., "Evaluating Structural Equation Models with Unobservable Variables and Measurement Error," *Journal of Marketing Research*, Vol. 18, No. 1, Feb. 1981.

[38] Frisbee, W.R. and Madeira, K., "Restaurant Meals – Convenience Goods or Luxuries?" *The Service Industries Journal*, Vol. 6, No. 2, pp. 172–192, Jul. 1986.

[39] Goyal, A. and Verma, P., "Do It Yourself Effect on Restaurants – The Pandemic Effect: Driven by the Fear Appeal Theory," *Journal of Hospitality and Tourism Management*, Vol. 48, pp. 76–87, Sep. 2021.

[40] Gupta, N., "Extent of Susceptibility to Interpersonal Influence and Price Sensitivity among Indian Youth: Is There a Relationship between These Two Constructs?" *Young Consumers*, Vol. 12, No. 4, pp. 361–369, Nov. 2011.

[41] Gursoy, D. and Chi, C.G., "Effects of COVID-19 Pandemic on Hospitality Industry: Review of the Current Situations and a Research Agenda," *Journal of Hospitality Marketing & Management*, Vol. 29, No. 5, pp. 527–529, Jul. 2020.

[42] Hakim, M.P., D'Avoglio Zanetta, L. and Da Cunha, D.T., "Should I Stay, or Should I Go? Consumers' Perceived Risk and Intention to Visit Restaurants during the COVID-19 Pandemic in Brazil," *Food Research International*, Vol. 141, Mar. 2021.

[43] Han, S.H., Nguyen, B. and Lee, T.J., "Consumer-Based Chain Restaurant Brand Equity, Brand Reputation, and Brand Trust," *International Journal of Hospitality Management*, Vol. 50, Sep. 2015.

[44] Hoang, T. and Suleri, J., "Customer Behaviour in Restaurants before and during COVID-19: A Study in Vietnam," *Research in Hospitality Management*, Vol. 11, No. 3, pp. 205–214, Sep. 2021.

[45] "Investigation of the Effects of Corona Virus Pandemic and Social Isolation on Psychological Symptoms in Terms of Psychological Resilience and Coping Styles (Tur)," *Journal of Clinical Psychiatry*, 2020.

[46] Jeong, E. and (S.) Jang, S., "Price Premiums for Organic Menus at Restaurants: What Is an Acceptable Level?" *International Journal of Hospitality Management*, Vol. 77, pp. 117–127, Jan. 2019.

[47] Kaiser, H.F., "The Varimax Criterion for Analytic Rotation in Factor Analysis," *Psychometrika*, Vol. 23, No. 3, pp. 187–200, Sep. 1958.

[48] Kang, Y. and Park, S., "The Perfection of the Narcissistic Self: A Qualitative Study on Luxury Consumption and Customer Equity," *Journal of Business Research*, Vol. 69, No. 9, pp. 3813–3819, Sep. 2016.

[49] Kim, W.G., Lee, Y.-K. and Yoo, Y.-J. "Predictors of Relationship Quality and Relationship Outcomes in Luxury Restaurants," *Journal of Hospitality & Tourism Research*, Vol. 30, No. 2, pp. 143–169, May 2006.

[50] Knight, D.W. *et al.*, "Impact of COVID-19: Research Note on Tourism and Hospitality Sectors in the Epicenter of Wuhan and Hubei Province, China," *International Journal of Contemporary Hospitality Management*, Vol. 32, No. 12, pp. 3705–3719, Nov. 2020.

[51] Krosnick, J.A., "Attitude Importance and Attitude Change," *Journal of Experimental Social Psychology*, Vol. 24, No. 3, pp. 240–255, May 1988.

[52] Kwun, D.J., Hwang, J.H. and Kim, T., "Eating-Out Motivations and Variety-Seeking Behavior: An Exploratory Approach on Loyalty Behavior," *Journal of Hospitality Marketing & Management*, Vol. 22, No. 3, pp. 289–312, Apr. 2013.

[53] Lakshmi, R. and Shareena, P., "Impact of COVID 19 on the Restaurants," *Journal of Interdisciplinary Cycle Research*, Vol. 12, No. 8, pp. 1327–1334, 2020.

[54] Lee, J.H. and Hwang, J., "Luxury Marketing: The Influences of Psychological and Demographic Characteristics on Attitudes toward Luxury Restaurants," *International Journal of Hospitality Management*, Vol. 30, No. 3, pp. 658–669, Sep. 2011.

[55] Espinosa, A. *et al.*, "I'll Have the Usual: How Restaurant Brand Image, Loyalty, and Satisfaction Keep Customers Coming Back," *Journal of Product & Brand Management*, Vol. 27, No. 6, pp. 599–614, Sep. 2018.

[56] Fornell, C. and Larcker, D.F. "Evaluating Structural Equation Models with Unobservable Variables and Measurement Error," *Journal of Marketing Research*, Vol. 18, No. 1, Feb. 1981.

[57] Frisbee, W.R. and Madeira, K., "Restaurant Meals - Convenience Goods or Luxuries?" *The Service Industries Journal*, Vol. 6, No. 2, pp. 172–192, Jul. 1986.

[58] Goyal, A. and Verma, P., "Do It Yourself Effect on Restaurants – The Pandemic Effect: Driven by the Fear Appeal Theory," *Journal of Hospitality and Tourism Management*, Vol. 48, pp. 76–87, Sep. 2021.

[59] Gupta, N., "Extent of Susceptibility to Interpersonal Influence and Price Sensitivity among Indian Youth: Is There a Relationship between These Two Constructs?" *Young Consumers*, Vol. 12, No. 4, pp. 361–369, Nov. 2011.

[60] Gursoy, D. and Chi, C.G., "Effects of COVID-19 Pandemic on Hospitality Industry: Review of the Current Situations and a Research Agenda," *Journal of Hospitality Marketing & Management*, Vol. 29, No. 5, pp. 527–529, Jul. 2020.

[61] Hakim, M.P., D'Avoglio Zanetta, L. and Da Cunha, D.T., "Should I Stay, or Should I Go? Consumers' Perceived Risk and Intention to Visit Restaurants during the COVID-19 Pandemic in Brazil," *Food Research International*, Vol. 141, Mar. 2021.

[62] Han, S.H., Nguyen, B. and Lee, T.J., "Consumer-Based Chain Restaurant Brand Equity, Brand Reputation, and Brand Trust," *International Journal of Hospitality Management*, Vol. 50, Sep. 2015.

[63] Hoang, T. and Suleri, J., "Customer Behaviour in Restaurants before and during COVID-19: A Study in Vietnam," *Research in Hospitality Management*, Vol. 11, No. 3, pp. 205–214, Sep. 2021.

[64] "Investigation of the Effects of Corona Virus Pandemic and Social Isolation on Psychological Symptoms in Terms of Psychological Resilience and Coping Styles (Tur)," *Journal of Clinical Psychiatry*, 2020.

[65] Jeong, E. and (S.) Jang, S., "Price Premiums for Organic Menus at Restaurants: What Is an Acceptable Level?" *International Journal of Hospitality Management*, Vol. 77, pp. 117–127, Jan. 2019.

[66] Kaiser, H.F., "The Varimax Criterion for Analytic Rotation in Factor Analysis," *Psychometrika*, Vol. 23, No. 3, pp. 187–200, Sep. 1958.

[67] Kang, Y. and Park, S., "The Perfection of the Narcissistic Self: A Qualitative Study on Luxury Consumption and Customer Equity," *Journal of Business Research*, Vol. 69, No. 9, pp. 3813–3819, Sep. 2016.

[68] Kim, W.G., Lee, Y.-K. and Yoo, Y.-J., "Predictors of Relationship Quality and Relationship Outcomes in Luxury Restaurants," *Journal of Hospitality & Tourism Research*, Vol. 30, No. 2, pp. 143–169, May 2006.

[69] Knight, D.W. *et al.*, "Impact of COVID-19: Research Note on Tourism and Hospitality Sectors in the Epicenter of Wuhan and Hubei Province, China," *International Journal of Contemporary Hospitality Management*, Vol. 32, No. 12, pp. 3705–3719, Nov. 2020.

[70] Krosnick, J.A., "Attitude Importance and Attitude Change," *Journal of Experimental Social Psychology*, Vol. 24, No.

# Analysis of Switching Intentions of Customers between Click and Brick Using Machine Learning Approach

**Anuradha Yadav and Vijay Prakash Sharma**
Assistant Professor, IILM University, Gurugram, India

***ABSTRACT:*** *Consumer buying behavior is a set of actions done over time. In this period consumer buying decisions sometimes are not based on any logic. Although there are always some factors like emotions, offers, trust, and cultures that play an important role in buying decisions. In the present era when there is the availability of multichannel, consumers have lots of buying mode options. This leads to switching behavior from one channel to another depending on convenience and other factors. The goal of the current study is to identify the variables that influence consumers' behavior while purchasing apparel either through the online method or in a traditional manner, as well as the potential causes of any behavioral change. These external elements, which have an impact on both types of shopping ways, include technical, behavioural, perceptual, and neural aspects. Though technology is an integral part of online shopping, there are always some issues with technology acceptance. Likewise, customers' age, gender, etc. also affect their purchase behaviour. With the use of supervised machine learning techniques, the study will also look at how socio-demographic factors and other influencing factors affect customers' switching patterns and satisfaction with their purchasing decisions for both traditional and online modes of distribution.*

**Keywords:** Machine Learning, Online Shopping Behaviour, Switching Behaviour, Technology Adoption, Traditional Shopping Behaviour.

## 1. INTRODUCTION

Marketers face challenges in delivering faultless customer experiences, crucial in today's virtual market (Tareq *et al.*, 2020). Creating delightful online shopping experiences is paramount (Kesharwani & Sharma, 2020), while traditional purchase models also encounter similar hurdles (Yadav, 2019). Businesses are adopting newer technologies, like machine learning (ML), to gain insights into customer behaviors and purchase intentions (Dewalska-Opitek *et al.*, 2022). ML techniques integrate customer insights, enhancing both online and offline shopping experiences (Visconti-Caparrós *et al.*, 2021). Factors influencing switching to online shopping include product availability, discounts, and convenience (Kennedy *et al.*, 2022; Zhao *et al.*, 2022; Klaus *et al.*, 2022). AI-powered solutions enhance customer loyalty and shopping experiences (Zhao *et al.*, 2022). Internet buying trends are increasing due to global pandemic conditions (Tran, 2021; Kesharwani & Sharma, 2020). ML modeling examines consumer behavior's impact on decision-making, facilitating transitions between traditional and online purchasing modes (Sharma *et al.*, 2021; Klaus *et al.*, 2022). Researchers utilize the technology acceptance model and consumer behavior theories to understand switching behavior in integrated markets (Tareq *et al.*, 2020).

## 2. LITERATURE REVIEW AND HYPOTHESIS

Artificial Intelligence (AI) and Machine Learning (ML) have become integral to modern marketing strategies, revolutionizing consumer behavior modeling and decision-making processes. Analyzing consumer credit and transaction risks through ML techniques has been acknowledged in literature (Khandani *et al.*, 2010; Breeden, 2021), highlighting their role in enhancing business decisions. ML has transformed the understanding of consumer shopping behavior from a costly, time-consuming process to the development of domain expert models (Chi-Hsien & Nagasawa, 2019), opening new dimensions in consumer behavior research.

Customer behavior modeling involves predicting how similar customers will behave under comparable circumstances, a process facilitated by ML (Yadav, 2019). Data mining techniques are employed to extract insights from large datasets, with regression being a commonly used ML algorithm (Roselin *et al.*, 2014; Maulud, 2020). This allows marketers to understand the complex interplay of factors influencing consumer decisions.

Despite the rise of online shopping, many consumers still prefer traditional modes due to various factors like anxiety and quality concerns (Klaus *et al.*, 2022). Multichannel retailing is emerging as a dynamic shopping approach, with consumers utilizing different channels at various stages of the buying process (Arora *et al.*, 2017). Socio-demographic factors, such as age, gender, and income, significantly impact consumer shopping behavior (Hasan, 2010; Dominici *et al.*, 2021).

Switching behavior between traditional and online modes of purchase is influenced by several factors (Sharma *et al.*, 2021; Gupta *et al.*, 2004). However, research on these dynamics is still limited (Klaus *et al.*, 2022; Yadav, 2019). Therefore, we hypothesize:

H1: Socio-demographic factors significantly impact traditional and online shopping behaviors.

H2: There are significant factors affecting switching intentions of consumers from traditional to online buying.

H3: There are significant factors for choice satisfaction between traditional and online modes of purchase.

Recent studies have employed supervised ML techniques to examine consumer behavior in various contexts (Jose, 2019). However, research specifically focusing on switching behavior and choice satisfaction in online shopping remains scarce (Sharma *et al*., 2021; Yadav, 2019). This study aims to fill this gap by identifying variables influencing switching behavior and choice satisfaction through ML algorithms.

In conclusion, AI and ML are reshaping marketing strategies and consumer behavior research. By leveraging these technologies, marketers can gain deeper insights into consumer preferences and behaviors, ultimately enhancing decision-making processes and optimizing customer experiences.

## 2. METHODS AND MODELS

This research utilized a cross-sectional analysis employing survey methodology to gather data from the Delhi-NCR region. Measures from previous social media studies were adapted to fit the context, with a survey questionnaire employing a seven-point Likert scale. Convenience sampling was employed, as described by Bujang *et al*. (2012), with data collected from December 2021 to February 2022. The sample comprised 200 respondents chosen due to the region's diversity, technological advancement, and representation of online users. Data analysis methods ranged from basic to advanced statistical tools.

### 2.1 Empirical Analysis

#### *Respondent's Profile*

The study had a sample size of 200 participants, with 109 of them male and 91 females. The age range of the participants was 18 to 58 years old, with 110 being married and 90 being single. The participants represented various professions, such as businessmen, salaried employees, researchers, and homemakers.

#### *Reliability and Validity*

The responses were collected through a questionnaire, which was tested for both reliability and validity. The reliability of the measurement scale was assessed using Cronbach's Alpha, which was reported as 0.919. The validity of the questionnaire was determined through factor analysis. The Kaiser-Meyer-Olkin (KMO) value for the questionnaire data was calculated as 0.788, indicating that the data was appropriate for factor analysis. The KMO measures the adequacy of sampling. The factor analysis was performed to reduce the number of variables in the study and identify the most critical factors in analyzing the online and traditional behavior of consumers. From this we aim to the objective:

*To identify the factors that influence shopping behavior for both traditional and online apparel shopping.*

The study only considered factors with values greater than 1. To group variables with high correlations, an exploratory factor analysis was conducted using SPSS version 23. The data for the study was collected through a structured questionnaire that included 52 variables, which were categorized into five main groups based on their relevance: Technological Factors, Perceived Benefits (Traditional & Online), Perceived Risk, Socio-Cultural Factors, and Behavioral Factors.

The exploratory factor analysis results, indicated that 15 items had a significant impact on both traditional and online apparel shopping behavior. The next objective of the study is:

*To examine how socio-demographic factors influence both traditional and online shopping behaviors.*

Multi Group Analysis was employed to test the hypothesis, given its efficacy in identifying differences within and between groups (Deng & Yuan, 2015; Dominici *et al.*, 2021). Specifically, the study aimed to discern variances in the impact of socio-demographic variables on traditional and online shopping behavior in the Delhi-NCR region. Four key variables - age, marital status, expenditure, and occupation - were examined to understand their influence on apparel shopping behavior across both traditional and online platforms. The analysis sought to elucidate how these socio-demographic factors shape shopping behavior in each context.

### *Impact on Online Shopping Behaviour*

To accomplish this, a path analysis model was created in SPSS AMOS for multi-group analysis. The purpose of this model is to investigate how socio-demographic factors, including age, marital status, occupation, and expenditure, impact the online shopping behavior of consumers.

The researchers utilized maximum likelihood estimates in SPSS AMOS to analyze the data and identify differences within the group. The results, suggest that the initial model is a suitable match for the sample data, as indicated by the goodness-of-fit indices. The following are the regression weights between socio-demographic factors such as age, marital status, occupation, and expenditure, and online shopping behavior.

Based on the results, age was found to be insignificant in relation to online consumer behavior, as the p-value of age & expenditure 0.405 is greater than 0.05. As a result, age and expenditure have not any significant effect on online consumer behavior. In contrast, marital status and occupation is deemed significant with a p-value of 0.007 & 0.06, which is less than 0.05, and marital status and occupation significantly affects online consumer behavior. The findings indicate that marital status and occupation have a significant influence on online shopping behavior, while age and expenditure do not impact consumer behavior for online purchases.

### *Impact on Traditional Buying Behaviours*

The same analysis was conducted to determine the impact of socio-demographic factors on traditional shopping behavior in Delhi-NCR.

The model fit indices indicated that the model had a good fit with the sample data. The regression weights between the socio-demographic factors and traditional shopping behavior are shown below:

The analysis reveals that age, occupation and expenditure are not a significant factor in traditional consumer behavior, with a p-value of 0.997,0.379 & 0.272 respectively which is greater than 0.05, leading to the rejection of null hypothesis H01. On the other hand, marital status has a significant effect on traditional consumer behavior, with a p-value of 0.027, less than 0.05, resulting in the acceptance of null hypothesis H02. As a result, it can be concluded that only marital status has a significant impact on traditional shopping behavior in Delhi-NCR, while age, occupation, and expenditure do not have any significant influence.

The next objective of the study is:

*To analyze the impact of various variables that influence the switching behavior and choice satisfaction of consumers when making purchases through traditional and online modes.*

Through internet, customers have gained a lot of information and decision-making power. The abundance of information available on the internet has changed the way customers interact with companies and has shortened their decision-making process, leading to an increase in online purchases. This change in behavior is due to the convenience and ease of making a purchase with just a few clicks (Al-Mashraie *et al.*, 2020). We proposed the hypotheses as:

$H_{3a}$: There are significant factors for choice satisfaction between traditional and online mode of purchase.

$H_{3b}$: There are no significant factors for choice satisfaction between traditional and online mode of purchase.

To capture switching behavior stepwise regression technique was used, out of 52 variables, 4 variables for each (i.e., switching to online shopping and choice satisfaction) were found significant. Regression models were formulated to interrogate the relationship between switching to online shopping and other variables. The model estimation show that the adjusted R is 0.69 and R-squared is 0.67. The Durbin Watson value of 1.81 falls within the range of 1.5 to 2.5, indicating that there is no evidence of first-order autocorrelation. The highly significant F value suggests that the model has a significant impact on the variation in the switch from traditional to online shopping behavior.

The model is influenced by several factors, including user-friendly navigation flow (β=0.024, $p<.05$), the availability of more offers in online shopping (β=0.786, $p<.05$), process of transaction is easy (β=0.024, $p>.05$), and the importance of friends and family opinion (β=0.007, $p<.05$). With an R-squared value of 67%, it can be concluded that the model is a good fit for the data. Therefore, based on the analysis, the alternate hypothesis is accepted.

### *Model for Choice Satisfaction*

The regression analysis found that the model accounts for 68% of the variance in the data, with an adjusted R-squared value of 0.68 and an R-squared value of 0.64. The Durbin Watson value of 1.95 falls within the acceptable range of 1.5 to 2.5, and the F value is highly significant. The model is influenced by factors such as no waiting time, availability of more offers/discounts in online shopping, difficulties in judging product quality, and access to information from store personnel having ($p<0.05$). Despite having a slightly lower R-squared value of 64%, the model still fits the data well as indicated by the adjusted R-squared value of 0.68.

## 2.2 Findings

The analysis reveals a significant difference in the online and traditional apparel shopping behavior of customers, with various factors impacting both types of shopping behaviors. The current study builds on previous research findings from Hansen & Jan (2009), Bagozzi (2007), and Yadav & Mahara (2019), providing a comprehensive overview of the variables that influence these behaviors. Additionally, the analysis highlights that socio-demographic factors such as gender, occupation, age, and marital status also play a role in shaping online and traditional shopping behavior in Delhi-NCR (Dominici et.al, 2021).

According to the model, marital status and occupation have a significant impact on online shopping behavior, while only marital status has an effect on traditional shopping behavior in Delhi-NCR. This suggests that the factors influencing the two modes of shopping behavior are distinct and that businesses should take into account these differences when developing marketing strategies targeting these groups of consumers.

According to the regression model suggested for switching to online shopping customers switch mainly because of more offers available online.

Market and consumer behaviour has been impacted by covid 19. Pandemic has made everything online and it is the time when people who didn't want to shift from offline to online have also been forced to shift. (Opitek *et al.,* 2022; Tran, 2021). During pandemic people shifted from traditional to online marketing because of its health and safety benefits. (Tran, 2022) This shows that fear is also one of the influence factors for change. There are many factors that attract online modes of shopping, one of them is the easy transaction process.

The model for choice satisfaction in online mode highlights the importance of two variables: no waiting time and the availability of multiple options. Consumers prefer to be able to shop at any time without having to wait in line. Additionally, the availability of more options increases their satisfaction with the online mode of purchase. The presence of discounts and offers also contributes to choise satisfaction in the online mode.

For choice satisfaction in the traditional mode, the model points to two factors: product quality and access to information from store personnel. Consumers are often unable to judge the quality of a product when shopping online, but in traditional shopping, they can physically inspect the product before making a purchase. Additionally, having access to information from store personnel helps to increase choice satisfaction in the traditional mode. Therefore, it can be concluded that there is a gradual shift in behaviour from traditional shopping to online shopping or vice versa, depending on the level of choice satisfaction experienced in each mode of purchase.

## 3. CONCLUSION

The introduction of technology has greatly changed the way consumers buy products. Customers have progressed from being occasional online buyers to becoming regular online purchasers. There are various factors that influence customers' decision-making when it comes to online purchases, and these factors differ from traditional shopping behaviors. Research shows that there is a noticeable distinction in the behavior of online and traditional apparel shoppers, and this variation is affected by socio-demographic elements like gender, age, occupation, and marital status. To cater to the needs of buyers, it is crucial to develop a demographic-based information system that considers factors like marital status and occupation for online shopping and just marital status for traditional shopping. (Jamal & Ahmed, 2007, & Dominici *et al.*, 2021).

Due to the widespread use of the internet, customers are constantly being inundated with information, leading them to gather information both online and in physical stores, and make purchases through either channel. This study uses new data and a machine learning technique to explore the variables affecting both traditional and online shopping behaviors. This has resulted in an elongated decision-making process, as consumers switch between online and physical shopping based on their level of satisfaction with each mode. Online shopping is becoming increasingly popular because it allows for easy ordering at any time of day and is more time-efficient compared to traditional markets (Stefko *et al*, 2022; Zhao *et al.,* 2022). The present study employs a basic machine learning approach, but with the advancement of digitization and artificial intelligence, future studies will be even more advanced and capable of analyzing consumer behavior on a larger scale.

## Future Scope

There are several limitations to the study. One of them is research design; future researchers can do experimental research. Secondly, covid has helped to change consumer online shopping behavior, and there is a need to study in that direction. Many researchers have shown that covid impacted the decision to buy online. The pandemic is not over and there is a need to study the influence of covid 19 after a few years (Optiek *et al.*, 2022; Tran, 2021). Thirdly this study can be studied by different methods of research for triangulation such as Qualitative study (Kennedyd *et al.*, 2022). Future researchers can study attitudes (cognitive and behavioral) components that might help consumer attitudes towards AI (Zhao, 2022). Sentiment analysis has also become an important tool for e-commerce giants to capture user sentiment toward their products and use such analysis to attract users to purchase products (Yadav *et al.*, 2022). There is a need to study whether health and safety influence shifting behavior.

## REFERENCES

[1] Al-Mashraie, M., Chung, S.H. and Jeon, H.W. (2020). Customer switching behavior analysis in the telecommunication industry via push-pull-mooring framework: a machine learning approach. Computers & Industrial Engineering, 106476. doi:10.1016/j.cie.2020.106476.

[2] Albesa, J.G. (2007). Interaction channel choice in a multichannel environment, an empirical study. *International Journal of Bank Marketing*, 25(7), 490–506. https://doi.org/10.1108/02652320710832630.

[3] Arora, S., Singha, K. and Sahney, S. (2017). "Understanding consumer's showrooming behaviour: Extending the theory of planned behaviour", *Asia Pacific Journal of Marketing and Logistics*, Vol. 29, No. 2, pp. 409–431. https://doi.org/10.1108/APJML-06-2016-0111.

[4] Breeden, J. (2021). A survey of machine learning in credit risk. *Journal of Credit Risk,* 17(3).

[5] Bujang, M.A., Ghani, P.A., Bujang, M.A., Zolkepali, N.A., Adnan, T.H., Ali, M.M., … Haniff, J. (2012). A comparison between convenience sampling versus systematic sampling in getting the true parameter in a population: Explore from a clinical database: The Audit Diabetes Control Management (ADCM) registry in 2009. *2012 International Conference on Statistics in Science,* Business and Engineering ICSSBE). doi:10.1109/icssbe.2012.6396615.

[6] Chi-Hsien, K., and Nagasawa, S. (2019). Applying machine learning to market analysis: Knowing your luxury consumer. *Journal of Management Analytics*, 1–16.

[7] Chi, T. (2018). 'Understanding Chinese consumer adoption of apparel mobile commerce: An extended TAM approach,' *Journal of Retailing and Consumer Services*, 44, 274–284.

[8] Deng, L. and Yuan, K.-H. (2015). Multiple-Group Analysis for Structural Equation Modeling With Dependent Samples. *Structural Equation Modeling: A Multidisciplinary Journal,* 22(4), 552–567. doi:10.1080/10705511.2014.950534.

[9] Dewalska-Opitek, A., Bilińska, K. and Cierpiał-Wolan, M. (2022). The Application of the Soft Modeling Method to Evaluate Changes in Customer Behavior towards e-Commerce in the Time of the Global COVID-19 Pandemic. Risks, 10(3), 62.

[0] Dominici, A., Boncinelli, F., Gerini, F. and Marone, E. (2021). Determinants of online food purchasing: The impact of socio-demographic and situational factors. *Journal of Retailing and Consumer Services*, 60, 102473.

[11] Gupta, A., Su, B.C. and Walter, Z. (2004). An empirical study of consumer switching from traditional to electronic channels: A purchase-decision process perspective. *International Journal of Electronic Commerce*, 8(3), 131–161. https://doi.org/10.1080/10864415.2004.11044302.

[12] Hasan, B. (2010). Exploring gender differences in online shopping attitude. Computers in Human Behavior, 26(4), 597–601. https://doi.org/10.1016/j.chb.2009.12.012.

[13] Jamal, A.S. and Ahmed, A.F. (2007). Socio-cultural factors influencing consumer adoption of online transactions. *8th World Congress on the Management of E-Business,* WCMeB 2007 - Conference Proceedings, (WCMeB), 1–6. https://doi.org/10.1109/WCMEB.2007.60.

[14] Jose J. (2019). Predicting customer retention of an App-based business using supervised machine learning. Technological University Dublin.

[15] Kennedyd, S.I., Marjerison, R.K., Yu, Y., Zi, Q., Tang, X. and Yang, Z. (2022). E-Commerce Engagement: A Prerequisite for Economic Sustainability—An Empirical Examination of Influencing Factors. Sustainability, 14(8), 4554.

[16] Kennedyd, S.I., Marjerison, R.K., Yu, Y., Zi, Q., Tang, X. and Yang, Z. (2022). E-Commerce Engagement: A Prerequisite for Economic Sustainability—An Empirical Examination of Influencing Factors. Sustainability.

[17] Kesharwani, S. and Sharma, N. (2020). Swaying between qualitative information and customers' expectation: An assessment of online shopping sites in India. *International Journal of Information Technology*, 1–7.

[18] Khan, I., Hollebeek, L.D., Fatma, M., Islam, J.U. and Riivits-Arkonsuo, I. (2020). Customer experience and commitment in retailing: Does customer age matter? *Journal of Retailing and Consumer Services*, 57, 102219. doi:10.1016/j.jretconser.2020.102219

[19] Khandani, A.E., Kim, A.J. and Lo, A.W. (2010). Consumer credit-risk models via machine-learning algorithms. *Journal of Banking & Finance*, 34(11), 2767–2787.

[20] Klaus, P. and Zaichkowsky, J.L. (2022). The convenience of shopping via voice AI: Introducing AIDM. *Journal of Retailing and Consumer Services*, 65, 102490.

[21] Muzayyanah, M.A.U., Putra, A.R.S., Syahlani, S.P. and Dewi, N.H.U. (2020). 'Consumer perception on selecting marketplace for livestock products food,' *IOP Conference Series: Earth and Environmental Science,* Volume 637, *The 7th International Conference on Sustainable Agriculture and Environment,* 25–27 August 2020, Surakarta, Indonesia.

[22] Maulud, D. and Abdulazeez, A.M. (2020). A review on linear regression comprehensive in machine learning. *Journal of Applied Science and Technology Trends*, 1(4), 140–147.

[23] Sharma, R. and Yadav, A. (2021). Switching Behaviour for Traditional and Online Mode of Purchase: Analysis of Choices for Switching Consumer Behaviour. *In Data Driven Approach Towards Disruptive Technologies* (pp. 269–285). Springer, Singapore.

[24] Sharma, Yadav (2018). 'Critical Evaluation of Traditional and Online Theories of Consumer Behaviour: Review and Setting Stage for Future Research,' *IJAIR*, Vol. 5, issue 4(VII), Pg 1–13.

[25] Stefko, R., Bacik, R., Fedorko, R. and Olearova, M. (2022). Gender-generation characteristic in relation to the customer behavior and purchasing process in terms of mobile marketing. Oeconomia Copernicana, 13(1), 181–223.

[26] Suhartanto, D., Kusdibyo, L., Chen, B., Dean, D. and Setiawati, L. (2020, April). Predicting consumer behavior in the tourism industry: Comparing Structural Equation Modelling (SEM) and multiple regression. *In IOP Conference Series: Materials Science and Engineering* (Vol. 830, No. 3, p. 032090). IOP Publishing.

[27] Tareq, S.U., Noor, M.H. and Bepery, C. (2020). Framework of dynamic recommendation system for e-shopping. *International Journal of Information Technology,* 12, 135–140.

[28] Tran, L.T.T. (2021). Managing the effectiveness of e-commerce platforms in a pandemic. *Journal of Retailing and Consumer Services,* 58, 102287.

[29] Visconti-Caparrós, J.M. and Campos-Blázquez, J.R. (2021). The development of alternate payment methods and their impact on customer behavior: The Bizum case in Spain. *Technological Forecasting and Social Change*, 121330.

[30] Yadav, V., Verma, P. and Katiyar, V. (2022). Long short term memory (LSTM) model for sentiment analysis in social data for e-commerce products reviews in Hindi languages. *International Journal of Information Technology.*

[41] Zhao T, Cui J, Hu J, Dai Y, Zhou Y. Is Artificial Intelligence Customer Service Satisfactory? Insights Based on Microblog Data and User Interviews. Cyberpsychol Behav Soc Netw. 2022 Feb.; 25(2): 110–117. doi: 10.1089/cyber.2021.0155. Epub. 2021, Dec. 17. PMID: 34935458.

# Author Index


**A**

Abheeti ........ 136

**B**

Balagopal, Bindu ........ 58
Banu, Neha ........ 86
Bassi, Sania ........ 136

**C**

Cirappa, I.B. ........ 109

**D**

Diksha ........ 136

**H**

Harshith, M. ........ 23
Hemamalini, T.D. ........ 179

**I**

Iyer, Santha Ganesh ........ 23, 28

**J**

Jagtap, Manisha Vikas ........ 124
Jose, P. Chacko ........ 58

**K**

Kamaraj, M. ........ 179
Katti, Pratima ........ 47
Kaur, Manjeet ........ 171
Kavitha, G. ........ 148
Khosla, Rekha ........ 171
Kiran, L. ........ 28
Kumar, S. Ranjith ........ 86

**M**

Manisha, G. ........ 23

**N**

Neha, K. ........ 28
Nilaish ........ 3

**P**

Patil, Prachi ........ 195

**S**

Sharma, Vijay Prakash ........ 216
Shivanna, J. ........ 109
Shwetha, M.K. ........ 72
Siddiqui, Masood ........ 171
Singh, Alka ........ 158
Singh, Avnare ........ 158
Singh, Suma ........ 72
Suryadevi, P. ........ 148

**T**

Tiwari, Bhupendra Bahadur ........ 3
Tripathi, Jyoti ........ 35

**U**

Unnisa, Farhatnida ........ 3

**Y**

Yadav, Anuradha ........ 216

# Applauds

***Dear Vice-Chancellor Prof. Raghavendra Sir***

We have attended many Conferences and Seminars. The Present Conference is one of the well organised academic event. We take with us sweet memories about the Conference which we will cherish for long time to come. We congratulate you and your young, dynamic and active team led by Prof. B.B. Tiwari for successfully organising the Conference under your guidance. We pray God to give you strength to organise many more such International events to serve the Society and make India one of Super Power by 2047.

With best wishes

**S. Indrakant,**
*Visiting Professor,*
Centre for Economics and Social Studies,
Begumpet, Hyderabad-500016

Thanks Prof Tiwari for your kind hospitality. I returned to Delhi after a useful trip to Bengaluru. Best wishes and kind regards, sincerely yours,

**Prof. Prem Vrat**
*Pro-Chancellor,*
The NorthCap University, Gurugram
Chairman, BoG, IIT (ISM) Dhanbad

***Dear Tiwarisahab,***

A very good morning as I reach my home in Ahmedabad after an exhilarating experience at the CMRU international conference. Having participated in many conferences and a few in foreign country as well, I have to say this was an extremely pleasant experience. In all departments and functionalities your teams performed A-Star. Congratulations to you and your team for putting up such a great show—a benchmark difficult to reach is thus established.

Best regards Hemant

**Hemant Trivedi**
*Director CVMU-MBA*
VVNagar Anand

***Dear Prof. Tiwari***

Congratulations for organising the conference successfully. You attracted many scholars and had many good papers. Arrangements were superb. I have attended many conferences and seminars. This is one of the best conferences. We cherish sweet memories about the conference for long time to come. Your school has lot of potentiality. You have capacity to organise many more international events. Congratulations to you and your young and dynamic members like Balaji, Ranjit, Eshwar Reddy, Ravi Kumar, Shareef, Nilesh and many others. Convey our Regards to your VC Prof. Raghavendra Sir.

Once congratulations to all of you.

**Prof. S. Indrakant**

*Visiting Professor,*

Centre for Economics and Social Studies,

Begumpet, Hyderabad-500016

# SOCIAL-MEDIA

**raghavendra hadadi** · 1st
VC CMR University, Bangalore, Former VC Chandigarh ...
6h ·

CMR University SOEC School successfully conducted International Conference on Economics, Finance Management and Technology Conference on 5th and 6th April 2024. The smooth running of conference with more than 200 papers selected for presentations from all over India and abroad is an indicator of success. . The excellent remarks from the Guest and Delegates are testimony to the team work of CMRU SOEC under the Directorship of Dr BB Tiwari. I appreciate the team along with others of CMR University for fantastic coordination and hard work. We are indebted to the Sponsors of the conference. Dignitaries include Prof. Premvrat and Padmasree Prahlada Rao Eminent Scientist with many others leading sessions and tracks. The picture with Padmasree Prahlada Rao during concluding ceremony is also shared.

# NEWS PAPER COVERAGE

**CITY READ**

## CMR University's international conference concludes

The School of Economics and Commerce at CMR University, Bengaluru, conducted an international conference on 'Recent Advances In The Field Of Economics, Finance, Management & Technology (ICREFMT-2024)'. Held over two days, at the university's OMBR Campus, this event gathered renowned personalities from various sectors, enriching the discussions with insights and experiences. The conference showcased the expertise of over 244 delegates from India and abroad, with more than 150 full-length research papers submitted by paper presenters from both national and international spheres, participating in the event both online and offline.

ಸಿಎಂಆರ್ ವಿಶ್ವವಿದ್ಯಾಲಯದ ವತಿಯಿಂದ ನಡೆದ ಅಂತಾರಾಷ್ಟ್ರೀಯ ಸಮ್ಮೇಳನದಲ್ಲಿ ಐಐಟಿ ಧನ್‌ಬಾದ್‌ನ ಆಡಳಿತ ಮಂಡಳಿ ಅಧ್ಯಕ್ಷ ಪ್ರೇಮ್‌ವ್ರತ್ ಸಮ್ಮೇಳನದ ಸ್ಮರಣ ಸಂಚಿಕೆ ಬಿಡುಗಡೆ ಮಾಡಿದರು. ನಿವೃತ್ತ ಐಪಿಎಸ್ ಅಧಿಕಾರಿ ಡಾ.ಕೆ.ಸಿ ರಾಮಮೂರ್ತಿ, ಕುಲಾಧಿಪತಿ ಡಾ.ಸಬಿತಾ ರಾಮಮೂರ್ತಿ, ಉಪಕುಲಪತಿ ಡಾ.ಎಚ್.ಬಿ.ರಾಘವೇಂದ್ರ, ಕುಲಸಚಿವ ಡಾ.ಪ್ರವೀಣ್ ಇದ್ದರು.

# ತಂತ್ರಜ್ಞಾನ ಆಧರಿತ ಸಮ್ಮೇಳನಗಳು ದೇಶದ ಪ್ರಗತಿಗೆ ಪೂರಕ

ಬೆಂಗಳೂರು, ಏ.7- ಅರ್ಥಶಾಸ್ತ್ರ ಹಣಕಾಸು ನಿರ್ವಹಣೆ ಮತ್ತು ತಂತ್ರಜ್ಞಾನ ವಿಷಯಾಧಾರಿತ ಅಂತಾರಾಷ್ಟ್ರೀಯ ಸಮ್ಮೇಳನಗಳು ದೇಶದ ಪ್ರಗತಿಯನ್ನು ಅವಲೋಕಿಸುತ್ತವೆ ಎಂದು ಗುರುಗ್ರಾಮ್‌ನ ಐಐಟಿ ಧನ್‌ಬಾದ್ ಆಡಳಿತ ಮಂಡಳಿ ಅಧ್ಯಕ್ಷ ಪ್ರೊ.ಪ್ರೇಮ್ ವ್ರತ್ ಹೇಳಿದರು.

ನಗರದ ಒಎಂಬಿಆರ್ ಲೇಔಟ್‌ನಲ್ಲಿನ ಸಿಎಂಆರ್ ವಿಶ್ವವಿದ್ಯಾಲಯ ಸಭಾಂಗಣದಲ್ಲಿ ಸ್ಕೂಲ್ ಆಫ್ ಎಕನಾಮಿಕ್ಸ್ ಮತ್ತು ಕಾಮರ್ಸ್ ವಿಭಾಗಗಳು ಆಯೋಜಿಸಿದ್ದ ಅರ್ಥಶಾಸ್ತ್ರ ಹಣಕಾಸು, ನಿರ್ವಹಣೆ ಮತ್ತು ತಂತ್ರಜ್ಞಾನ ಕ್ಷೇತ್ರದಲ್ಲಿ ಇತ್ತೀಚಿನ ಪ್ರಗತಿಗಳು ಕುರಿತ ಅಂತಾರಾಷ್ಟ್ರೀಯ ಸಮ್ಮೇಳನದಲ್ಲಿ ಅವರು ಮಾತನಾಡಿದರು.

ಚರ್ಚಿತ ವಿಷಯಗಳು ಇಲ್ಲಿ ಪಾಲ್ಗೊಂಡಿರುವ ಆರ್ಥಿಕ ತಜ್ಞರು, ಉದ್ಯಮಿಗಳು, ಸಂಶೋಧಕರು, ವಿದ್ಯಾರ್ಥಿಗಳು, ಪ್ರಾಧ್ಯಾಪಕರುಗಳಿಗೆ ಉತ್ತಮ ವೇದಿಕೆಯಾಗುತ್ತವೆ. ಭಾರತ ಸರ್ಕಾರದ ಮಹತ್ವಾಕಾಂಕ್ಷೆಯ ವಿಕಸಿತ ಭಾರತ ಸಂಪೂರ್ಣ ಸಾಕಾರಗೊಳ್ಳುವ ನಿಟ್ಟಿನಲ್ಲಿ ಇಂತಹ ವಿಷಯಾಧಾರಿತ ಅಂತಾರಾಷ್ಟ್ರೀಯ ಸಮ್ಮೇಳನಗಳು ವಿಶ್ವವಿದ್ಯಾಲಯ ಮಟ್ಟದಲ್ಲಿ ಜರುಗಬೇಕು, ಹೆಚ್ಚು ಹೆಚ್ಚು ಸಂಶೋಧನಾ ಪ್ರಬಂಧಗಳು ಮಂಡನೆಯಾಗಬೇಕು ಎಂದು ಅಭಿಪ್ರಾಯಪಟ್ಟರು.

ಆನ್‌ಲೈನ್ ಮತ್ತು ಆಫ್‌ಲೈನ್ ಎರಡು ಹಂತದಲ್ಲಿ ಆಯೋಜಿಸಿದ್ದ ಈ ಅಂತಾರಾಷ್ಟ್ರೀಯ ಸಮ್ಮೇಳನದಲ್ಲಿ ದೇಶ-ವಿದೇಶಗಳ 244ಕ್ಕೂ ಹೆಚ್ಚು ಪರಿಣಿತರು, ಉದ್ಯಮಿಗಳು, ಸಂಶೋಧಕರು, ವಿದ್ಯಾರ್ಥಿಗಳು, ಪ್ರಾಧ್ಯಾಪಕರು ಭಾಗವಹಿಸಿದ್ದರು. 150ಕ್ಕೂ ಹೆಚ್ಚು ಮೌಲ್ಯಾಧಾರಿತ ಸಂಶೋಧನಾ ಪ್ರಬಂಧಗಳು ಮಂಡನೆಯಾದವು.

ಗುರುಗ್ರಾಮ್‌ನ ಸ್ಟಾರೆಕ್ಸ್ ವಿಶ್ವವಿದ್ಯಾಲಯದ ಮಾಜಿ ಉಪಕುಲಪತಿ ಪ್ರೊ.ಎಂ.ಎಂ. ಗೋಯೆಲ್, ಅಲಹಾಬಾದ್ ವಿಶ್ವವಿದ್ಯಾಲಯದ ವಾಣಿಜ್ಯ ವಿಭಾಗದ ಮಾಜಿ ಡೀನ್ ಪ್ರೊ.ಪ್ರಹ್ಲಾದ್ ಕುಮಾರ್, ಮಾಜಿ ರಾಜ್ಯಸಭಾ ಸದಸ್ಯ, ಸಿಎಂಆರ್ ಸಮೂಹ ಶಿಕ್ಷಣ ಸಂಸ್ಥೆಗಳ ಅಧ್ಯಕ್ಷರಾದ ಡಾ.ಕೆ.ಸಿ.ರಾಮಮೂರ್ತಿ, ಸಿಎಂಆರ್ ವಿಶ್ವ ವಿದ್ಯಾಲಯದ ಕುಲಾಧಿಪತಿ ಡಾ.ಸಬಿತಾ ರಾಮಮೂರ್ತಿ, ಉಪಕುಲಪತಿ ಡಾ.ಎಚ್.ಬಿ.ರಾಘವೇಂದ್ರ, ಕುಲಸಚಿವ ಡಾ.ಪ್ರವೀಣ್ ಆರ್., ಸ್ಕೂಲ್ ಆಫ್ ಎಕನಾಮಿಕ್ಸ್ ಮತ್ತು ಕಾಮರ್ಸ್ ನಿರ್ದೇಶಕ ಡಾ.ಬಿ.ಬಿ.ತಿವಾರಿ ಮತ್ತಿತರರು ಉಪಸ್ಥಿತರಿದ್ದರು.

# 2 ದಿನಗಳ ಅಂತರಾಷ್ಟ್ರೀಯ ಸಮ್ಮೇಳನ

**ಬೆಂಗಳೂರು:** ನಗರದ ಪ್ರತಿಷ್ಠಿತ ಸಿಎಂಆರ್ ವಿಶ್ವವಿದ್ಯಾಲಯದಲ್ಲಿ "ಅರ್ಥಶಾಸ್ತ್ರ, ಹಣ ಕಾಸು, ನಿರ್ವಹಣೆ ಮತ್ತು ತಂತ್ರಜ್ಞಾನ ಕ್ಷೇತ್ರದಲ್ಲಿ ಇತ್ತೀಚಿನ ಪ್ರಗತಿಗಳು ವಿಷಯ ಕುರಿತು 2 ದಿನಗಳ ಅಂತರಾಷ್ಟ್ರೀಯ ಸಮ್ಮೇಳನ –2024 ಯಶಸ್ವಿಯಾಗಿ ನಡೆಯಿತು. ನಗರದ ಒಎಂಬಿಆರ್ ಲೇಔಟನಲ್ಲಿನ ಸಿಎಂಆರ್ ವಿಶ್ವವಿದ್ಯಾಲಯ ಸಭಾಂಗಣದಲ್ಲಿ ಸ್ಕೂಲ್ ಆಫ್ ಎಕನಾಮಿಕ್ಸ್ ಮತ್ತು ಕಾಮರ್ಸ್ ವಿಭಾಗಗಳು ಏ.5 ಮತ್ತು ಏ.6 ಆಯೋಜಿಸಿದ್ದ ಅರ್ಥಶಾಸ್ತ್ರ, ಹಣಕಾಸು,ನಿರ್ವಹಣೆ ಮತ್ತು ತಂತ್ರಜ್ಞಾನ ಕ್ಷೇತ್ರದಲ್ಲಿ ಇತ್ತೀಚಿನ ಪ್ರಗತಿಗಳು ಕುರಿತ ಅಂತರಾಷ್ಟ್ರೀಯ ಸಮ್ಮೇಳನ – 2024 ಕಾರ್ಯಕ್ರಮವನ್ನು ಮುಖ್ಯ ಅತಿಥಿಗಳಾಗಿ ಭಾಗವಹಿಸಿದ್ದ ಪ್ರೊ. ಪ್ರೇಮ್ ವ್ರತ್, ಐಐಟಿ ಧನ್ ಬಾದ್ ಆಡಳಿತ ಮಂಡಳಿ (ಬಿಒಜಿ) ಅಧ್ಯಕ್ಷರು ಮತ್ತು ಗುರುಗ್ರಾಮ್‌ನ ದಿ ನಾರ್ತ್ ಕ್ಯಾಪ್ ವಿಶ್ವವಿದ್ಯಾಲಯದ ಪ್ರೊಚಾನ್ಸಲರ್ ಉದ್ಘಾಟಿಸಿ ಸಮ್ಮೇಳನದ ಸ್ಮರಣ ಸಂಚಿಕೆ ಬಿಡುಗಡೆ ಮಾಡಿದರು.

ನಂತರ ಮಾತನಾಡಿದ ಪ್ರೊ.ಪ್ರೇಮ್ ವ್ರತ್ ಅವರು ಅರ್ಥಶಾಸ್ತ್ರ, ಹಣಕಾಸು ನಿರ್ವಹಣೆ ಮತ್ತು ತಂತ್ರಜ್ಞಾನ ವಿಷಯಾಧಾರಿತ ಅಂತರಾಷ್ಟ್ರೀಯ ಸಮ್ಮೇಳನ ದೇಶದ ಪ್ರಗತಿಯನ್ನು ಅವಲೋಕಿಸಲು ಮತ್ತು ಚರ್ಚಿಸಲು ಆರ್ಥಿಕ ತಜ್ಞರು, ಉದ್ಯಮಿಗಳು, ಸಂಶೋಧಕರು, ವಿದ್ಯಾರ್ಥಿಗಳು, ಪ್ರಾಧ್ಯಾಪಕರುಗಳಿಗೆ ಉತ್ತಮ ವೇದಿಕೆಯಾಗುತ್ತದೆ ಎಂದು ಅಭಿಪ್ರಾಯಪಟ್ಟರು.

ಅಂತರಾಷ್ಟ್ರೀಯ ಸಮ್ಮೇಳನದಲ್ಲಿ ಪ್ರೊ.ಎಂ.ಎಂ. ಗೋಯೆಲ್, ಗುರುಗ್ರಾಮ್‌ನ ಸ್ಟಾರೆಕ್ಸ್ ವಿಶ್ವವಿದ್ಯಾಲಯದ ಮಾಜಿ ಉಪಕುಲಪತಿ ಮತ್ತು ನೀಡೋನಾಮಿಕ್ಸ್ ಸ್ಕೂಲ್ ಆಫ್ ಥಾಟ್‌ನ ಸಂಸ್ಥಾಪಕರು, ಪ್ರೊ ಪ್ರಹ್ಲಾದ್ ಕುಮಾರ್, ವಾಣಿಜ್ಯ ವಿಭಾಗದ ಮಾಜಿ ಡೀನ್, ಅಲಹಾಬಾದ್ ವಿಶ್ವವಿದ್ಯಾಲಯ. ಇವರುಗಳು ಮುಖ್ಯ ಅತಿಥಿಗಳಾಗಿ ಭಾಗವಹಿಸಿದ್ದರು.

ಮುಖ್ಯ ಅತಿಥಿಗಳಿಗೆ ಡಾ.ಕೆ.ಸಿ ರಾಮಮೂರ್ತಿ, ಐಪಿಎಸ್ ನಿವೃತ್ತಿ, ಮಾಜಿ ರಾಜ್ಯಸಭಾ ಸದಸ್ಯರು, ಸಿಎಂಆರ್ ವಿಶ್ವವಿದ್ಯಾಲಯ ಮತ್ತು ಸಿಎಂಆರ್ ಸಮೂಹ ಶಿಕ್ಷಣ ಸಂಸ್ಥೆಗಳ ಅಧ್ಯಕ್ಷರು ನೆನಪಿನ ಕಾಣಿಕೆ ನೀಡಿ ಸನ್ಮಾನಿಸಿದರು.

ಸಮ್ಮೇಳನದಲ್ಲಿ ಸಿಎಂಆರ್ ವಿಶ್ವವಿದ್ಯಾಲಯದ ಕುಲಾಧಿಪತಿ ಡಾ.ಸಬಿತಾ ರಾಮಮೂರ್ತಿ, ಉಪಕುಲಪತಿ ಡಾ.ಎಚ್.ಬಿ.ರಾಘವೇಂದ್ರ, ಕುಲಸಚಿವ ಡಾ.ಪ್ರವೀಣ್ ಆರ್, ನಿರ್ದೇಶಕ ಸ್ಕೂಲ್ ಆಫ್ ಎಕನಾಮಿಕ್ಸ್ ಮತ್ತು ಕಾಮರ್ಸ್ ಡಾ.ಬಿ.ಬಿ.ತಿವಾರಿ, ಉಪಸ್ಥಿತರಿದ್ದರು.

# CMR University's ICREFMT Concludes with Grand Success

Published on April 8, 2024

Bengaluru – The School of Economics and Commerce at CMR University, Bengaluru, conducted an International Conference On Recent Advances In The Field Of Economics, Finance, Management & Technology (ICREFMT-2024). Held over two days, on April 5th and 6th, at the university's AV Hall, OMBR Campus, this pivotal event gathered renowned personalities from various sectors, enriching the discussions with profound insights and experiences.

The conference was honored by the presence of distinguished guests, including Prof. Prem Vrat, Chairman of the Board of Governors at IIT (ISM)-Dhanbad and Pro-Chancellor of North Cap University, Gurugram, who graced the occasion as the chief guest who had inaugurated the conference. Joining him were Dr. K. C. Ramamurthy, IPS (Retd), former Member of Parliament, Rajya Sabha and chairman of CMR University & CMR Group of institutions, and Prof. Prahlad Kumar, Ex-Dean, Faculty of Commerce, University in Allahabad, Uttar Pradesh, adding significant prestige to the proceedings.

Prof. M.M. Goel, the pioneering former vice-chancellor of Starex University, Gurugram, and founder of the Needonomics School of Thought, served as the conference host, guiding the event towards a platform for groundbreaking research and innovative discussions. Dr. Sabitha Ramamurthy, the Chancellor of CMR University, delivered the keynote address, offering invaluable insights and guidance to the attendees. Along with the dignitaries Dr. H.B.Raghavendra, Vice Chancellor, CMR University, Dr. Praveen.R, Registrar Presented the report of conference, Dr B.B.Tiwari, Conference General Chair and Director, SOEC,CMR University presented vote of thanks at the event.

The conference showcased the expertise of over 244 delegates from India and abroad, with more than 150 full-length research papers submitted by paper presenters from both national and international spheres, participating in the event both online and offline. Dr. Hemakshi Chokshi, Deputy Head, Guildhall School of Business and Law, London Metropolitan University, UK participated in the Conference. Dr. Chokshi chaired the Panel Discussion on Viksit Bharat 2047. Research scholars from Taylors University, Malaysia presented their papers. The conference acted as a melting pot of ideas, fostering discussions spanning the latest trends and challenges within the realms of economics, finance, management, and technology.

Prof. Prem Vrat, in his address at the conference, had emphasized the importance of nurturing academic spaces that promote creativity, innovation, sustainability, and entrepreneurship, urging students to cultivate a positive mindset conducive to achieving their envisioned dreams. He had also launched the ICREFMT-2024 souvenir.

The esteemed guests were honored with the mementos as the token of gratitude from CMR University. ICREFMT 2024 successfully fulfilled its mission as a catalyst for innovative thinking and cooperative dialogues. It not only brought together academics, researchers, business professionals, and policymakers from around the globe but also paved the way for future collaborations and advancements in these critical fields.